# How to survive your own gay life

AN Adult Guide TO Love, Sex, AND Relationships

by Perry Brass

*Belhue Press*

Published in the United State of America by:
Belhue Press
2501 Palisade Ave., Suite A1
Bronx, NY 10463
Electronic mail address: belhuepress@earthlink.net

Cover and overall book design by M. Fitzhugh
Cover photo by Vince Gabrielly

ISBN 0-9627123-9-6
LIBRARY OF CONGRESS CATALOGUE NUMBER: 98-70408

---

**Publisher's Cataloging-in-Publication**
*(Prepared by Quality Books Inc.)*

Brass, Perry.
    How to survive your own gay life/an adult guide to love, sex, and relationships/by Perry Brass, 1947. — 1st ed.
    p. cm.
    Includes index
    Preasigned LCCN: 98-70408
    ISBN 0-9627123-9-6

    1. Homosexuality, Male—Social aspects. 2. Gay men—Conduct of life. 3. Bisexual men—Conduct of life. 4. Gay men—Social life and customs—Handbooks, manuals, etc. 5. Bisexual men—Social life and customs—Handbooks, manuals, etc. I. Title.

    HQ76.B73 1998       306.76'62
                           QB198-607

"The human heart is vast er

— ...p.. Conrad, *Lord Jim.*

For Hugh, who has helped me more than anyone to survive this life. And also for Richard LaBonte, Walter Vatter, John Orcutt, Norman Laurila, Dan Seitler, John Alvord, and so many other people who are working to bring books like these to the growing numbers of readers who want them. And for Patrick Merla, and, as ever, for Mimi. And of course to my brothers and sisters in the gay tribe, whose survival and happiness means everything to me.

Other books by Perry Brass:

**Sex-charge** (poetry)

**Mirage**, a science fiction novel

**Circles**, the sequel to *Mirage*

**Out There**: *Stories of Private Desires. Horror. And The Afterlife.*

**Albert or The Book of Man**, the third book in the *Mirage* series

*Works and Other 'Smoky George' Stories,* Expanded Edition

**The Harvest**, a "science-politico" novel

**The Lover of My Soul,** *A Search for Ecstasy and Wisdom,*
(poetry and other collected writings)

# How to Survive Your *Own* Gay Life

- How to have the *adult* gay relationships you want and need.

- How to attract and keep relationships.

- How to survive and thrive, no matter what age you are, in the difficult—and exciting—years ahead.

# Table of Contents

"Many gay men . . . are stuck between child*lessness* and child*ishness*.
It is a complete dead-end that has become for them what the 'gay world'
is all about."

"Walt Whitman often nursed the psyches of men as well as their
physical problems. He wrote extensively in his journals of holding the
hands of dying men, of kissing them good-bye as their eyes closed for the
last time, and of writing letters for them—acting, therefore, as their scribe,
another part of the gay work."

"What you want to do . . . is re-establish the nakedness of sex: sex which
has been over-clothed in intimacy, in fact, may even be strangling in it."

"We went from being unmentionable to *sellable*."

"We enter the tribe alone and naked, without a previous personal history.
And yet our own history is a part of the history of the tribe."

"It is important for us to deal with the generalized depression around
us and survive."

"I believe in the 'Gay Feast,' the inner banquet for gay men."

"There are still so many things to understand about our own gay
stories. Each of us has one, and we have really only scratched the
surface of them."

# Even Before We Begin–6 Do's and 6 Don'ts

1)   Realize that only you can change things for yourself. Some change may consist of just opening yourself up to what is already inside you. Your therapist can't do it—in fact, *some* therapists have an interest in keeping you unchanged (it's called their hourly fee!). In the long run, your lover, your family, or your friends cannot bring about changes, either, although having their help along the way can be very important.

2)   Realize that there are things about you that may not need changing, that may be authentically right for you. That the warm, loving, tender feelings you have inside are natural and beautiful. Those of us who were a part of the fabled 60s "love generation" now feel as if we are living through a bitter reaction to it: a period of open, even encouraged hostility and hatred. Even though these are the "cutting-edge" emotions that much of our commercialized culture ("gay culture" as well) spits back at us, that does not mean we have to buy this venom at market value.

3)   Allow yourself a regular dose of self-love every day. It should be taken on a "medicinal" healing basis. This person whom you've been living with—yourself—has had to live through an awful lot, bear great burdens, and for the most part invent a "lifestyle" that was unknown thirty years ago. Many of us, no matter what age we are, have had to do this alone. Give yourself credit for the courage and endurance you have shown.

4)   Love someone (or *something*) for the sheer wonder and beauty of it. As we get older, it becomes more "comfortable" (my favorite b.s. word from this period) to become more isolated and insulated from feelings, risk, and hurt. We associate love with all of these things, even while chasing after sex more avidly than ever. The most important thing about loving someone or something else is that it breaks us out of the isolation we settle into and makes us see again with greater depth and feeling. This takes risk on our part, but the rewards are equal to it.

5)   When necessary, push off on your own. Allow yourself time to recuperate from the stresses of "gay life," as well as a "straight" world.

6)   Realize that *honesty* is supportive, not simply "brutal" and "critical." Your own honest needs are important. Don't let people strip you of this honest connection with yourself, in the name of their version of honesty.

## Now, 6 DON'TS

1)    Don't make up rules that you can't follow: "In my next relationship, I'm going to be monogamous." "When I fall in love, it shall be *forever*!" "Any relationship after thirty has to be a *serious relationship!*" "I'll never trust you or anyone else *ever* again." These are the sort of rules that were thrust on you as a kid. You don't need them.

2)    Don't allow other people to label or define you: "You can always tell gay people by the way they dress (or, that they like opera, love disco, or are flaky and have no integrity, etc.)." "You're too old to feel that way!" "You're too old (or young) for that kind of idea." Tell all the labelers and definers to go do something ingenious with a rear part of their body.

3)    Do not hesitate to be different—you will *not* be lonely if you do. There are an amazing number of gay men who do not follow the gym crowd, the drug crowd, the club crowd, the political crowd, or any crowd. Believe it or not, they would love to find you.

4)    Do not apologize for your feelings. They add color, depth, interest, excitement, and passion to your life. Without them, life becomes as colorless as what we see around us today. (And if you wanted to live with that drabness forever, you wouldn't be reading this book!)

5)    Do not let other people—any people at all—destroy you. They will, if allowed. This includes jerks on the Right, who think you are less than human for being gay, and "friends" on the Left, who seriously want to tell you *how* to think.

6)    Do not let other people put you down because you want to break out of the very molds that hold them. Some of the usual lines you will hear are: "We're only telling you this for your own good." "If you had any sense!" "Only your *friends* will let you know." Yeah, sure.

(And one last *don't*: Don't stop reading here!)

"So, how do we survive all this?"

This book is for every generation of gay men. For men just coming out into their "gay careers," as sociologists used to say, and for men who've been around the block many times and are just as confused each time they make the trip. It is for men who are in relationships and are trying to figure out how to make them work, for men who are working to be in a relationship, and for men who never want to be in one. Despite its title, it is often not so much a "how-to" book, as a "why-is-it?" book. That is: it deals with *why* are we doing so many awful things to ourselves, things that you probably see around you every day; and then how can we change this.

A lot of people will ask why I did this. How could I presume to write a book like this? I don't have a Ph.D. I'm not a social worker or a psychologist. Unfortunately, the gay market has been flooded with books by well-meaning social workers and psychologists, who often (despite being gay themselves) have only recently been able to come out. But they are sure that, with a bit more therapy, their gay patients and clients will be able to have the kind of lives that they as "professionals" could not. And, "mental health-wise" (on some planet I've not been able to imagine so far), they'll be able to cope—but not in the bruising, difficult "gay world" that most therapists still have very little handle on. Likewise, as an unaccredited sociologist, I have not interviewed hundreds of gay men to find out "how they tick." (Usually the result of this is finding out how the interviewers tick!)

So why did I do this? Mostly because I have been very much "out" in the gay wars now for about thirty-five years and have been writing about them for thirty. I have been involved with the modern gay movement since 1969, when I joined the Gay Liberation Front in New York and went on to become an editor of *Come Out!*, the first gay liberation newspaper in     13 the world. In 1973, with two other friends, I helped establish the Gay Men's Health Project, the first health clinic for gay men on the East Coast. We strongly advocated condom use fifteen years before the AIDS crisis, and realized that gay health would become the most pressing issue of our time. I have been in a relationship with one man for eighteen years and feel that my deepest, most intimate gay relationships have been, for the most part, successful. They have given me the support and nourishment I have needed to keep on functioning and working. I feel that these relationships, these close, working, passionate friendships with other gay men, are vital for us. Their place in our lives is one of the cornerstones of this book.

I have not done "therapy" with gay men. In fact, one of the ideas that I bring forward is that gay men have become too attached to therapy—and to their relationships with therapists. These "therapeutic relationships" are fairly easy and artificial ones. Often they take the place of the frank relationships we have with friends and lovers. Therapists are "paid friends" and as long as we're happy to do the paying, they are just as happy to do the listening.

In many ways, the gay therapy "habit" only mirrors the larger, mainstream culture's obsession with "professional friends." This obsession has resulted in the breakdown of other intimate friendships, as well as throwing a great deal of phony "talk-show intimacy" out as bait. How many times do we go to parties and have a stranger "open up" to us completely, only to realize that two days later he wouldn't be able to recognize us in a line-up?

This is part of our therapy culture that says that it does not make a difference what you say to someone—no matter how painful or destructive—since you can always come back next week, write out another check, and keep on talking.

Another problem with therapists and gay men is that for a long time therapy was the only place we *could* go for the sort of validation (or advice) that heterosexuals went to their parents, relatives, and friends for.

If you were unhappy and straight, you could go to a friend or relative. He (or she) would not bring into question your whole existence, which happened as soon as the "gay problem" was brought up. Usually, this was in the form of a confession, as in: "I have to tell you, I'm homosexual. . . ."

Straights did not have to do this: they did not have to confess to being *straight*.

But for us, "coming out" became a terrifying obstacle that we could best jump over with therapists. (A good example being the famous *Ellen* "coming out" episode, where she ends up quickly in therapy, with Oprah Winfrey as her therapist.) Therefore, to many self-doubting gay men, therapy seemed such a natural outcome of our difficult "sick" lives that one result of coming out was going *in*—to therapy.

This is not to say that there is no place in the lives of gay men for therapy—or to deny the necessary role of therapists. Often in times of crisis, a *good* therapist *can* save your life.

But, although thousands of gay men go into therapy, very few of them get any grip on the problems that are keeping them at odds with "the gay world." Often this comes about from the homophobia of straight therapists or the *internalized* homophobia of gay ones. At this point *internalized* homophobia may be the greatest enemy facing gay men, as we finally confront what several thousand years of social hatred, oppression, and violence have done to us. Therefore, even gay-friendly therapists rarely manage to work through how their clients will fit into a highly commercialized, competitive, alienating environment of bars, clubs, and cruising situations (now often sanitized under the term "networking") of various sorts, that we call—for want of a better term—"gay life."

The reality is that this public commercialized "iceberg" tip of our world does nothing to feed our inner lives, that deeper, more wondrous element necessary for our own survival. At most, it can give us some strained opportunities for meeting each other. But it does not give us the strength and support necessary to survive an inner and outer environment of homophobia, as well as the intense emotional, spiritual, and psychological *deprivation* of contemporary society.

Although gay men are not the only ones experiencing this deprivation (or even worse, not experiencing it but internalizing it as "normal"), we are often more victimized by it.

This is because we do not fit the advertising and media images around us which dictate what is cool, acceptable, and, to many people (strangely enough), "real." Although a part of the new "queer consciousness" has been to question some of this—and sometimes laugh at it—for younger gays, especially, there is nothing out there other than what is offered in today's two main focal points: TV and our shopping mall culture.

In other words, if you can't *sell* it on television or *buy* it at the local mall, it does not exist.

For younger gay men who will not see themselves represented in either place, this means *they* don't exist.

But I want to counter this. We do *exist*, and on a very important level. I want to counter this non-existence with two ideas, that I want to let out the bag right now.

The first is that it is possible for gay men to connect with a great source of strength inside us. Why "queer" or gay men can do this is probably that we have been excluded from the rigid patterning heterosexual society has imposed upon itself. This does not mean that *all* gays are spiritually advanced. Any visit to a gay gym, disco, or hard-as-nails cruising area will argue against that. But inside we do have the power to connect with this wondrous inner source of strength. Walt Whitman described it simply as "adhesion"—the ability of men to come together in love and support, with an imaginative and erotic undercurrent to it.

The second idea is that most of us will never *fully* come to terms with the depth of homophobia around us. It is literally a sleeping monster out of our worst nightmares. No matter how much we try to close it out of our lives, it wakes up often enough, spits its poison right into our faces—and then we see it for what it is. We try to rationalize these moments: "Well, that's life. This much hostility can't possibly be directed towards *me*—they must be talking about somebody else!" And if we're lucky, really lucky, the monster goes back to sleep until the next time. But our awareness of its existence is so emotionally draining that most of us will do anything to forget about it.

Whether the homophobia is external—and we see it in its most blatant forms as gay-bashing, hate legislation, and other campaigns—or internalized, in the obsessive physical body culture that is turning many gay men into steroid-androids, the results are the same: a society that is both rejecting of gay men and a *gay* society that is self-rejecting.

The strangest thing is that this rejection now eats inside us: it has become like a very efficient computer virus openly working its way through us. We see it even in gay magazines and gay media, and in the most "openly" gay situations. The result has fostered a synthetic, shallow, gay *sameness*. It can be the sameness of Republican "invisible" gays—who want to be like "everybody else," even when they can't—or the sameness of the buffed Chelsea-boy clone look. But it is always done to keep the big, scary monster of internalized homophobia somewhat at bay.

The feeling runs: if we just swallow a little bit of its poison (in the form of rejecting or ridiculing other gay men) the big poison (humiliation; rejection from our families and straight society) won't hurt us. Wrong.

All we are doing is *slowly* swallowing the same poison that will destroy us.

We must survive this. We must recognize *internalized* as well as external homophobia to survive it. It is very much a part of surviving your *own* gay life. And that is what this book is about: surviving your own gay life. Not somebody else's. Not some fashionable, politically correct line you've been fed and then told to believe is what you *are* about. Nor some gay Never-Never Land of high consumerism and gym-clone models that is supposed to represent you, your feelings, and your so-called "lifestyle."

It is not about AIDS, although the AIDS struggle has influenced many aspects of our lives, and has made our own survival, both physical and psychological, more questionable.

It is not a sex guide, but sex figures often into this book: both our own, very *important* needs for sex and the limitations of sex as far as intimacy is concerned.

It is not about making yourself smarter, sharper, or fabulously attractive. In other words, giving you that all-important edge in the dog-eat-dog, man-eat-man "gay meat market." It is about realizing what *strength* you have, and then helping you find a lot *more* of it in yourself.

Above all, it is about gay tribalism and gay individuality, about connecting with something deep and ancient in yourself and in other men. It is also about dealing with the very important "straight," or mainstream, world, and the interplay between you and it.

Finally, it is about finding happiness and depth in life, and security within yourself. This is important in an "Information Age" culture that tends to get flatter, more shallow, and more disconnected as we go along. This culture has made the myth of the "gay market" more important than the reality of any single gay life.

So, how do we survive all this? How do we survive the distortions and lies handed to us by both straight society as well as the new, very mainstreamed gay "movement" and its newest allies, the corporations and gay marketers who see us as a willing and usable market? How do we deal with our lives as adult gay men with *adult* gay sexual and emotional needs? These are questions I want to deal with openly in this book, openly and honestly. I want to do this because many of the men I see around me are looking for the answers, and I have come across enough of them to help.

In the long run, *help* is what we need to do for each other. I hope these answers work for you as much as they have helped me. And also I hope they bring you back to the adventure, the power, and the excitement of our lives. This is something that we need to bring back into the "gay world"—along with the power and excitement of love—and we need it *now*. We need a lot more of it. To survive our *own* gay lives.

"The important thing is to keep your mind, soul, and imagination open."

CHAPTER I

# Realizing Your Intentions:
## Clearing the Way for What You Really Want

Many gay men feel that their lives are ones of *unrealized* intentions. They intended to have a lover, but never did. They were sure that the *right* man ("One day he'll come along, the man I *love!*") would never come along, or that any man who did would never come up to their fantasies of what a lover (". . . and he'll be big and strong, the man I *love!*") should be. They wanted deeper gay friendships, but could never work them out, either. They wanted to be more open with their families, but could not even imagine how to do this—how to begin talking about themselves. They wanted to have a more sexually exciting, fulfilling life, but their bashfulness and repression cut them off, also, from this.

The only thing they could imagine were the brutal consequences of being open. These consequences were shaped for the most part by internalized homophobic feelings of guilt, fear, hurt, and repression. Having lives of unrealized intentions has become for many of us part of the gay landscape—and despite several decades of "gay liberation," it is often the only landscape we see for ourselves. A landscape that gets smaller and more depressing after an initial, sometimes euphoric "coming out" period.

So we come out. Then we hit a solid "blank wall" of unrealized intentions.

The blankness is caused by one simple fact: realizing our desires and intentions is something we cannot even *imagine*. Our imagination is stopped by an atmosphere of jaded cynicism (How many of us want to be the next Oscar Wilde?), or by commercialized sexual images that say, "You are never going to be *this* guy, so why bother?" or, "He's never going to be the man of your dreams, so why bother with *him*?"

This brings me to an early lesson in my life.

Years ago, when I first came to New York, like many young men I took acting lessons. I was a very shy, repressed kid from Savannah,

Georgia, and one of my friends, a would-be actor, said that at the very *least* acting lessons would decrease my shyness. At my first lesson, my coach, who was of the "Method" school, declared: "An actor's first work is to realize his intentions on the stage." I looked at him dumbly, so he explained: "Just learn to get done what you *want* to do! If you need to pick up a coffee cup at the end of the stage, make sure you do that. Even if you have to jump over a wall and two tons of scenery to get to that cup!"

When I asked my coach how was I going to be able to do that—jump over all that scenery, I meant—he answered: "First you have to imagine—deep in your mind—what the cup means to you. How important it is to you—and the play. And, of course, that you are *supposed* to get it. After that, everything gets a lot easier!"

I never did become an actor. But I did become much less shy, and my coach's words have stayed with me for almost thirty years, especially in what we call "gay" settings. Too often gay men, to begin with, are frightened of their own intentions. We cut ourselves off from them as quickly and neatly as possible. We are ashamed of them. We have been made to feel that they are not "legitimate." That realizing them is not "work," but getting away with something that is, at best, "unnatural" and at worst, criminal.

Our intentions are often put down as "just sex," and from childhood we have been made to understand how severely erotic/emotional/sexual intentions will be squashed. We are made to feel—at the very least, that they are unnecessary, that they are options we can live without. Or, at the most, we are made to feel that our intentions are so *revolting* that we will be made to pay for them for the rest of our lives. This revulsion has been drilled further into us by the AIDS crisis. Now sex is not only illegitimate, but highly "risk-laden." So gay men face each other with more fear, and push their intentions farther back. And straight society, even after more than a decade of AIDS education, can still whip up enough anti-gay hostility to put down the warmth and connectiveness of sex between men, whenever it feels threatened.

What many gay men do not understand is that we are paying for our intentions by *not* realizing them. We are paying for them with our own unhappiness, alienation, and hurt. Our intentions are real, and very important. In fact, they may be among our most *real* parts.

Among our foremost intentions: The intention to have *authentic* emotional involvements. The intention to have a deeper connection with life. The intention to allow openness, kindness, and warmth into our lives. And the intention to show feelings that may not *always* be welcome—in other words the intention *not* to show that smiling little face at all times. This intention is often pushed aside by men who feel that they have to "buy" their gay selves by always being "perfectly" nice, bland, or agreeable. (You probably know some of these men yourself.)

But how about sex?

Why can't we just be open about our sexual intentions?

Sure, why not? Meeting men and having sex—if we honestly face it—is very important. Let's don't hypocritically play that down! Sex is an important part of life in general, and our own lives in particular. The need to subvert this intention—and all the basic human needs under it—in the name of "maturity," "political correctness," "mental health," and other types of b.s. is one of the oppressions gay men especially face today. As gay sex has had to carry a huge weight of heightened anxieties and taboos behind it, our honest attractions have had to be steered into a direction that is not *honestly* sexual. Hypocrisy is winking at us the whole time, and saying: "Your intentions are unworthy, so let's pretend they don't exist."

Wrong!

They do exist. And by not dealing honestly with our intentions, we are again subverting them, and ourselves.

But how do we "realize our intentions," these intentions on the "stage of life," whether it be a social stage, a sexual stage, or an emotional one?

First, we have to face our own *internalized* homophobia. Internalized homophobia works like a sponge, absorbing every negative feeling we experience, both from within and from outside. These negative feelings cut us off from our own tenderness, closeness with ourselves, and sources of strength. We also have to add to this "sponge" of homophobia the effects of an increasingly repressive culture that robs us of any feelings we have of personal security (and privacy), while at the same time exposing us to open expressions of bigotry and hatred.

Along with internalized homophobia comes another thief in the night—the fear that steals from us our imaginative lives and with it much of our courage as well. I consider this *imaginative* life our connection with our own deepest feelings—and our pathway to other gay men. Why this imaginative life seems so natural and organic a part of gay men is something that we've been trying to figure out for years (perhaps centuries!). But basically gay men have been forced to work outside the "normal" male-female patterning that limits much of the imaginative process. This process is directly related to what we call the "soul" or "creativity." It is an extremely important aspect of human life—Albert Einstein once said, "Intelligence is nothing. Imagination is everything!" But it is an aspect that we denigrate terribly, even as we try to Prozac our way out of the depressed, imagination-starved environment around us.

This soulfulness, playfulness, and genuine *lightness* is a natural antidepressant, yet one that we block at every possible moment in what passes now for "normal" life.

How is it blocked?

One important way is by blocking avenues for sexuality. By making even the most casual interactions between strangers virtually impossible—so much so that breaking down alone in your car has become a terrifying situation. And by making the act of trusting anyone (except in a useful "networking" way) suspect and harshly open to judgment. (This has brought us to an interesting definition of "contemporary marriage": six hours' worth of hard work with the "pre-nup" lawyers, followed by a quick, fifteen-minute ceremony.)

As our society becomes more alienated, techno-driven, and closed-in on itself, creativity is something that is increasingly relegated to "artists." So you either specialize in "creativity," or you can look for it in a very canned, pre-digested version, such as Martha Stewart's "Home" line at K-Mart or the latest super-hyped, over-budgeted movie. The soul, this recharging, nurturing part of human beings, is only seen within a stock, commercialized, religious context. It is reduced to lines on a drugstore greeting card. The soul as a living, creative part of us, something that reaches out openly towards other men, terrifies most people. It terrifies *us*.

We can see "having sex" as another detached advantage in a consumer economy. (Hot, hip, successful people look good, buy "designer" clothes and have "lots of sex.") But we are frightened of the idea that our sexuality—something we are so defensive about—can actually make us feel warmer and closer to others. That it can allow us to see other men as soulful, more human—more warmly beautiful—and react to them in a normal, trusting way. We are frightened, in short, of the disarming, close aspects of homosexual attraction and sexuality. We can accept its cruel, cynical, commercialized aspects—smart drag queen waiters in chic restaurants; vacuous porn stars on drugs—but not its genuinely endearing ones.

So how can we change this? That is, of course, a big question, but since you are reading a book about change and survival (with the two working very hard, hand in hand), let's begin this right now.

Here are some ways to deal with opening up your intentions (instead of clamping down on them)—and then realizing them.

— We can open our intentions by *imagining* them in a deeper, more personal and satisfying way. This means facing that part of the gay self that we have been rejecting and becoming closer to it.

— We can also stop externalizing (and commercializing) our sexuality. It is no longer something that we have to keep buying from a stock set of cardboard images.

Sadly, as homoerotic images—from Calvin Klein underwear ads to near-naked hunks in sitcoms—have become more blatant, lookalike, and openly sold, our responses to our own sexuality have become more closed down. (A perfect example of this: going into a gay bookstore and seeing fourteen men glued to gay porno magazines, while ignoring each other.) These sexual responses are now narrowed down to what is "buyable." We either *buy* a guy, or don't. He is either within a very narrow range of fantasies, or not. At the same time, we *void* the natural area of eroticism around him, an area of playfulness in which we can put ourselves, so that sexuality is seen as something that is "take out," "brought in," "porn-originated," "center-folded," but not an organic part of us. So we end up feeling that we can either "buy" our sexual success and happiness—or it's just not available for sale at a price we can afford (i.e., our bodies—ourselves—are not marketable).

It is important to understand that "None of this is *really* what I am." *I am not one of these images.* They may be cool. They may be fun. But they are not what I am about. They have nothing to do with me, but only with getting me to buy something associated with a product. *And I am no longer buying it.*

At this point I want to suggest an exercise. Stop looking at the men around you—whether in a bar, in social groups, even men you find interesting in the most casual way—as "types" or set images. Stop hearing the words inside you that are rejecting the possibility of you with them—such as, "I don't know them. They can't possibly be interested in me. They can't (this). They won't (that)."

Now, start looking at them as parts of a story (which can be a simple, "everyday" story, or a romantic or erotic one that has special interest to you) that *you* are telling. Put yourself into that story. In your mind's eye, you are talking to a particular man, interacting, smiling at him. You don't have to act physically on this, but don't be afraid of going into it imaginatively. As you experience this story on a deeper, more imaginative level, you will see how much closer other men will seem to you. They are now part of an imaginative *reality* that you are allowing yourself to participate in. Instead of starving yourself—and feeling that you cannot even imagine them being close to you, you are allowing them to become a part of "your story."

They are now a part of your own warmth and feelings, and not completely separate from you. Like I said, don't be afraid of making the story up (after all, you don't know the men), but don't let other people tell the story for you ("They all hate you. How could they find you interesting or desirable?").

How do these men fit into *your* story?

An example: "I would like to imagine that man (the one over there; you know, that I've seen on my street or at the gym) talking with me. In my mind, I'm smiling at him. I'd like him to come over and we'd talk. I'd tell him about my day and he can tell me about his. He's been having problems or situations just like I have. I can see him smiling, too, as he recognizes how much we have in common. If I work deeper at this, I can see him wanting to spend time with me. Even deeper, I can see him wanting to hold me, just as I want to hold him. On a deeper level, I can see the two of us making each other happy—even if I'm only seeing it right now.

"I'm sure he doesn't see that he's a part of the story I'm telling. But he is."

Although in reality, none of this may actually happen—he may not come over to you and you may not—at least yet—go over to him, you are opening yourself up to the possibility of this happening on a *real*, imaginative level.

I know this sounds like a contradiction: real <u>and</u> imaginative. How can we have both? But many men cannot even imagine having these things happen. They have starved themselves of the *possibility* that they can realize their own intentions. Their intentions are, at every moment, off their imaginative maps, maps which are now crowded with "porno" images, but not with real men.

So once you can imagine these things happening, facing someone, smiling at him, and initiating contact becomes much easier—in fact, it becomes possible. It also means that the real payback for your actions is *realizing* your intentions. Don't let anyone deny you this: that you have *realized* your intentions. You have put yourself into the center of action, and that is very rewarding in itself. I know that for many men this seems like only putting yourself in line for rejection. But rejection, as you become more and more the master of your intentions, becomes far less threatening and hurtful than the state you started out in: never beginning to face—or realize—an intention.

Finally, another question: how would you get them (or him) to listen to your "story"?

You might be amazed to find out how pleased and fascinated men are to know that you've been thinking about them, that they have figured into your imaginative life. Men are, for the most part, ignored in our society. Just saying, "Hello, I thought about you. You look interesting," is giving something to most men—your time, involvement, and interest—that they do not normally get. It is giving them a rare gift in our stressed-out, time-budgeting world.

But would you get them to listen to your story through seduction, flattery—or simple honesty?

One approach, *honestly*, would be to be yourself. It is not something that is tried often; but—often enough—it does work.

But what about *their* story? Even though we are making up the story imaginatively—you might find that *their* stories and yours are quite similar. So many of us have been through similar experiences—leaving home, trying to establish lives on our own—that gay stories have an amazing universality to them. So it is possible that unconsciously, in a similar way, if *he* attempted this exercise, he would find you fitting easily into his own imaginative story.

This means that in his own way—if *he* could honestly realize his intentions—he would be telling you about his day, his cares, problems, and desires. And, to be honest, his fears. And always, in the story, we would find some of the same themes: trying to love ourselves, and others. Trying to get to know someone else, as difficult as that is. Trying to get over our fears of strangers, rejection, pain, violence, and ridicule.

The object of this exercise then is simple: one thing bringing other men into your story does, is to get you away from your *own* fears.

Most gay men in social situations now operate on fear: after the last decade and a half of AIDS, heightened homophobic violence, and techno-emotional meltdown (translation: we spend too much of our lives involved with technology, in order not to have genuine emotional lives at all), fear has become a more natural response to us than sexual feelings. Fear has become, in fact, the dominant feeling of the 90s. So the question is, how do we get past this generalized atmosphere of fear—your own fears and those of other men—and connect?

Bringing men towards you imaginatively is a good way to start. Later in this book, I will go into how your own imagination will find parts of you that you've lost. These are deeper, kinder, genuinely self-loving parts. But for right now, just begin to think about other men in a warmer, more rewarding way. Hold them closer to you, even on this imaginative level. Often, if you let yourself "go ahead" with this, you will start to smile. You will start to like that feeling of trusting your own imaginative self with other men. Of simply allowing yourself, imaginatively, to hold them closer to you. This feels very good—and if it causes you to smile in front of someone you might be interested in (without being on one of the several "designer" disco drugs that many men now take for this express purpose)—what is so terrible about that?

The answer: smiling is always a good way to open barriers, even if only slightly.

Despite our lip-service intentions of leveling every playing field, most of us still feel huge divisions of generation, race, class, body type, politics, and attitudes between us and other men. So now we look for things we have *in common* (the currently fashionable "networking" goal so many gay situations have turned into), and dismiss men with whom we feel we have no commonalities, who are not, in short, "usable" to us. This puts us into a smaller and smaller box of sameness, which, for many of us, the "liberated," contemporary gay world is all about. But actually our external differences can add meaning and excitement to our meetings—once we become open to them. Once we realize the astounding array of gifts gay men have for us. That is, once we decide that we'd like to learn things from other gay men, and find out things about ourselves as well.

My best friend, Jeff Campbell—who unfortunately died of AIDS five years ago—and I had very little in common, except the fact that we were both open to loving one another. I was too "intellectual" for him. He loved basketball, smoky gay bars, discos, and high-energy younger guys. We had a tremendous amount of fun together, and I learned a great deal from him. He allowed me to express things about myself that I could not with other people. I could be raunchy, funny, irreverent—and also angry, pissed off, and honestly in pain. He had been through all of that, and knew exactly where it was all coming from. Yet, when people met Jeff and me, they would ask, "*What* do you two have in common?" And I would answer, "Only the fact that we can love each other."

We met in April of 1986 at an early AIDS demonstration in Washington, in front of the White House. People were picketing in a circle around us, and he walked up to me and smiled. I quickly realized that we were both from the South—something we had in common—and that we had no problems meeting people we wanted to talk to. Obviously there was some kind of imagination—a "gay" imagination—working there. Jeff and I could imagine liking each other. We could imagine putting aside the usual reservations people have and establishing a friendship. It was something we intended to do; and we could realize that intention.

Men often ask me, "How do I meet guys? How do I enter the gay *cruisarama* and come back with an experience that does not make me feel like *shit*? In other words, how do I meet men in an atmosphere that often feels *designed* to reduce my self-worth?" They want to get off the merry-go-round of rejection that the gay world has become. (A perfect example are the "circuit parties," which now screen men for muscularity and youthfulness, giving birth to a new tribe of hairless, pumped up, aging *youth* impersonators: our successors to an older version of *female* impersonators.)

These men are afraid to make the first steps towards their own self-acceptance and the acceptance of others. They feel no alternative to the culture of rejection, to the gay shopping mall mentality that very much seems to surround us.

What can they do? How can they do it?

The answer is we *will* have to strengthen our own imaginations, our imaginative powers to connect with other men. We need to use the kind of imaginative exercises actors use even before approaching a script and then an audience. Any actor will tell you that stage fright is a real part of acting, and the adrenaline it produces can add excitement to the play. In this case, the "play"—which does have its own script (although not always a set, formal one) is meeting strangers. But we don't want our stage fright—and all the other fears behind it—to destroy completely our ability to "play."

So we need to prepare. This can be done through imaginative exercises. Through approaching a "script" that we are writing in our minds. One that says we are now a living, important part of the action. We are no longer on the sidelines, a "by-product," lucky only if we score. But we are truly coming into contact with a richer, more voluptuous part of ourselves.

In doing these exercises, we will have to build our imaginations back up, like a set of weakened muscles. Just as many suburban kids have

26

almost forgotten how to walk, we will have to relearn how to meet, listen to, and engage each other. We now have a new generation of puny Charles Atlas wannabees silently posing and kicking sand in the faces of other queer "loser weaklings," only to feel (under their steroid attitudes) even more rejected than the previous generation. So why not build up an imagination that connects us with other gay men? Why not strengthen it with the same kind of determination many of us have invested in our bodies? Why not go back into that wonderful, private room of our sexual feelings—before it became so dense with fears and anxieties, so crowded with impossible cardboard "porno" figures—and see what kind of unexpected space is in it for others?

This is the real sexual "holy of holies"—that place porn writers always want to hand us on a plate. But, in reality, it is that private chamber of our most basic sexuality, the unclothed "chat room" of our own primal lives. The place where we contact both ourselves and other men. It is us— naked, direct, and whole. Some of us remember it as the first time we ever had sex; the first time we ever fell in love, or knew we could be excited— maximally—by another man.

You may remember it, physically, as a room with showers in it. Or a room in a distant dorm, or in an apartment that you can see completely, down to the sheets on the bed. (I always associate it with chlorine, since one of the first, full-bodied turn-ons I ever had was at an old "Y" swimming pool in Savannah.) This is a room from our memories, or dreams. Others may see it simply as an orgy room, with no inhibitions at all—just the wonder of gorgeous gay sex itself.

Now we might find, when we return imaginatively, privately, to this room, that there is *more room* in the room than we thought. If—and that *if* is important—we can return to it before we became turned off by fear. But if we can, *imaginatively*, turn the fear aside, we will find this room is once more private, warm, and very . . . very sexual.

Suddenly, the room—*our* room—is as wild, raunchy, and thrilling as our deepest fantasies. And, most wonderful of all, there is room for a lot of *different* men in all of our room's secret places.

The men are older—and younger. And if you let yourself go down deeper (and even deeper), you'll find guys of a whole range of different body and character "types." They are not just your "public" type—the airbrushed, centerfold dudes you might drool to your friends about—but men who don't look like they just crawled out of a gym. Or a Gianni Versace ad. Or even a "Bear" calendar.

These are the private men whom you tucked away, because your bar "friends" (all of your buddies whom you're sure are staring at you—and inhibiting you) would never approve. These are the same men who want just as deeply as you want. And they feel equally as deeply. They are gorgeous and fabulous, and, too often, like you, they are very much *forgotten*.

They also bust out of whatever you thought your "type" was. (As an ex-porno writer, I'm always amazed at guys who tell me they could not "get into a story." "He wasn't *my* type." The imagination does not have a *type*. It breaks open and celebrates *all* types.) So there are men in your private room (the room you are now decorating to your own taste—with bodies and faces, as well as extra places to fuck) who may be physically remote from your past fantasies and self-limited experiences, or physically disabled, or physically/sexually in a direction you might have wanted to explore but censored yourself away from. These men have also pursued very interesting, not always public, sides of themselves, and they want you to discover that as well.

They are all in your room. Waiting.

These are the men who *want* to become a part of your story, and imaginatively they are already in it. This is your own room, and it is getting wilder, warmer, and more satisfying by the minute. And the only thing that is holding you from it is your own fear of walking in.

We have to go back to this wonderful primal "sex room" of our imaginations to find men, meet them, and then bring them back to the "real" world—where they do exist. But without strengthening this imaginative ability and seeing the depth and richness of many men—and what they have to give us—meeting anyone becomes more difficult, tense, and fearful. The very situation in which we find ourselves already.

I have often said about homosexuals that I can't stand the "professionals," only the gifted amateurs. Part of realizing your intentions is finding out what gifts other men have to give *you*. In other words, giving them credit for their own inner resources. Too often because of internalized homophobia, we feel that we are the ones doing all the giving. I hear repeatedly: "What a great catch *I* am," and then I wonder why nobody is catching him!

This feeling comes from the idea that other gay men are incapable of doing anything except criticizing or testing us. We either pass the test (score) or fail (are rejected). So realizing that other men have things to give us is important. That we can explore and enjoy other gay men, without miserable rejection anxieties, without playing rejection games (who is smarter, bigger, richer, etc.), is a gift. And knowing this—that you are *not* there to play games—is an important part of realizing intentions.

As you have seen, one of the ideas I will talk about in this book is the *culture of rejection* we live in. It is part of our shopping mall mentality: either we buy or refuse *everything*, and since the cost of buying anything in our information-glutted age becomes higher and higher (something else to deal with; something else to evaluate and then toss out), it becomes easier to reject it all at once. *Next!* This attitude joins our own internalized homophobic feelings, so approaching men becomes harder and harder. Yet, amazingly, we want to keep on meeting people, especially meeting other gay men.

Why? Why do we want to keep on meeting other men, despite the problems, fears, rejections, and the gathering stigma around strangers? Or, to be more specific, a stigma that is re-gathering: meeting strangers has always been fairly taboo in American Anglo-Saxon society. Meeting strangers leads to "adultery," and we know what kind of scarlet letter that leaves you with.

(At this point, we have the *Scarlet Q*, the letter that says you are a "queer" who *still* wants to meet other men.)

The answer is that meeting people is a normal, exciting part of human existence. Like homosexuality, it is something that Judeo-Christian societies want to control; but inside us we maintain a normal, desirable curiosity about others. It is something that wants to be satisfied. Strangers have become suspect and terrifying to us, inflated to Godzilla-evil by the mass media that loves finding a serial killer behind every tree. So we have turned to safer, cardboard celebrity figures as the "strangers" we want to meet. The cult of celebrity and the sales-generated "Celebrity Interview" have taken the place of meeting new people and talking to them. But this does not satisfy the need we have to meet others. To see new people—to find fresh faces in our "village." And, frankly, to see them sexually.

This is a need that we play down. To most, it is embarrassing. In a pre-TV era, there were places—bars, squares, taverns, the beach—where the entire town went out to "cruise." You went there to look at people, admire them, gossip, and see who and what was new. It was part of civilization and an accepted part of civilized society. Civilized people could look at each other with a sense of trust. Uncivilized ones were still cooking each other on spits.

Lately, even the vocabulary of meeting new men—"Hello, how are you. I've never seen you here. Would you like to join me?"—seems stilted and unnatural. It frightens us. "What do I say?" you ask yourself. He's looking at me. What do I say? Even smiling seems stressful, even though smiling is a normal facial expression. (Fact: It is easier, muscle-wise, to smile than to frown.)

This is mostly because we have come to expect rejection. That *he* will pass us by in the shopping mall. And we are not sure that what we have to offer—muscles, money, youth, etc.—will give us the ticket to ride home in his car.

The real sin of Sodom and Gommorah, contrary to Pat Robertson, was not "sodomy." Sodomy had been going on in the lands of the Fertile Crescent way before there was a Sodom. Sexual intercourse with men had a language of its own, and just as with intercourse between the sexes, it all depended upon the setting to determine its meaning. In other words, there was good fucking (between friends) and bad fucking (humiliation, rape). It was as simple as that. You did not have to be a Sodomite to know it. The Old Testament's problem with Sodom was that by blurring the line between good sex (which embodies a promise of caring) and bad sex 29 (translation: male rape), the Sodomites were really guilty of a violent transgression against the ethics of hospitality. They took violent advantage of strangers; they were not offering real protection. They could not imagine treating strangers warmly, affectionately, and decently. We find this same situation towards strangers repeated too often now. So today, in America we are *all* Sodomites, with not nearly enough sodomy going on!

---

Nuts & Bolts Department:
Eight (Fairly Easy) Ways to Meet Strangers
(translation: Pick Up Men, Instead of Just Standing There.)

---

"Can you help me with — (*moving my car; tying my shoe; lugging this huge five-pound bag of groceries*)?" When you find the *right* man, being helpless is a great invitation. His response is also a good indicator of how open he is to you revealing your desire to meet him. His openness, in fact, is a lovely gift he is giving you, just as you are giving him one with yours. So, if he cannot stop to help you at all, he's probably the wrong guy. (Or else you will have to work even harder to overcome his shyness.)

"I like the way your (*shirt, pants, eyes, teeth, hair, shoulders, chest, or crotch*) looks." Despite everything, flattery has not gone out of style.

"I had no idea I could do this here." ["Do what?"] "Come over and talk to you."

"Sorry, for a moment I thought you were my cousin (*Vinny, Alfred, Abner?*). You look just like him." I've been told Gregory Peck and Cary Grant both used this line often.

"Would you mind if I bought you a drink?" [Often one of the best investments you can make. Now that smoking and drinking are *over*, how do strangers ever meet? "Can I buy you a Big Mac?"]

"I thought this place would be a lot more (*empty, crowded, fun, hot, cheap, expensive?*)." If he looks at you like you're too dumb to deal with, then don't worry. You can always tiptoe out.

(Smile, then say:) "This is a dumb thing to say, but I would really like to (*meet you, ask you back to my apartment, get your phone number?*)" Direct. To the point. But smile a lot while you do it.

"You remind me of someone I used to know." (World's oldest line: but it works.)

Finally, best bit of how-to: words are not as important as *sincerity*. If he cannot see that—if your sincerity is completely off his imaginative map (which, unfortunately, is crowded with put-downs and self-loathing)—then you just picked a *lemon*. It does happen. Gay men are often mirrors for each other: our put-downs are for the most part self-put-downs. But remember: now that you have imagined what it would be like to have your intentions realized, know that any rejection is not nearly as bad as

believing you *cannot* realize your intentions.

That is rejecting yourself, before you even start.

When meeting a man in the flesh for the first time, either from a Personals ad, the Internet, etc. Try: "I never expected you to look this good"; or, "You are much more interesting in real life." And don't be afraid of being nervous. Nervousness is *real*, and reality is, despite all the media b.s. to the contrary, wonderfully fresh, exciting . . . and seductive.

Another bit of advice (which I will talk about often): believe in the total *magic* of unbidden (or freewill) offerings. Something wonderful that comes to you without asking for it. (Or, as we used to say in the old days, is "laid on you.") Many men question these unasked for gifts, because they question their own worthiness. But in our own, very important gay mythos (the feelings and beliefs that shape us; what I call the "gay cosmology"), the *right* man will see your own worthiness, so don't deny it when it comes. And it will if you invite it by your own kindness, which, as an attitude, in many contemporary gay settings seems almost shocking, but which should be there.

Kindness, as something to be practiced, takes strength and a recognition of purpose—which, once more, is to realize your own intentions. To make them *real*. To show that you are a feeling, valuable man.

Too often, we are led to people only by their "usefulness" in our lives. When we cannot see this usefulness, we cannot see them. But having kindness and love brought to you, without asking, is one of life's great gifts. And often it will be dropped at your feet by smiling, by being kind yourself, and showing interest in another person.

Another exercise: Look around you. Keep your eyes open and see others. Notice them. You don't have to stare, but you can take them in. Start looking at men with *kindness* (this may be a hard one: we are too used to looking at them like layouts in men's magazines). Let their humanness start to appeal to you. This is part of the story that *they* are telling, that you are making a part of your *own* story. Younger men are fresh and vulnerable; older men are poignant—they (okay, *we*) have been through a lot. We have a lot of stories inside us. A lot of testimonies to give. Seeing men this way is a delicious, wonderful feeling. Men become immensely sexy. Even with all their clothes on.

As a writer, I do this as a matter of course—and think it's sad that I have to use a professional excuse to do it. Often I pretend that I am in a foreign country, and I am looking at everything as a tourist, a visitor. In New York, that's easy. The city is constantly foreign. But I do it as well when I leave New York, and it is then that I find that adventures take place. I become open to others. This takes a certain amount of courage, and I, too, close down at times, and become like anyone else. But the important thing is to keep your mind, soul, and imagination open. You are telling a story—your own—and there should be others in it. That is your intention: to realize your *own* story. But the question is: How will you realize it?

In some of the other chapters, I will deal with rejection, that most difficult, deflating, and disappointing of feelings. The one thing I can say at this point, though, is that if you are going to let out and use your imagination—one of the deepest components of your *soul*, in other words—there must be room in it for this. Don't invite it—or expect it (rejection gets enough invitations already). But you have to leave some room for it and know that your own *particular* beauty—in that larger, more wonderful room of your own life—can contain rejection. It can watch rejection do its own little nasty dance, and, with the right strategy, take care of it.

"The absence of tricks desexualizes a situation, and brings a kind of good 'clean' fun to it. But maybe tricks weren't meant for that."

CHAPTER 2

# The Holy Trick

This chapter is about something that many (okay, most) gay men feel they are experts on: tricking. Or, quick, casual (and what I like to call "spontaneous") sex. Usually performed with someone whom you have hardly known for any amount of time. If at all. To begin at the beginning: I am always—and I do mean *always*—amazed that even the most upright, p.c., and "enlightened" of gentlemen, the kind who would never, *ever*, let even the least racial, ethnic, or class epithet slip their unsullied lips will— at the drop of a Kleenex—condemn someone for being a trick.

I am sure you have probably heard these remarks yourself: "He's some stupid trick I met." "*She* [as in male or female] came to dinner and brought one of her tricks!" "You're not the sort of person I would treat like a trick."

Sure. There they go again, mouthing off about "tricks" as if they had never been one. And never would be, either.

Now, a trick, unless you've been sleeping under toadstools for the last century, is a casual, throwaway, sexual encounter. The term *trick* first came about, sex-wise, via the slang of prostitutes. A trick was a "john." A man who expected sex, got it, and then either threw you out or you got rid of, but not before he threw a little green your way. A trick came into your life for a specific purpose. You fucked him. Blew him. Got him off— then got him out. Gay-wise, he might do the same thing to you, but the idea was that whatever you did was designed not to have any more per- manent effect on you that a quick Egg McMuffin.

A *trick*—in short—*was gay fast-food.*

For young men of my own generation, in the 1960s, not being a trick was paramount. A lot of us must have gotten our cues from our older sis- ters, who were told not to put out until they got the ring, or at least a box of Godivas, a fox stole, and some nice jewelry.

In short, *men* should work for it. You just did not give sex away, 33 whether it was of the female or male variety. And if you did, then you were cheap. You were trash. You were the sort of person even *you* did not want to bring home to dinner.

So not being a trick was important. And at that time, among men of the more polite classes, not treating each other like a "trick" was considered excellent manners. We are not talking here about "gay manners"; these were straight manners. Queers treated each other like tricks. Straight men who just "happened" to be queer (at least were queer some-*times*, like when their mommies weren't looking) never treated one another like tricks. So there was a very involved etiquette involved with tricking, in order *not* to give the impression to a trick that he was . . . a trick.

First, you had to exchange names. Get one point for using your entire name. Not a fake name. Not just a nickname. But a real, whole name. "Hello. I'm Edward Foofyard Van Gleason IV. *How do you do?*"

Second: You invited the trick home. There, you put out your best towels (no tacky little "trick towels" for this trick). Two points.

Next, offer the trick a drink. A real drink. No bar scotch for our new friend. Then maybe even a bite to eat. Okay, a quick bite. One more point.

Now things heat up. And you have white-hot, over-the-top, trick sex, the kind of sex you might expect to have with the *perfect* stranger. Wild, non-stop. One hundred percent and still counting. You do this when everything about "said stranger" is still dewy, rosy, full of good Scotch and stark naked desire.

Yep. You know this might not be the most romantic sex in the world, but is it HOT! So you pulled out about 98% of your sexual repertory, and you did all this with (ohhhmygod. . . ! ) a *trick*.

Now, you get five more points *if* in the morning you offer the trick (okay, your new buddy, Carter Wilson Avery Hipplewhite III) a decent breakfast, a shower, the use of the guest toothbrush—and, finally, you exchange phone numbers.

Now, at last, here is where two gentlepersons distinguish themselves from the scum around them. At the doorway, they pledge that they will call each other soon. They will keep in touch. They won't be just *tricks*. And then they part.

And, of course, the host throws the trick's name away and the trick throws away the name of his host. Because they've already done everything that was necessary to do to each other; and they  probably will see each other again (at some old watering hole where the discreet elite greet). But there's no need to carry it further, even though they both had an abso-fucking-lootly *fabulous* time. . . . but, nobody treated anybody like he was . . . (Hell, can we say it?) . . . a **trick**.

(Or, as Cole Porter, who knew a lot about high-society tricking, said: "It was great FUN, but it was just ONE of those things.")

34    Being a trick is low. It's *schmutzy*. It's redolent of dirty towels and old

jars of Lube. It's an extension of that "gay contract" that said that we can have hog-heaven sex behind closed doors, but out in the real world we'll have to pretend to be casual acquaintances. Maybe even pretend to be strangers once more.

In the old days, in fact, learning to be a stranger with a trick was part of Gay 101. You *tricked* with a trick. You did not go to bed with social equals—that was really tracking crap across Grandma's Persian carpets. That *was* shitting where you ate. The tricking relationship was casual and embarrassing. It was like scooping up poop from the gutter and bringing it into your house. Homosexual sex and whore sex were considered on the same par. Except that whore jokes were funny, and queer jokes were too threatening ever to be funny. One of the worst things you could do, in the closet, was get a queer joke too fast. The other worst thing you could do was recognize a trick.

After tricking, tricks were supposed to be invisible.

This last bit of folk knowledge has remained, like a remnant of Jim Crow racism, in gay life to this day. I remember reading in *Metrosource*, a trendy New York gay magazine, that the institution of *brunch* was for friends, not for tricks. "You never bring a trick to brunch. You brunch with your friends."

Yeah, sure. Since when? Since at least a few of your gay friends may start out as tricks, this seems like a strange statement. But the concept is to elevate brunch—and the kind of gayish restaurants that serve it—to a coy level outside of vulgar tricking. To take it to a place where queers go and check their dicks at the door, along with their coats and wallets.

The absence of tricks, then, desexualizes a situation, and brings a kind of good "clean" fun to it. But maybe tricks weren't meant for that.

### Tricking As Ritual

What takes tricking out of the gutter is when another "agenda" is involved. *Agenda* is a twenty-cent word for any activity that either introduces, adds to, or temporarily gets your mind off tricking. Say, you go out bowling with a bunch of friends. Suddenly in the middle of a spare, you notice an attractive man in the other lane. Eyes meet. He's on another team. You know who he is. But you haven't looked at him in a sexual way before. Like I said, you know who he is: you've heard about his story. You've been introduced and now, suddenly, he's there. A sexual green light is going on, and you can't keep your mind off him.

You can't treat him like a trick, but you do want to seduce him. You want to do this very badly. You can, in fact, as they say, "taste him."

The radar you are sending out definitely has sex in it. It's like you are suddenly sending out a giant searchlight, originating from a very phallic source of power. (Okay, maybe even the *original* phallic source of power.) Even more amazing, your *radar* has become more intensified because he—let's call him Arthur—has become more *real* to you. Its signals have hit something you can connect with on an authentic, emotional level, if you let yourself.

You know something about him. Perhaps, say, that he's been through a hard time lately. You feel, oddly, softened in your feelings toward him. Your heart has gone out to him, and now the strangest thing has happened: your *dick* has followed it.

Frequently sexual feelings follow other intense feelings, as much as we try to neaten them up with a pretty little bow. It is not uncommon for two men at a memorial service to suddenly find themselves unbearably sexually attracted to each other, and feeling like rotten shit about it. "This can't be happening! Ralph's dead! And now all we want to do is jump into the sheets with each other! What *sort* of people are we?"

The old homophobic answer was: "What else? Queers sexualize everything!" But the reality is that intense *sexual* feelings follow other feelings. This of course confuses many people, and adds a lot of bewilderment and guilt to their lives. The Yiddish writer Isaac Bashevis Singer reported that a huge amount of plain, unvarnished *fucking* went on in the concentration camps during World War II. People of every sexual stripe crawled into bed with each other. Whether the cause of this was fear, misery, hunger—no one can tell—but nothing stopped sexual feelings. This is something that "enlightened" Western bourgeois civilization has tried to squelch for the last century, and it led Freud to declare that "normalcy" was being able to keep a job, get married, and have children. In other words, to keep "trick" situations as far as possible away from *normal* life.

Getting back to our friends at the bowling alley, the question is: how will they have sex with one another as acquaintances—who know something about each other—and not end up as "tricks"? Will the trick sex put an end to any friendship that can happen? Or, will they bypass spontaneous, hot trick sex and go on to a more formalized, romantic relationship—which neither of them may be interested in? Much of the answer to this will depend upon how much our friends—and we—still stigmatize tricks. And how much room we will allow in our lives for spontaneous, hot trick sex, even if we don't admit that it comes from "tricks."

Gay men, rather than deleting the inherent sexuality from life, often eroticize men who take "normal" or mundane roles in their lives: firemen, policemen, auto mechanics, soldiers. These are men that gay men, as outsiders, often see in a power position, even though those inside these positions might deny it. Since we often think of ourselves as being outside a "normalcy" which forbids tricking, we see "normalcy" itself as an erotic (or "trick") situation.

Likewise, gay men who are involved with a certain part of a culture will eroticize other men who are active in it: thus servicemen may find other servicemen attractive—they have shared the discipline of military experiences and many forms of hell itself. Out of this has emerged a hardened, often homophobic sexual mythology in which both gay military men and their straight peers play a part. (An old line dating back to World War II which, despite all of our recent turmoil about "gays in the military," aptly describes this is: "Half the Navy's queer and the other half is glad!")

Gay yuppies find a man in a business suit exciting. He represents the power that they want and that they are usually trying hard to swim through, without "making waves." There is something subtle then—and commanding—about office drag, so that recently it has figured in porn scenarios that twenty years ago would have ridiculed men in suits.

Being *inside* the "culture" keeps the "trick" feelings that we associate with throwaway sex *out*. You cannot denigrate men with whom you have sexual feelings as "tricks," if you'll see them again and again in a formal or work setting. In short, there are deep, conflicting—and enticing—feelings working here.

Any form of shared experience under duress can bring out these feelings. Often we try hard to control them, since control is the *essence* of the male role in society. Sometimes the aura around the experience becomes so intense that it produces a special "safety island," free of "trick" guilt and anxiety.

An example of this is fisting, which has such an aura of danger and specialness to it, that the trick role in it becomes lost in its rituals and preparations. This creates a special intimacy for the people involved, but an intimacy which is enclosed in the act itself: you reveal more of yourself in fisting (and other forms of "fetish" sex) than in more routine sex, but only within this environment. In other words, a trick you fist is much less "throwaway" than a trick you just blow, fuck, or jerk off with. There is a kind of "grit," or difficulty, involved with fisting and other fetishistic forms of sex, and grit provides a degree of friction—and closeness—that "smooth" sex, or what S & M people called "vanilla sex," does not.

Fisting and other forms of S & M also allow—dramatically—for more of the "submission/surrender" transactions that I will describe later as vital parts of the gay mythos to take place. This, in turn, adds an emotional depth to sex that keeps some of the more casual, trick element from it; although some of the more formalized structures around S & M sex (the working out of "contracts," for instance) can work to keep its emotional content from running away with you.

Other situations like this are "Body Electric"-type courses, in which emotions are revealed in a controlled way, and gay "Outward Bound"-type tours, in which gay men get together under rugged outdoor situations, often exposing themselves to a type of duress that kindles sexual feelings, even if they are not acted upon. Heavy romantic buttons are pushed this way, which can play havoc with plain old "trickiness."

During the 70s, for the first time, multitudes of very nice middle-class men started going to "down-and-dirty" on-site sex bars whose attractions were a kind of staged, amusement park sleaze. These bars combined working-class roughness with S & M scenarios, which previously had seemed like only the flip side of most standard gay environments. (A kind of "Yesterday's drag queen is tomorrow's Leather Boy" attitude.)

So sex there became "serious." It might have been the same trick sex that happened in a bathhouse or at home with a stranger whose name would only appear a week later on the back of a matchbook cover. But it was negotiated underground, with an inch of bilge water at your feet in the midst of men wearing real dirty T-shirts and who'd gone out without a drop of cologne on. For many men, these experiences were absolutely liberating. They took them out of the "trick experience," which used to be part of gay bars with foofy music and twinky waiters, and brought them into a ritual of real men and real environments, which had not been devised by uptown decorators (although they might have been engineered by downtown ones).

By "de-tricking" these environments, many men felt a brotherhood and tribal closeness with other gay men that they had not allowed themselves to feel before. They felt that they were connecting on a more serious, raw level. In reality, they may not have been connecting any closer than men who had met in twinkie-foofy bars, but the aura of seriousness and "reality" in these on-site sex bars (manufactured as it might have been) opened up more than a throwaway, "trick" attitude towards gay sex for many men.

To the ancient pagans, tricking—hot, wild, and spontaneous—was considered part of life. It fed a respectable appetite, just like food did. Just as you would have to pay for your daily bread, sex was an expense that you *would* have to pay for. It would not just drop off the trees. The gods, who could playful—and horny—as well as serious, made sure of that. If you wanted a little *nookie*, you had to leave something in return. There was absolutely no getting around it: every pleasure had its expense. You got what you paid for, but you could—eventually—get it.

Or—if you were *really* cursed—you paid double for it.

Later the humorless, monotheistic One God did this as well, although payment to Him exploded out of all previous proportions. He was not going to let your Crayons wander out of His rigid lines at all. This may be the reason why tricks to this day have taken on such a bad name.

The Bible *is* filled with examples of tricking: of hot, spur-of-the-moment sex—that must be paid for, often, as we say, "in spades." In the tight, cause-and-effect world of the Old Testament, the result was humiliation and devastation. In the story of Sodom and Gomorrah, Lot, a stranger who has settled in Sodom, is visited by two angels. He invites them into his house as part of his natural custom of courtesy, because he knows what it means to be a stranger himself. The men of Sodom, hearing that he has two new "tricks" in his house, come to him demanding that he hand the strangers over to them, and that their sexual use of these two men will be part of Lot's price for staying within the walls of their town.

The men of Sodom see that Lot, himself a stranger, has invited these strangers into their midst. Therefore, the townsmen—checking their own domestic morals at Lot's door—want to have sex with them, since they are sure they will not see them again. In ancient Mesopotamia, this sort of casual sexual relationship with strangers (male or female) was not uncommon, although—as in our day—it was not particularly smiled at, since it denied the contracts and duties that more regulated sexuality demanded. Often this type of sexual gratification was part of the "price" of taking people in—of giving them food and drink. The only protection from this was to say that you, as a stranger, were "family." You would have to prove that you were part of someone's kinship network (and therefore, not just a trick). In a time of small, walled towns isolated on a desert, this would not be all that difficult: everyone was someone else's cousin.

God, of course, being vengeful, punished the wicked Sodomites (as well as their kids and wives) for a practice that seemed fairly normal to them: wanting "free" sex from strangers (in other words, taking advantage of their availability), instead of offering them the simple kindness of shelter. Free sex without guilt, history, or strings attached was even then a rare commodity. You had to pay for sex with your wife by providing for her and your children. Sex with relatives was unthinkable, going against incest taboos. And sex with neighbors, as you can guess, was as difficult then as now.

The only opportunity open, then, was sex with strangers.

Or, as we'd say, "trick" sex.

The other form of "free" (i.e., unmarried) sex that was common in the ancient Middle East was temple prostitution. Ishtar, the goddess of both war and beauty and Astarte, the serene goddess of the moon and fertility, employed droves of prostitutes in their temple compounds. Often these prostitutes were men who dressed in drag and performed ritual fellatio with worshipers, who paid them a "sacrifice" of coinage which went in part, legally, to the temple. The ancient Hebrews swore off temple prostitution, but on occasion returned to the practice, probably because it was the only way single women (who had no property or herds to sacrifice) could give to the Temple. Some Hebrew texts show that men also engaged in sexual temple work, but this was spoken of harshly, since it meant that men were engaging in the same practices as unpropertied, cast-off women.

To the ancient Jews casual sex was thought of in the same terms as rape, since sex always carried such a high price: marriage and involvement with kinship. With this in mind, the Levitical law against "man lying with man as if with woman" makes sense, since there was no way that a man could make another man "pay" the price he would have to pay with a woman. He could not be forced to make the man his wife; he could not swear to protect him and his kin forever, etc. Since sex in the Bible was often used as a tool of humiliation, this injunction prevented

Hebrew men from "humiliating" strangers in their midst, that is, by "tricking" with them.

In my novel *Mirage*, I wrote about the male temple prostitutes of Inanna, the earlier Sumerian name for Ishtar. I was impressed that harlots and priests in ancient Sumerian texts were often spoken of together. In the famous "Inanna texts," which are the oldest writings in the world, sexual practices are talked about with amazing frankness. One idea that is repeated in many ancient texts is that the harlot was considered, basically, another specialist. Her (or in some cases *his*) specialty was sex. It was an honorable profession, and any association with her/him was considered not at all degrading.

This idea did not completely evaporate through Western history. Kings had their courtesans, and queens their male favorites, and sometimes kings, too, had male "favorites," or lovers. This was, however, denied in public, and the idea of going to see a sexual "specialist," one who is not treated as a *pervert* or an expendable object, cast off like a used rubber, has completely died out. He's gone.

Except in one instance. He has re-emerged, to a degree, in the gay persona of the *trick*, the creature who enters our life solely for sexual purposes—and then leaves it, with all his sexual magic intact. And ready, soon enough, for his next act of magic—the next "trick"—which we realize, despite all of our reservations and the situation's fairly predictable tawdriness, will thrill us.

That is, if we give the "trick" the respect his performance deserves.

It always amazes to me that this "trick" is not the most honored persona in the gay pantheon. In this hall of the gay gods we already have the diva goddess—whether she's Maria Callas, or Judy, Barbra, or Madonna. We have the bitch next door, who has all the dirt on you and your boyfriend and a tongue that would make an adder wince (she might be Bette Davis or any of the women from *Melrose Place*). We also have the tired George Sanders queen who talks in Oscar Wildean epigrams ("No good deed goes unpunished!"), and who's been everywhere and done everything. And the blushing virgin boy fresh from any current Fox network series, whom everyone wants at the party, and the Jonathan-and-David couple who are the current role models of the age (*Rod and Bob?*—oh, well).

But where is the "trick"? Where is the holy man who comes in as the soul of sex, who delivers himself to you, purely for sexual reasons, and then leaves after making you—and himself—feel really satisfied? Or even blessed?

Sorry. Our friend *Trickie* is still in the closet.

He is put down as a bimbo. A slut. A worthless peckerhead who's only good between the sheets—as if this were such an odious position. Our daily language is now pepper-gassed with homophobia and anti-sexuality. A worst, kids' put-down is, "It sucks," like a great blow-job is the twentieth century's vilest act. The fact that Hugh Hefner was the ultimate heterosexual "trick," who showed straights how to get fabulously laid—and made a fortune doing it—completely escapes the gay world. We have no Hef. Instead we have Gore Vidal, Quentin Crisp, Andrew Holleran, Larry Kramer, David Leavitt, and Michelangelo Signorili: none of whom have exactly given sex a great name.

The closest we have come to the "holy trick" in the gay book trade has been Boyd MacDonald of the famous "Straight to Hell" books and Pat Califia—who truly honors every sexual bend and alley. But I think that the late John Preston (master of the S & M story and an unashamed "pornographer") came closer to it than anyone. I knew and liked Preston and saw him as an underestimated messenger from the divine, who came into our lives bearing only the gift of sex. He wrote about it in a wonderful, meat-and-potatoes language: simple, nourishing, and very hard-on provoking. It's sad that we have given sex such a bad name that simple porno stories have to be hyped up as "literary erotica," but being a holy trick has never been easy.

The closest we came to holy tricks on the screen were some of the porn stars of the late 70s-early 80s, such as the great Richard Locke, Michael Kearns, or Al Parker, who started out either as "real" actors or "real" gay men (unlike Jeff Stryker, they would not have to wake up, hogtied, to get fucked; it was part of their character to begin with). Neither did they feel that working in porn was a step down. But, as exciting as they were, they were always denigrated as *just* porn stars, or had to go legit to make it, or were swept aside by age, the AIDS crisis (which left us with ever drearier porn flicks), or an atmosphere of shame that has washed its way back over sex like so much sewer water.

I would like to see more holy tricks. I want them out of the closet, to bless us with glorious, scrumptious sexuality. I would like them to spread sex like fairy dust. Yes, I want a little night music right now, and I would like men with magically available penises to make it. The kind of dicks that are, in themselves, magic wands light years away from any canned, sanitized Disney version.

And even if you're *not* in the mood for it at this very second, I think these tricks of the future should be *generously* thanked.

"One of the joys of your *own* gay life should be that having a relationship with another man, besides your lover, should not be suspect."

CHAPTER 3

# Is My Lover My Best Friend?

A strange occurrence happened to heterosexuals sometime in the middle of the twentieth century. Men decided that they had to become best *friends* with women. After several thousand years of the War of the Sexes, your closest ally was no longer another man, but a woman who had to be desexualized into being your buddy. This was, for the most part, an American phenomenon. America had gone from a country where women were looked upon as a special interest group (found strictly on the *Women's Page*) to a place where women became looked upon if not as equal in all ways to men, then at least as an equal threat.

At this point, of all things, a man's best friend became . . . his wife.

There were many reasons why this change took place. Part of it was the escape into suburbia, which had no separate culture of its own and which gave people no opportunities to establish the richer social lives that cities did. Most suburban couples meet other couples through their children, at PTA or other school meetings. In other words, they become friends with the parents of the kids their children get along with—a strange way to choose your friends, but then suburban living also gave us the drive-in church. In the suburbs, the church or synagogue became one of the main places for adults to meet. This meant that all your friends had to sing the same moral and social songs that you did. So friendships with strangers—even the most casual ones—became charged with the threat that any revelation of your private life could be dangerous to your status in a small community.

As I said in the previous chapter, strangers themselves became "suspicious," as the social venues of the city, where a variety of people could easily meet, became suspect. Some of this attitude came about as America's World War II mentality (when people became hospitable to soldiers and other friendly strangers at home) gave way to the Cold War, then the push into faceless suburbs. During the Cold War, numerous demagogues equated homosexuality with subversion, so fearing and hating queers and Commies became an attitude expected of "normal" Americans. At that point, meeting any new people in "questionable" (city) situations (bars, parks, clubs, etc.) became even more undesirable.

Civility with strangers became foreign to us, even as waves of immigrants, who might have made us more aware of human difference, rushed in. But civility could also lead to any number of activities, most prominent among them being sex. Life in the suburbs, therefore, meant that couples had to look to themselves as their main means of emotional support. Friendship networks outside work, church, or school tightened. They tightened even further as couples moved around frequently for career purposes, which meant that suburbs filled with (of course) *strangers* became the norm. So we became frightened of strangers, and became strangers even quicker. Because of this newcomers often had to resort to socializing with other couples from work. This meant that any interaction carried with it the threat of being reported back into the work situation.

Suddenly the husband and the wife were thrown solely onto each other, like two sailors cast overboard, clinging to one another out to sea. (In a recent study in *The New York Times*, seventy-eight percent of the husbands queried said that their wives were their best friends; almost double a poll taken twenty years earlier.) In this case, our lonely shipmates might take several years just to swim off, as either their marriage dissolved (remember: first marriages are now called by sociologists "trial marriages") or they clawed each other to bits as the relationship became so stagnant that the couple became merely two roommates with kids attached.

But the other reason why his wife became a man's best friend was that homosexuality had been pushed as far out into the open as it has ever been in our culture. Therefore, any sensitive, intimate relationship between men—the sort of relationship men have had with other males for thousands of years—was pushed under a cloud of suspicion.

Men can no longer gather with each other, either in pairs or in larger groups, without the fear that there is something "unnatural" about it. It now, *per se*, has a "gay" undertone to it. The pleasure of male company stays in question. In fact, any man actively seeking the company of other men would have to explain it first. The most he can say is that he is doing it professionally, for "networking" purposes. Or, as in the case of the new right-wing Christian "Promise Keepers" movement which packs stadiums with crowds of men, he is doing it on religious grounds, to "atone," and then go back to his wife and family a better, more *forgiven* man.

Male companionship has become undesirable. It is almost unthinkable. In countless TV commercials, same-sex company is looked upon as stupid, worthless, or ridiculous. The promise of (or threat of being a failure at) heterosexuality sells products. The idea that a man can actually enjoy himself, his own company, and that of other men, is made to seem "immature" and pointless.

Men who prefer a life of friendship and self-exploration are referred to as "Peter Pans," which carries with it the coded message of "fairyism." What they have done, by not "growing up," is to postpone their participation in the hetero couple market; or they are hiding their own "latent" homosexuality, which itself is considered a sin, in that serious women should have the right to be warned away from closeted men (no matter how much they have to offer) and not waste important, husband-hunting time on them.

Any declaration that the enjoyment of male company might be healthy is quickly made to seem a sick joke. Men who like men are losers. On Jerry Seinfeld's recent popular TV sitcom, *Seinfeld*, Jerry's male friends who associated with other men were either fat, stupid, or socially inept *geeks*. They constantly repeated that something was missing from their lives: the necessary "babe" factor, which worked instantly as soon as a woman walked in. The women, always gorgeous compared with Jerry's pathetic friends, were then presented like dandruff shampoos or mouthwashes. After they were used, personal problems cleared up and the result was momentary happiness. That is, until the end of the episode, when the girls left and Jerry's friends began the babe hunt again.

Not only are men who like men losers, but male company is not even seen as a consolation prize. Rather than have to be with other men, the "normal" man would rather stay home with his computer or play video games. Time with other men is not seen as "quality time." Today people would question why Ralph the bus driver and Ed the plumber spent so much time with each other on the old *Honeymooners* series. The new buddies on TV are men and women, usually husbands and wives. In commercial movies, which are aimed squarely at fourteen-year-old boys, male pairing ("buddyness") is marked by constant violence, competition, aggression, and action. Men can barely touch, except to have their faces kicked by another man. The idea being that at no time can two men actually enjoy each other, except in scenarios that are too "hot" and explosive for women to tag along.

At the same time that men and women are now being paired off in a way that allows no private time for either, homophobia is used openly by many industries, especially those based on communicating "commercial concepts" (translation: something else rather than what is in the product itself) as a selling tool. The main "concept," of course, is for you to keep buying and consuming a lot. But the underlying concept, which is done with a not very subtle twist, is that it is possible to be an avid consumer—to be *consumed*, in fact, by your interest in clothes, cosmetics (i.e., men's grooming lines), furniture, home accessories, music, magazines, etc.—and not be a queer. Whereas in the old days a *real* man disdained clothes shopping as a chore he'd do once a year, dragged around by the wife, now you can be a real man and still buy. And buy. And buy.

A perfect example of this was recently cited by Amy M. Spindler in a *New York Times* article on the new trend-setting English men's fashion magazines *Arena* and *The Face*, that were trying to make an inroad in the American magazine market, despite the fact that their content might have been viewed in this country as too "gay."

"There is a very simple general operating principle for mainstream fashion magazines for men," Spindler says. "Exploit fears. And a fear of forward fashion is among them." What "forward fashion" is easily decoded to mean is explained by Peter Howarth, the editor of *Arena*, and the former fashion editor of British *GQ*, who tries to represent his slant on fashion as "punk," but not *queer*. "The straight-guy phenomenon is all linked to Condé Nast and Hearst. They are so scared in their fashion coverage, and this is where I think they've got it wrong. Over here, there is a tradition of British men dressing up, usually related to music culture. Punk wasn't a gay scene, even if there were some gay punks."

(Basically, this is the same old: "Yeah, I may look like a fag, but I ain't one" story.)

In the fashion world, this has spawned a trend towards "anti-gay" clothes. These span from the ever blander offerings of catalogues like J. Crew, which do 90s versions of grandma and grandpa's WASPy country club *schmattas*, to Hip Hop's baggy oversized T-shirts and pants. Hip Hop's body concealment gets its origins from prison fashions, where showing any body definition was an invitation to gay sex. In the same way, kids now label skin-tight Speedo swim suits and muscle-revealing Lacoste shirts as "fag wear." To wear them means to show a body consciousness that is dangerous, even as our commercial culture sells the male body now as just a piece of fashion. You can have muscles. You can have good skin. You can furnish your apartment so it doesn't look like a dork lives there. And if you play the constant "babe" card, you don't have to be a *queer*.

So men and women, as husbands and wives, have become best friends, as much as they detest it. At a certain age (usually when being single is no longer acceptable to the corporate world that discriminates against the unmarried or the never-married), a man will have to leave his social male friends, and "grow up." This means that through marriage he will have to join what is now the very commercialized world of women (a world that TV makes no bones about playing up to): of constantly improving his house and his family, and both of their values. And during those few hours that a man has to himself (when he is not working, or improving himself through Adult Ed), you will find him with his wife.

Most probably they will be shopping at a mall or going to a mall movie. They may be with other friends or relatives who are coupled up in exactly the same way. This lockstepping of the couples in a way that would have embarrassed Noah finds its most amazing consequence in the idea that single people are considered undesirables in modern hetero coupledom. Since she is now looked upon as her husband's best friend, a wife looks upon a single woman as a threat to her marriage. This is not simply because a single woman might seduce her husband, but suppose an outside woman suddenly became *his* friend? Single men are also a threat because they are considered losers, although they have more value on the couples market than women. The role that single men used to play—that of the adored uncle from the city, the teacher, the adventurer who had stories to tell—is over. He is now either the closet queen or someone who, if he "gets his act together," will grow up and take a wife—that is, if he is not at the moment between marriages.

The reason why I'm bringing all this up is that gays for the most part model their expectations and relationships on straights. This idea seems to be more current than ever because so many gay men want to "universalize" their lives. They want to see that there is no difference between them and the straight world. They want to fit in. Even though they may be more open about the homosexual aspect of themselves than men were a generation ago, they do not want the *sexuality* of their homosexuality to embarrass others. As Larry Kramer recently expounded in a famous *New York Times* op-ed piece, they want to lead "calm, orderly lives."

They want to be a part of a couple and they want this couple to be like their straight neighbors down the corridor in their co-op. They are looking for the one man who will be everything to them the way that a woman is now supposed to be—God help her—everything to a man. They want a man who is their best friend, buddy, intellectual equal, sexual fantasy, career complement ("He makes as much money as I do and his career is something I can take an interest in!"), and who shares their interest in hobbies, musical taste, restaurants, etc. The two of them, in short, should be a living commercial for what straights might believe a gay relationship should be. In many ways, this new couple has been produced by the "mainstreaming" of gayness. They have literally been spawned by Ellen DeGeneres, although in their predictability they would probably be Ellen's nightmare.

This "new" lover situation (now called the "partner") has become more of a networking situation than a romantic one, since the partnership will become a much more public one than gay relationships in the past were. Your new lover will have to pass muster with your friends, family, and even your business acquaintances. These in turn will take on a special patina of intimacy as they become allowed into your own "gay" life. This translates to mean: you introduce your business friends to your same-sex "partner." Your "gay life" then is supposed to start and end with him. Anything else might be considered embarrassing, and your straight friends would have a hard time understanding it.

The seriousness of this pursuit of the "new" lover is exemplified in so many "Personals" ads we see that ask not only for a man of a certain race, size, and sexual categories ("top," "bottom," etc.), but also that he be "straight appearing," "financially solvent," and "a regular guy." Basically: that he should not be a source of discomfort to you on the streets, or at your Aunt Bertha's house, where that very next Sunday after you meet him, he'll be passing the meat loaf.

Please do not feel that this means I think we should all take our boyfriends back into the closet and have a good time with them there. But there are two problems with the New Lover who will be all things to all people.

First, no matter how suitable he is and no matter how good his suits look on him, you may not fall in love with him. This is either because there is nothing there that you can attach your own inner feelings to, or because *he does not know how to appeal to those feelings you are looking to have satisfied*. These feelings are related to what I refer to as the "gay mythos," a working consciousness that affects (but does not control) gay men. I will be speaking about this important gay mythos and its aspects often.

And second, that unlike the straights who are stupid enough to believe that a wife must mean everything on earth to a husband and vice versa (as witnessed by our huge divorce rates), gays should realize that a same-sex lover relationship is a *special* relationship that does not take the place of other important relationships—but should not conflict with them, either. In other words, you don't toss out your relationships with a best friend, other friends, or your family, when you find the person who will be, hopefully, your significant other. Nor will you allow your best friends, other friends, and your family to pass judgment on him.

This is your call and your relationship. So keep it that way.

A lover relationship, in short, is different from a relationship with a friend. Although there may be more tension in a sexual/romantic/lover relationship due to the demands of intimacy, there is also more room for conflict. Very few friendships can stand the stress that a *good* lover relationship can. The emphasis is on good: a lover relationship is not a friendship, in that it is not based on common interests but on *shared* inner feelings. There is an intimacy and sharing of feelings in this form of closeness that can and should stand a lot of slings and arrows—and very few friendships can stand this. (When they do, they are among life's great blessings, but, again, they cannot take the place of having the special person we call, for lack of another name, a lover. Okay, some men are going back to that great word, *husband*.)

Now, one problem many gay men have is that they do put this sort of stress on friendship relationships. Friendship relationships, unfortunately, are rarely this "special," and, for the most part, are more generalized. When two men become lovers, they find that their friendships ebb and flow as their relationship becomes more established. Men who find that their "lovers" come and go while their other friendships remain somewhat more stable, are doing something wrong: they are trying to put the

stresses of an intimate love relationship onto their friends. This is very difficult and for some friends quite bewildering. After the third or fourth attempt at this, some of them may start to ask you to "get a life." In other words, find someone else to become the center of it.

Conversely, these same men often try to make their lovers into their "friends." They want lovers who are "regular guys," "good sports," "pals." They want them to be an extension of either the fuck-buddy or the disco partner. So they generalize and neuter a very specific, important relationship. This takes the passion and commitment needed to cement these important relationships out of them.

The end results are stressed, difficult friendship relationships and shallow, phony lover relationships. Repeat: the lover relationship is a *special* relationship. It does not come about instantly. It requires more energy and it should be able to take more stress. This stress is a normal part of patterned heterosexual relationships ("in sickness and in health, for richer or poorer, till death . . ."); but it is usually considered an ultimate test of gay ones. Very few gay men allow themselves the seriousness of a relationship, one that will develop and mature and that can take a normal lifetime's stress.

Instead, they go about expecting everything they can—in a "Personals" ad, shopping mall way—from many quicker, failure-bound relationships. They expect to find, somewhere out there, the man who will satisfy *all* their needs in a lover, as long as these needs are fairly flat and fulfill a wish list that won't conflict with real human limitations, such as the possibility of illness or a sudden lack of desire that might *not* reflect love, or the loneliness that can come into any relationship, even the most "perfect."

So if your lover is not your "best" friend (in fact, he may not even be a friend, in the scheme of friends being people who come and go in your life: as in work friends, social friends, political friends, etc.), then who is he?

The answer is your lover is a person who satisfies your deepest needs for intimacy, needs that are not only deep in that their roots go back to childhood, but also needs that are broad enough to need satisfying very often, perhaps even every day. These needs may include a variety of problems as well: in short—as I talked about in the chapter on realizing your *intentions*—you will not be putting on a happy face for him every day. But it can't mean using your lover to recycle all those childhood dramas that never got resolved. Part of this intimacy scheme is allowing yourself to grow with him. You will both need to grow in this special way of two men who are open to each other, and yet respectful of one another's need for privacy. (Or what we call, currently, "space.")

## Privacy: A Necessity

Privacy is an important part of any intimate relationship: there should be real privacy involved in a lover relationship that you do not invite 49 your friends to invade. You should feel that this relationship is not really open for their commentaries or suggestions, although in keeping this attitude you don't want to isolate yourself so much from them that it breaks off a needed closeness to them as well. It is a hard call. It is a balancing act, but one that is important to maintain.

The reason for this is that many of your friends may never be able to establish a strong, intimate, sexual relationship. They may have "girlfriends" they can have dinner with (and complain to for hours about what *shits* men are). They may have platonic friends to whom they can show off their knowledge of chintz and china. They may have quick sexual encounters (enter, again, the tricks; now sometimes referred to as "affairettes") who satisfy their needs for attention and adventure. But they will not have the kind of sensitive, committed, resilient, tough, passionate, important connections you will have with a lover.

So of course they would *love* to snap your connection to yours.

They will tell you that he's "not worth it." That he is "using you." That your situation is "dysfunctional," "codependent, "etc. and perhaps bring out other bits of jargon stylish at the moment and that they've heard in the Twelve-Step programs that are (too often) giving them the only relationships they can maintain. (Which leads me to the question of the moment: why are there no Twelve-Step programs for people who are dependent on Twelve-Step programs?) In other words, they would love to wreck your relationship, and are just waiting for a little foot in the door to do it.

They will do this to *prove* their love for you.

Take this advice. Don't let them.

Conversely, your lover may feel threatened by your friends, and he may make your relationship with him contingent upon your increasing isolation. I refer to this as the "It's-just-you-and-me-in-the-same-boat-babe!" complex. This is often caused by insecurities on his part, or, even worse, by his own internalized homophobic feelings. He is sure that all of your friends are out to hurt him—after all, most of the evil people in the world are faggots, right? Your straight friends won't approve of him because, well . . . he's gay. And your gay friends: well, forget them.

So the privacy thing is important both ways. You should demand it from your friends as regards your lover relationship, and you should demand it of your lover regarding your friends. In the beginning this may be very difficult. There are few easy ways around it. After all, you had your friends before you met your lover. They feel that you expect them to like him. Stress number one.

He feels that *you* expect *him* to like them. Stress number two.

They feel that for them to be there for you, they have to solve *all* your problems. Isn't that kind of them? Bingo: number three!

Since you will be spending a lot of time with him in the beginning, the chances are that as your feelings for him make themselves known, you may jettison some of your friends in his favor. Sorry: fact of life.

Your need to have this person in your life—despite the risks involved—will supersede your needs to have X, Y, and Z as friends, even if X, Y, and Z were there when Jurassic Park was a playground. If the thing with Joe (as we'll call him) piffles out, it will be a test of your connections to X, Y, and Z to see if they come back. Sometimes people expect this to happen, and often they will allow you a certain amount of "credit" in your friendship account to allow for these "rainy day" emergencies. (*The Man of Your Life*, for whom you gave up the throne, turns out to be a dud.) But don't expect this to happen too often. Don't expect them to stick around if Joe makes an encore, then another quick exit, then returns with a bunch of wilted daisies and a month-old box of chocolates. Loyalty is lovely; being a patsy—someone used over and over again—is not.

But that sense of privacy that you develop around your relationship, that beautiful little hedge of thorny roses that you have started to cultivate so carefully, can expose something else in the clearest way. Now that you have that very special person who is satisfying your deepest needs for intimacy, your feelings about your friends may really change.

You may see some of them, in fact, as "enemies." Real enemies. As in the old saw, "With friends like these, who *needs* enemies?" Of course you needed them as friends at one time, because your own feelings about yourself were so bad. You were sure that no one else would have you, and they bought you very cheap—simply by paying attention to you.

For years these sort of "enemy-friends" were endemic to gay life. They were the jokes and gist of hundreds of plays and stories, from the acid-faced George Sanders in *All About Eve* to *The Boys In The Band* and then some. They were always giving you a good kick in the teeth of "reality" because only they knew what was good for you. Only *they* were honest enough. Gay friendships were supposed to be based on the lives of Tallulah, Bette, and Judy. When they weren't putting out their cigarettes on your hide and inviting you over to have a fourth martini washed down with a couple of Valium, they were offering to come over and mop up after your latest suicide attempt. In other words, they *loved* your misery. It made their own shit taste so much better.

These were the little darlings who told you (in the nicest way), "Sugar, we love you, but you don't have a *lick* of talent. Give up all those ideas and come down to Earth with us." Or, "Who needs a boyfriend, when you have *pals* like us to stick with you?"

In *Camille*, Marguerite tells her young lover that only her parasitic low-life friends understand her, so she can't give them up no matter how bad they are. In John Cheever's great short story, "The Black Widow," an old friend always comes in to console a failed writer as he sinks into alcoholism and despair. She always appears at the worst moment, until he realizes that she is sucking off his misery. Living on it.

These enemy-friends are the most insidious types, and they despise competition. They will see anyone who deeply loves you as exactly that. Competition. Once you see this dynamic going on between them and the man you've picked to be there for you, resign them to the Late Show. And *don't* tune in often.

Before we wrap this chapter up, one more question:

Now that you realize that your *lover* may not be your "best friend," what happens to that need *for* a best friend, for someone that you can spend time with in a nonsexual but intensely intimate, even passionate way? The answer, I'm afraid, is *it does not go away*. Straights often try to satisfy the need for a best friend with children. This is dangerous, since kids have lives of their own, and most kids at some point will come to feel that Mommy and Daddy are among the world's stupidest people; that is, until they live long enough to know better.

What happens with this need for a best friend is that as your lover starts to satisfy some of it, you can let go of *some* of it as well. And you can generalize the need onto several other men—men who share your interests the way your lover does not. Or men who may be the opposite of your lover, who allow aspects of you to come out that your lover does not. Your lover may have no religious feelings. Then you meet Bruce, who is in contact with this part of himself. Suddenly all of your own spiritual needs spill out to him: a very charged situation.

Bruce becomes the "best friend" to you that your lover is not. But be careful: the intensity of your spiritual needs may not be matched by the depth of Bruce's invitation for you to fill them. It's easy to mistake his invitation to come play for a genuine call to love. We call this "infatuation with a purpose." (Therapists call this "transference"; priests, teachers, and politicians similarly experience this all the time.) Your lover may give you no spiritual satisfaction, but Bruce does. But this does not mean that Bruce, whom you want to be *your* "best friend," can't return that same feeling—to six other men. You may feel that he's *your* best friend, but he does not. So don't make the mistake of inviting your "best friend" to take the place of your lover.

Instant intimacy is one of those things that our TV culture dishes out like Lean Cuisine. This has invaded the gay world in the form of sexual-*cum*-spiritual groups like the Body Electric, where intense intimacies are formed with strangers, who remain strangers after the experience is over. It's easy in the throes of these instant intimacies to "fall in love" with someone who is playing the game with you—who is "opening himself up" just like you are. But who may be much better, when the session ends, at sealing you up behind him. You have opened yourself up completely to him, and he is giving you a quick cheek-peck and a "So long!"

"Intimacy" itself, in this canned, instant version, may now become a weapon to be used against you.

Again, watch out. It may seem easy to try to replace your lover with
one of your new instant-intimate "buddies." After all, Jim, who has been

there with you for ten years, just does *not* understand the *intensity* of your feelings for Peter, the attractive, utterly sensitive star of a "touch-me-feel-me" weekend that left both of you gasping. What you might have found out during that weekend ("that we all spent with our clothes off, and where we all got more *naked* than I've ever been with anybody!") was that you did want somebody else in your life. Your lover is not your "best friend." But maybe you need to have several safer "best friendships" along with him.

How you are able to accomplish this will depend upon how satisfied and secure he is in your life together. And also how much privacy the two of you have allowed yourselves. One of the joys of your *own* gay life should be that having a relationship with another man, beside your lover, should not be suspect. Unlike the suburban straight couples who are now "best friends and absolutely *everything* to one another" and who cannot even be seen in the company of any other unattached adults, *you* can.

You can give yourself this right. You can allow room in your life for both of these relationships—for your lover as well as your best friend, or even best friends. But the important thing is not to confuse the space occupied by any of them. To honor them. Not to compare your lover to your best friend. It does not work. Even best friends have other "best friends," who may not be you.

But the relationship you have with your lover has a singular unique-ness, and if it does not, it is time to work on it and question it. In the chapter on "Gay Love and Gay Marriages," I will talk more about the work necessary to hold your gay marriage together and also how to identify when the marriage actually starts. It is not, as you may believe, when you start to register your pattern at Tiffany's.

*"Relationships* refer to a deeper intimacy, a closer bond than normally is
found even among friends. Your friends may come and go,
but your lover, that intimate, close person in your life, should remain,
should be there for you. And this, of course, is why his presence
in your life is so important—and problematic."

## CHAPTER 4

# Your Own Gay Relationships

All right. I think I should come right out and say it: Gays have pio-
neered what may be the relationships of the future.

You think I'm nuts, don't you? Many of your friends can't keep a man
around long enough to go through a load of laundry with him—and I'm
saying this. How can I?

Well, children are no longer the Number One priority of most heterosexual relationships. Certainly not those outside of "legal" marriage,
which now account for the majority of straight living patterns. In other
words, guys, the great majority of unattached (that is, *not* legally married)
heteros are living together in about the same way that we are. In couples,
without being legally married. Children are the not the Number One priority (which has done horrible things for children, and left much of our
society in turmoil). Expenses are often split down the line. And when one
partner decides that he or she has "outgrown" the other, the couple take
themselves to a "counselor," who for the most part has a limited stake in
keeping them together. This is in contrast to the olden days, when the
woman marched off to her parents and the man slunk back to his, and
both sets of parents warned: "Get back together, or consider yourselves
*dead!*"

In many ways this has left gays as rudderless out there in our choppy
relationship waters as heterosexuals, but at least with some sense of a
community behind us; which the straights at this point rarely have. What
straights (and I hate this term, but basically what I am saying are the
"non-gays") have is society's public relations campaign that says *they* are
"the norm."

Everything is set up for them: from the social pages of the morning
papers which report on their engagements, weddings, and *brisses*, to a
whole army of services and goods which go into a wedding and then into   55

marriage and the production of kids. Straight men have constantly conflicting needs for personal fulfillment (denigrated as the inability to grow up: "the Peter Pan complex") and for duty and responsibility (husband; parenthood; citizenship; etc.). They are made to believe that their success in life (which is measured by how many toys they have, and how big the toys are) depends upon fulfilling both of these needs virtually simultaneously. Nowhere is there a time or a place for that "other" person, the inner man—the "self"—who may have nothing to do with the strictly defined territories of family man and regular guy.

Gays to a great degree have given ourselves permission not to have this conflict. Because we are still very much outside the TV-image mainstream, we can explore our inner regions to a degree that many straights envy. We can get into contact with that figure that I will talk about later that I call the Male Companion; and we really do have some resources against the totally alienating, modern corporate world, although we often underestimate these resources. But this still leaves us with a large amount of territory unexplored. Since we've worked so much with our inner selves, our problem now is an "outer" self—and how this self works with our relationships.

I say "relationships" to refer to a deeper intimacy, a closer bond than normally is found even among friends. Your friends may—and actually should—come and go, but your lover, that intimate, close person in your life, your mate or partner, should remain; should be there for you. And this, of course, is why his presence in your life is so important—and problematic.

Lovers may start off as more casual friends, but a partner (or lover) is there for the longer haul, for thicker or thinner, richer or poorer, etc., not because it's "in the contract," but because his feelings for you are harder and even—something that we don't want to admit—more volatile and threatening.

A partner relationship does have a little fence around it and not everyone is invited to come in and play. If the fence is too high, the relationship may become painfully "incestuous" and neurotic. We see this with gay couples who start to talk alike, act alike, walk and dress alike (I know, memories of the old *Patty Duke Show!*). They are taking the powerful "twinning" myth that gay men look for, and are pushing it until sex within the relationship becomes redundant. It stops.

This situation mirrors many straight relationships where the husband, the wife, and the kids are set off on an island of their own, often called the suburbs, and the strangling that goes on on the "happy little island," if released to public view, would call for Emergency Medical Assistance. The people in it are suffocating, but by agreement, they cannot call out for help.

When this happens in a gay relationship, it either explodes or you are
left with two very bitter men. In straight relationships, you are left with

two people who have remained shackled together either *for the sake of the kids*, or a marriage pattern that has become an unbreakable mold into which they have poured themselves.

Much of the romantic inner feelings of gay men revolve around an "ideal partner." He is the sexualized version of the "ideal friend" who will give you everything, be everything you can't be (butch, rich, powerful, adult), and satisfy all your narcissistic needs to find someone whose value either reflects or increases yours. Although this is not at all limited to us (the aging executive's need for a trophy wife who is tall, gorgeous, and twenty years younger than the first wife is hetero narcissism), gay men often have a fear of going outside their narcissism: what they feel as "marrying" beneath them. Their own internalized homophobia makes it difficult to see someone else for what he is, and so they end up with a "type," a *template of desire* that turns them on like a light switch: every time. And it is from this template that they expect to find—every time—the "love of their lives."

I find this "love of your life" idea fascinating in that it expresses perfectly the gay need to find that mirror image, that narcissistic fulfillment, that keeps many gay men on a constant romantic merry-go-round. As with the heroines in old 1940s MGM two-hankie "women's" movies, we think of the *love of our lives* as the tall, dark, handsome stranger who finds us sitting out on a park bench, lonely, forlorn, with just a half pack of peanuts left. He gives us everything: the mink, the house, the car, the dick. He has it all. He excites and satisfies us—and asks from us (just as he would from any real movie heroine) the most complete, draining and one-sided love any testicled animal will ever get.

To put it another way: *we are prepared to love the living doody out of him.*

Millions of gay men will be looking for the "love of their lives" until they die. They will be sitting on that park bench, or cruising until four A.M., or complaining at brunch, and then gyming and shopping and dieting, and then cruising again. They will look and look and look, and never realize that *real* love might already have found them.

Why is that?

How could it happen right under their noses? Is it possible that this "great love" could originate from someone else? And in an amazingly open, touching, down-to-earth way? Is it possible that it could be there, and still escape them?

Uh huh: it's possible.

And it would escape them, because the truth is: they never, really find themselves lovable.

Loving someone else, being hurt by someone else, running after the next love-material and the next (and the next)—all of this is preferable to being *loved*. Why?

Because being loved means owning up to the responsibility of being loved, which is—in the long run—more difficult than asking for (or looking for) love. Although many of us love to be adored, being loved is different. Being loved on an *adult* level requires that you feel worthy of love, and also that someone else's feelings be responsibly respected. It also means looking into your own need for love and realizing how *vulnerable* that makes you, since we are sure that our own *unlovable* selves will be denied any love that is being offered to us, at any moment.

I refer to this chronic insecurity as "looking into the mouth of the volcano." Looking directly into that cavernous, frightening need we have to be loved; a need that goes back to childhood; a need that most people will spend their entire lives attempting to avoid. However, if we marshal the courage to look directly into the "the volcano," where so much inner turmoil lies—remember that volcanoes are actually weak spots in the earth's ancient crust—we will find the *love* that is ours: *ours to give as well as to receive.*

The love may come by uniting us with absent fathers, difficult mothers, rejecting brothers—by uniting us with all the painful, threatening fires within ourselves—but it is there. It is deep within the mouth of that volcano, that fearful place where our need for love is hidden. And there, if we can finally look into it, we can learn to accept love and, indeed, authentically (without histrionic "sacrifices") offer it. Loving will then be a natural part of our imaginative soul and personality. We will be able, in short, to *realize* the intention to love and be loved.

We will be able to say: "I am worthy of being loved, and of loving."

(The opposite, flip side, of this is the man who never feels that his love is worth having. "Why would he want *me*? What do I have to *give*?" Because he has felt genuinely unloved, he feels that his love is unworthy. This cycle is again broken when we realize how precious love is. By questioning a feeling that is presented, often unbidden, to us, we are demeaning ourselves. It is important to see love, then, as an ultimate gift. Or, as the poet W. H. Auden said, "If equal affection cannot be/ Let the more loving one be me.")

So one of the most direct ways of avoiding looking into this need (the "mouth of the volcano") is to spend your life "looking for love": for someone to invest your own narcissistic needs in, rather than accepting someone who, at that point in his own emotional development, can love you. What I'm asking for, then, is to be able to see and accept *emotional* richness in another person, rather than the other things that we have programmed ourselves to look for in a "Personals" ad way: that "template-of-desire" appearance (what is referred to, basically, as "my type"), manner, sexual technique, or position. We keep looking for these things more and more specifically ("smokes cigars; has a mustache; does not smoke; no facial hair . . ."), while rejecting men faster and faster.

Again, this harks back to the cruising games most of us have played for years. What makes cruising such a waste of time is our fear of rejection. After all, in cruising, everybody is out for the same thing, correct? But the sting of rejection becomes for most men much more painful than the pleasures of acceptance. This is especially true now in our culture of rejection, where we find ever more reasons to find men unacceptable.

So when you think of all the time you've wasted cruising because of your own fear of rejection, you may realize that some of that time went into your own fear that your cruised "object" just might not be "worthy" *enough* for you.

In a nutshell, he does not come up to your fantasy picture of what the *cruisable* object should be. (In an attempt to address any doubts, one of my favorite Castro Street T-shirts said: "Please don't think of me as an intelligent, sensitive human being. I'm also A GREAT HUNK OF MEAT!") To cruise and accept this guy would be the same thing as rejecting your own value, *if* you accepted him. So in a way, we're looking at a double rejection. First there is the fear that he just *might* reject you. And second is the fear that, even if he accepted you, his *unworthiness* (the paunch you noticed even in the dark; his tacky clothes; bad teeth; etc.) would only underscore your own.

Or, as Groucho Marx put it very aptly: "I wouldn't want to be a member of any club that would ask me to be a member!" (This feeling is reflected in many men's coming out fears: they are sure that other queers will be as despicable as they are sure *they* are. Other gay men will reflect their own paranoia and low self-worth. Usually, after wading into the gay waters a bit, they find that most gay men are blander and more acceptable than they expected, have almost no horns on their heads—and their feelings of self-worth begin an amazing, unexplainable rise.)

"True love," then, could be around the corner. It could very well be in someone else's *true* feelings about you. And although many of us have had relationships that "did not work out"—that is, another man did not give us everything we felt we deserved—we cannot deny that someone else might have loved us with an intensity that was palpable and indeed beautiful: with a veracity of love that was as deep as his soul was capable. But this was not the "true love" we wanted as a narcissistic ideal. This was not the place where we saw ourselves at the mirror, with Prince Charming staring back at us waiting to ask us in.

For many of us, this date with a Prince might be terrifying. After all, the first question is what *does* he see in us? Unless you've been trained in the "Famous Prince Charming School of Mate Material," a place that even the late Princess Di did not (to her own great misery) attend, you really don't have much of a chance.

But one thing you would have learned at old "Famous Prince" is that interest in another person—to any fairly well-adjusted Prince—is *immensely* sexy.

This is something that many gay men have a difficult time with, especially younger ones, who often internalize the idea that there is nothing interesting about them except their youth and bodies. For them, the idea that you're interested—or even capable of being interested—in any person beside yourself, comes with a little slip attached that says: "Beware, this guy has got to be as self-obsessed as I am. So how can he be genuinely interested in me?"

The flip side, once more, is the man who feels that since he is going to lose anyway, why bother? Either these men stay at home all the time, or in complete self-denial they refuse to make any concessions at all to others. Like the messy dorm rooms of college kids, filled with week-old pizzas and beer cans, they consider this their "authentic" selves. They enjoy being a "sonovabitch" that nobody wants to have around. And nobody does. An example are guys who feel that grooming (as part of the commercial "male beauty" package that gays are assaulted with) is "too queer" for them. So why not take a bath once a week, just to show people that you can?

Bad idea.

Just as we want to be attracted to other guys, we *do* want them to find us attractive. So why feel like the only kid left out of Christmas? Going directly into the "gay meat market" *au natural*—unwashed, unclipped, and with "problem" skin—is not a smart idea. It *is* a jungle out there, and none of us are dumb enough to think that it is suddenly going to turn into Romper Room. But learning—and perhaps you do *have* to learn this—to be interested in other people is a good way to get something out of your time spent in the "Garden of Extraterrestrial Cruising" that is, for many men, the gay world.

One of my favorite stories on this line is about the meeting of Wallis Simpson and the Prince of Wales, before he became Edward VIII and then abdicated the throne and they became the world-weary Duke and Duchess of Windsor. Right off the bat, she asked him: "How do you like your job?" Meaning, what in the hell did it mean to be the Prince of Wales?

Later the Duke confessed that this was the first time in his entire life that anyone had ever been interested in him as a working person, had actually thought that being the P. of W.—and appearing before millions of people, even when his hemorrhoids hurt, before TV, when he had to stand up and shake all those hands himself—was work. Mrs. Simpson, who went after the Prince the way Captain Ahab went after the White Whale, knew that every working man likes to talk about his work: it is often the one thing that identifies him. Even today, when real work (as opposed to making gobs of money) has been devalued, most men are delighted that you are interested in what they do to earn a living or keep themselves off the street.

Of course much of the problem about being "interested" in other men
is that we have lost so much of our language of interest (or, in other

words, of being *polite*). For that reason, I began this book with a little round-up of ways to break the ice with strangers. The hard, alienated, in-your-face, get-lost "street punk" look has become *in*. Along with "fats, fems, and freaks," many "Personals" ads in gay magazines actually call for "No gays." *Bi's* are okay. Bisexuals carry the promise of no complications. No messy feelings; only "cool" *bi* feelings. In a way, this is like repackaging the self-loathing, bitchy *Boys In the Band* queens of the 50s as the hard, cool "retro-punks" of the 90s. All I can say is: "Great step forward, boys. See you—alone—at the funny farm."

Seriously, this is sad. It is the same old problem: how to get over that gap of words and feelings from one man to another, when the gap is a moat filled with *in*ternalized homophobia, *ex*ternalized homophobia, and the "normal" fears people in general—and men in particular—have about opening themselves up. One technique I find effective for getting over that "moat" is what I call *taking your feelings out for a walk*.

In this exercise, you allow yourself the feelings you've been clamping down on inside—loneliness, rejection, anger, falling in love, grief—and you follow them. Instead of squelching them, you allow them to come out in a safe way. You have to keep them on a leash, because they're not easily "trainable" things—feelings—but you don't have to push them into the closet anymore. You can learn not be afraid of them, and also, difficult as it is to believe, to find joy in them. Your feelings, truly, add dimension to your life. The Greeks understood this, and thought of grief as being ultimately ennobling; falling in love was conspiring with magic. Each emotion then can have its own place. Taken too far, they can become madness; squelched, feelings become sources of terrible psychic pain.

Rejection, certainly, is one of the hardest feelings in the world. It brings to mind all the rejection we had as children, and those reactions of helplessness and pain it caused. But once you have let that feeling out, and seen it working among others, you realize that you can prevail over it. Rejection *itself* as a feeling will not kill you, but the pain of *rejecting* yourself can: the pain that comes from not owning up to what you are, as a valuable person, who has weathered so much, including rejection, including pain, grief, and hurt. This will not ever protect you from actual rejection. But it will strengthen you so that you will be able to go through the kind of normal risks that make life exciting and allow relationships to happen.

Risk and relationships go hand in hand. In the old days, gay relationships were automatically supposed to lose out. Everyone from Freudians to advice-divas like Ann Landers knew that gay couples could never *last* the way married couples could. Gays could never be a couple because they were never going to have the little rose-covered cottage, be true to one another, and not even *look* at anyone else. Gays could not be couples because everyone knew that for a couple to happen you had to have two     61 ingredients: one person (called a "wife") who stayed home and provided domestic stability for the other (called a "husband") to go forth each day, fight those dragons in the work jungle, and then come home exhausted, demanding dinner and his slippers.

This did not happen with gays because both of them were busy doing the same dragon fighting—and the popular theory among psychologists (and other "authorities") was that gay couples fought with each other constantly. (The shrinks of this period could not quite figure out that living under the pressures of a totally homophobic world might contribute to this legendary fighting—but then they were too busy either covering up their own queerness or committing us to "1984"-style mental institutions.)

Unfortunately, reality came to the rose-covered-cottage picture sometime in the mid-70s, when many married, hetero couples decided that to survive they needed *two* incomes. Today, the majority of women work outside the house. Their incomes are necessary for keeping their families afloat. In fact, there is often more emotional stress in single-income households where Daddy must do all the breadwinning, than in dual-income ones. So this sort of conventional husband/wife patterning has gone out of straight relationships and additional risk has come in.

In gay relationships, without the preset husband/wife patterning, risk was a regular part of our lives. An awareness of risk produced an openness to change that kept many relationships going. Although the down side was that with such a high level of risk (no laws to protect, or restrict, either party), breaking up was easy to do; the up side was that it became easier to go from one relationship to another without feeling marked as a "loser," which many divorced heterosexuals feel.

Although our relationships broke up quicker, they rarely had the added stress of joint property problems, kids, and sympathetic but nosy in-laws, etc. As gay relationships have become more complicated (in terms of three-partner households, gay parenting, joint property ownership, etc.), the difficulties in our own relationship patterns are now increasing to reflect the stresses in the most mainstream "hetero" relationships.

I will talk about several of these situations soon. I call them "models" for gay relationships. Since many of us model our gay relationships strictly after our parents, we usually see relationships *per se* as having only one model. We take our parents' relationships pretty much at face value, without seeing what they had to go through behind closed doors. Many straights also feel the same way: that *they* are trapped in one pattern. That is why these very compressed patterns (fidelity at all costs; the lonely, stay-at-home wife; the stressed husband who must appear in control at all costs) have—as our divorce rates witnessed—exploded in the faces of many heterosexuals. The backlash of this explosion has propelled some homophobic feelings even farther. Now that "the family" (and its "values") is in crisis, guess who is seen as its worst "enemy"? As we say in New York, this one of those pure "go figure" situations.

I felt, while coming out in the mid-60s, that I had one gay quest and it was the hardest thing for me to do: to find a man who did not hate himself so much that my own fragile sense of self-worth was not destroyed with his. I had been through so much damage growing up in a bigoted, homophobic South with a disturbed mother, that I was not about to connect with a man who showed me that even though he *hated* himself, he could still love me.

This "hating ourselves but loving you" model was prevalent then. (It also seems ready for a comeback, as internalized gay homophobia has come *roaring* back out of the closet.) You could not go out to a bar or a gay party and not feel it. It was to a great degree what the generation older than I was set on, and it set them apart from us, a generation that proposed to change the world through, of all things, *love.* Often I felt that men from the older, self-hating 50s generation had nothing to say to me, and this is a feeling that younger gay men now have: that we, men in our forties and fifties, are cut off from them, as they have cut themselves off from us. Yet I know that we are all looking for the same thing: some clue, model—or even a pattern—for how to survive our own gay lives.

### *Models for Gay Relationships.*

## The Homophobic Relationship

This relationship was very prevalent in the lives of pre-Stonewall, 50s-generation men who often paired off in order to exclude themselves from other gay men. It was the *good* gays versus the *bad* queers mentality: the good gays got into decent, faithful, monogamous relationships. The bad queers stayed out all night cruising, going to "toilet" bars, a term for sleazy Mafia gay bars in low neighborhoods, where gay men could, if they were lucky, dance together and meet others who were "out" enough actually to go to bars. The good boys went to respectable "mixed" bars where you dressed right and could pretend to date girls while you looked at other men. Even lower on the totem pole were men who went in for anonymous sex, which itself had not come out of the closet. (This period preceded that moment when Bette Midler would appear at the Continental Baths surrounded by men wearing only towels.) Interestingly enough, this 50s model of the good, safe, "careful gays" versus the bad, "sexually irresponsible queers" is returning. Such controversies as the Sex Panic! movement versus the rush for "serial monogamy," as espoused by Gabriel Rotello's *Sexual Ecology,* have brought this mentality back. (I will talk about the current version of the 50s homophobic couple shortly.)

One of the hallmarks of homophobic relationships was that once one was started you dropped your other gay friends like hot potatoes, unless 63 they, too, were in monogamous pairings. These relationships were labeled "mature" by the therapists and liberal clergymen of the time. They were what you were supposed to be on the lookout for. Basically, they were two men *out there* by themselves, but the premise was that the bars, the baths, the familiar cruising spots (places where you might meet other men and be strengthened by gay tribalism) were evil. They were underworld situations, filled with every sort of danger, sleaze, and illegality. The good gays "outgrew" them. They matured; they developed.

They also became further cut off from the tenderness and support of other gay men. This model, as I mentioned earlier, is being generously re-adopted by many younger gays, who feel they have "nothing in common" with other queers, only with married, "safer" couples (translation: straight) of their own generation. I hear kids spouting the same lines that I heard thirty years ago: "Being gay is no reason to be friends with someone." Or, "The two of us are the only gays we know; all our other friends are straight."

These earlier (1950s) homophobic couples ended up completely isolated within the "maturity" of their very tight relationships. They did not produce children, who often act as a window into the larger, mainstream world; and neither were other gay men invited in. Gay couples of the time were also frequently marked by being either apolitical or very conservative: they did not want to rock the narrow boat that they were holding on to for dear life.

This was especially true during the McCarthyist witch-hunts of the 50s which labeled every move they made "suspect." Under these circumstances, men in homophobic relationships did the best jobs they could, and it was a serious act of courage simply to realize the intention of a relationship with another man. But homophobic relationships resulted, for the most part, in becoming "enabling" ones, to borrow a term from Twelve Stepism: they promoted and stiffened the homophobia from within.

These duos repeated the mantra: "We're going to show the whole *queer* world we can make it, while they can't." To the homophobic couple, their togetherness was (and still is) a spit in the face of a gay world they can neither understand nor tolerate. Any feeling that they need other gay men, all types of gay men, not simply wealthy "professionals," but men they find attractive, warm, worthy, courageous—men who can cut through the defenses that the two of them are reinforcing and building higher—is something they will cast from their minds with the warning that: "All queers are like that! Gays are *only* interested in sex. They're not trustworthy."

Other statements you often hear from homophobic couples are: "We never socialize with gay men." "We don't believe in picking our friends because they're gay." And, "If any of our friends are gay, they don't act it."

Because homophobic couples (especially of the "older school") are so self-denying, they deny that other people can "detect" them. No one *knows* they are gay. They firmly believe that this part of their lives is invisible, even today—in our sexually hyped (but not hypersexualized) environment, when total invisibility for anyone bigger than a flea is impossible. Homophobic men build up around themselves an alter-ego act. If they live together, they will present themselves as "roommates," a throwback to that World War II period when men lived innocently with each other due to a national housing shortage.

If they don't live together, but spend a lot of time with each other, they are often "business associates," "consultants," or "pals." Although men in homophobic relationships pride themselves on being part of a "mature" world where sex is "unimportant" and social standing is the name of the game, they themselves often reside in prolonged adolescence (a *Boys in the Band* environment), since their own growing up brings up the ugly questions of marriage, family ties, and responsibility. They are still living in an environment very closely defined by these expectations, and the only way they can escape them is by staying within an artificial adolescence.

One homophobic couple I knew passed each other off as "my landscape gardener—I'm his client." They had been doing this for years, and sometimes Jeff, the gardener, would spend the night as they "discussed gardening." With another couple, one was "his accountant." With another, "my lawyer." Of course these acts become transparent, but as with any denial situation, the deniers feel that since they are working so hard to cover up the truth, everyone around them will also go along with the game.

Another constant homophobic mantra is: "It's nobody's business what you do in bed." This reduces the relationship to purely sexual, which it may not be, and demeans both parties: it keeps their relationship a shameful secret. Much of this feeling stems from the conservative 1950s, when homosexuality was taken to be a "subversive" element in American life and hiding was necessary for "patriotism." Simply stated, it was *un-American* to be queer. Not "red-blooded" enough, despite the thousands of gay men and lesbians who had fought honorably for their country in its wars.

So the best defense gay men and lesbians could come up with was "It's nobody's business. This is a private thing. I will not be judged by it." They could not be public enough to come up with a defense that said, "This is my life; I have a right to it, and I will defend that right." The "It's nobody's business" defense that stands at the core of many homophobic relationships was a watchword of the McCarthy period. The feeling was that as long as we kept this up, McCarthyism would leave us alone. But anyone who's ever been involved in a homophobic dragnet learns that homophobes are not out there to make your life comfortable. The higher you raise your defenses, the higher they'll aim their guns.

One element that still swears by homophobic relationships are what gays refer to (either derisively or enviously) as the "A-Gays." A-Gays are men with money and the power that goes with it. They are part of the invisible gay elite. Their names often appear in the society pages of local newspapers, or the Fashion section of *The New York Times*. Often they marry, have children, and keep a "gay accomplice" on the side, another man from their own social set who subscribes to the same A-Gay code: "This is nobody's business, so why should we parade it around like a bunch of *queers*?"

Sometimes their names are written in invisible ink on the Finance pages: that is, you will never associate them with being gay, unless they, for instance, die mysteriously of "pneumonia" at the age of thirty-eight. One of the myths of the commercially constructed gay world is that gay men have an inordinate amount of money, and the A-Gays are out there, just waiting to be "tapped." In other words, they are a latent source of power for our community. *Latent* here is the operative word; the rest is crap: the highest priority of the A-Gay is to keep his money and power intact. He is not going to risk it by coming out. A few, very high profile A-Gays have come out, but often they have done this rather than be "outed." (The absolute curse word among A-Gays is *outing*. Mention the "O" word in any A-Gay gathering and you'll find yourself "outed" pronto from their social set.)

One thing that has exploded—to a minor degree—the closed homophobic world of the A-Gay is AIDS. Before AIDS, A-Gays could "take care of themselves." They lived very covert gay lives, often in the bosom of discreet families and business acquaintances. Nothing about them ever got out into the papers or the community. AIDS changed that. It shook up their lives like nothing else. For this reason, even the A-Gays are starting to come out, but it is a mistake for most gay politicos to think that this part of the community is going to risk its power and money for any cause that does not augment both.

## The Agreement Relationship

Agreement relationships came up in the 1970s. Suddenly sexual freedom (or at least opportunities for gay sex) was all around us—due, to a great degree, to the American commercialization of sex itself. At the same time, men were coming out of their closets and forming couples. Agreement relationships are marked from the very beginning with certain "ground rules." They may be: "We can play around outside the relationship, but not bring anyone home." "We can take separate vacations and have all the outside sex we want, but never have any of this while we're together." "We can have quickie or 'trick' threesomes, as long as they include both of us, and neither of us feels excluded."

In other words, the agreement relationship is actually an emotionally monogamous relationship with some amount of sexual openness. The fact that the agreement is out in the open, gives both men a certain amount of permission to have a more satisfying sex life than they might have exclusively with each other. But for emotional depth they will return to one another. Agreement relationships do not allow long-term affairs. Honesty, at least in the direction of pushing a certain "openness," is usually part of the agreement. So any clandestine arrangement, one that might satisfy a partner's needs for privacy outside the relationship, is not allowed.

For this reason, agreement relationships often end up with some amount of "cheating," of sneaking around. When this happens, they start to approach "open" relationships, although agreement relationships are never *open* about this. By open, I mean a relationship that allows the maximum amount of freedom—and total openness about this between the two partners—but which may fall apart at any time as well. This is the great weakness of open relationships: if they are open to anyone and anything, then it is just as easy to dismiss them (despite the emotional commitments that go with them) and go over to "Choice B," whoever the new "open" partner of the time is.

Very few relationships last as *open* relationships, and I really wonder if they exist at all, for any extended amount of time, until they become "agreement" relationships. Open relationships are probably the hardest of all relationships to maintain, and sometimes when they do manage to survive for any length of time, a certain amount of coldness comes in. Both partners start to retract emotionally, on a commitment level. (A good example of this: Simone de Beauvoir and Jean-Paul Sartre, who kept an "open" relationship with each other for decades, ended up loathing one another!) How can you be committed to someone who is free to see anyone for any amount of time? Exactly where do you fit in to his sexual and emotional schedule?

The problem with privacy in agreement relationships (and privacy is an important part of any relationship, something that "liberated" 90s counselors rarely acknowledge) is that more experienced relationships (that is, relationships that have worked themselves into many areas of growth and commitment) do demand privacy. This goes for what happens between the primary partners in an agreement relationship, as well as for outside friends. The primary partners need this privacy because it adds a necessary closeness to what happens at home: home is not simply a preparation for going out. And these outside friendships, whether they start off as purely sexual, in a setting like the baths or a bar, or begin as social situations and end sexually, need a groundwork of privacy as well: they cannot simply be "material" to be discussed at home over coffee, a constant series of one-night stands to add spice to the primary couple's sex life.

If they are, a kind of routine settles into the primary relationship, so that each man's need for necessary emotional satisfaction and support outside the couple is not met. Often these needs can be met by best 67 friends or platonic friendships, and when this happens they can add support to the primary relationship if it is secure enough. However, many primary agreement relationships lack this security—which is the reason an "agreement" has been instituted in the first place—and many partners in this kind of relationship find quick "tricks" far less threatening than even the most platonic friendships.

## Monogamous Relationships

Although it may seem strange to place monogamous relationships after agreement relationships, in many ways they are simply another sort of "agreement," the agreement being not to allow outside sex in. How far you go in denying outside sex, though, can be up for grabs. Does it include masturbating alone? Some men in monogamous relationships feel guilty about this as well as even looking at other men and then masturbating while fantasizing about them. Another agreement aspect of monogamous relationships is that monogamy may not always be practiced through the duration of the relationship. You can decide that for the first year of your being together, you will try to stay monogamous, just to "check it out."

For some men this works beautifully: it means initially putting all of their energy, all of their emotional and sexual eggs, into one basket. For others, it means that if they slip off the monogamy wagon, the relationship is over. So a perfectly *good* relationship, one that includes love, commitment, openness, trust—everything that a promising relationship needs—will be destroyed because one partner is just not *able* to be monogamous.

I have witnessed the tragedy of this too many times in my life as so many friends' relationships have fallen apart, and years later one after another has said: "We could have made it, but I was *too* possessive." "*He* was too possessive." "If only we could have held out longer." "I wanted us to stay together, but it was not something I could control."

There are many theories about monogamy and how it works with human beings. One of the newer ones is that humans are *not*, unlike wolves and geese, monogamous by nature. We are more like whales, who can achieve sexual fulfillment in many different ways. But, biology aside, monogamy does have some very strong emotional payoffs. You love someone so much that the emotional fulfillment you get from him actually does expand. Instead of being limiting, monogamy can be thrilling, satisfying, rich, and extremely hot. However, it takes a lot of energy to keep it this way, and sometimes one partner in a monogamous relationship may fall short. He becomes tired of putting more and more energy into one person, not only of finding new sexual avenues but of finding new parts of this person to explore. There is also the long-term, always-present siren call of the New versus the security benefits of the Old. So the question is, which one will win out—and how much will each partner have to pay?

In straight relationships, monogamy is part of the patterning necessary to raise children. Husbands simply want to know that they are the fathers of their children. If they have to keep their wives locked up in a tower—or use a chastity belt—to do it, they will. This has not kept men from fooling around. The only thing that did that was fear of venereal diseases, and the fact that society's rules were often maintained by powerful women who needed some weapon to keep their husbands in line. (Men eventually reversed the situation, thus "getting even with all-powerful Mommy," by turning women into their exclusive property.) So in the final count, if monogamy has never really worked *naturally* for straights, how will it work for us?

The answer is monogamous needs should be respected, but not clamped down with the male version of a chastity belt. There are some men who are—or seem to be—naturally monogamous. Why this is so, I can't say, and I'm not sure anyone else can, either. It may be that they are using their parents' marriage (or some fantasy of it) as their model. It may be that they are made extremely insecure by any outside sex in a relationship, whether it is their own or others'. It may be that emotionally—who'da thunk it?—they really are monogamous.

The terrible rub is that very few of these straight-arrow guys mate with other monogamous men. They can advertise for them in "Personals" ads, and announce it as <u>Ground Rule Number One</u>. But that does not mean they are going to get it. Perhaps it is the attraction of opposites: the attraction being the seriousness and "purity" a monogamous man has for the hedonism of your average, totally charming gay *slut*. But when these matings do occur, the only answer is that one man's monogamy should be respected; but the other man's own sexual needs cannot be dictated to. Otherwise, again, you're allowing a good relationship to be ruined by monogamy.

Using respect for one another as a rule will (undoubtedly) mean sneaking around. It will mean that the monogamous partner will allow the other partner (okay, we'll call him the "slut" and get it over with: being enough of a slut myself, this name won't kill me or, most probably, you) the privacy to cheat. If he catches him, that will not blow things out of the water, and if the monogamous partner has any fantasies that his "slut" lover is as pure as the driven snow (yeh, in June . . .), he can allow himself to get over them.

Now, why would a monogamous person stand for such an arrangement, when he knows that his lover will "cheat" on him while he makes every effort possible to turn away as it's being done? Sometimes, simply enough, one man's sex drive is much higher than another's. Sometimes it is part of an agreement between a very horny younger man and a more settled older one (although you might be surprised how many older men are much more "slutty" than their younger boyfriends). Sometimes this actually gives the monogamous partner the freedom to pursue his career, to put his energy into other avenues that he would not be able to do, if he had to satisfy his partner more frequently. In other words, he knows that his partner is discreetly outside having an affair, and that he won't come home after twelve hours at the office and find him in their bed with another man, because he has allowed his partner enough freedom (and privacy) to go out and do this.

Although it may seem that an "agreement" is going on here, the agreement is simply not to bring it up. This is definitely *not* one of those "modern, contemporary, liberated" arrangements that TV and radio talk show counselors love, which end up blowing up in the face of the monogamous partner, hurting him again and again as he goes from one attempt at imposed exclusivity to the next. If he insists upon his own monogamy, he cannot insist upon another man's, but the two of them can honor the privacy of their own feelings and needs.

Of course this "agreement of privacy" can have its price as well. At some point the roaming boyfriend may decide that it is no longer worthwhile for him to sneak around. He wants to see somebody else. He wants to bring his "monogamous" partner into a more *open* agreement relationship. In a situation like this, I would ask: is it worth blowing this relationship up? How important is the outside relationship? Even if it is absolutely important, will it help for it to go "public" with your lover?

Perhaps what the roving lover needs is to be able to talk about it with someone, with friends, a therapist (yes, another time when therapists are important), or even a gay support group. How the third party in this situation feels is also important. Sometimes if that third is, say, Jerry, and he is seeing Frank, who is involved with Bill (who does not even know Jerry exists), Jerry may find this situation enjoyable. There are chances that he does not even want to deal with Bill—that Bill, the monogamous partner-really has no relevance at all to him. If Frank decides that Bill just *has* to find out about this, come hell or high water, Jerry may find that he's now up to his ears in a messy situation for which he had never bargained.

Although it is often said "In vino veritas," *in wine there is truth*, in monogamy the "truth" has to be a bit more elastic. The *truth* is that you love him; the *truth* is that he loves you. The *truth* is that your sexual makeup is not the same as his: so, will you sacrifice the whole thing on the alter of "truth," or will you "truthfully" work it out?

### The S & M Relationship

Many men consider S & M a series of sexual situations, rituals, fetishes, practices, costumes, etc., but not the groundwork or pattern for a relationship. But for men who find relationships themselves difficult to negotiate, the patterning of S & M can give them a structure with which to work. By patterning, I'm talking about "unequal" or differentiated roles with an element of submission in them. For "liberated" gays in the 70s the idea of roles was anathema. Straights had roles—they came male (superior) and female (inferior); man (on top), woman (on bottom). To a great degree, this was the patterning gays saw straights in, and the feminist line (which hordes of gay men followed as the true religion) did nothing to soften this. Any revelation that the "superior" male might be oppressed by his role as the family's sole breadwinner, that he might, in fact, be choking in a noose of responsibilities, was certainly kept under wraps.

S & M formats may be "Master/Slave," "Top/Bottom," or (as an S & M format, not meant simply to denote age:) "Daddy/Son. What this means is that you go into an S & M relationship with clear expectations that will be met. If you are in a Daddy/Son relationship, even though you are making three times the bread Daddy is, it is expected that Daddy will take care of you—whether it means making sure that you clean up your room (or it is cleaned up by ol' Daddy himself, who will then "punish" you), ordering for you at a restaurant, or telling you how to drive or put your taxes together, Daddy *does* know best. At least in this format, S & M patterning (as opposed simply to S & M sex scenes or acts) can inject a certain clearness to a relationship. You know *who* will do what to whom, and often *when*.

On the other hand, even Daddies need Daddies, and sometimes an older man may feel that it is time for him to be coddled, cared for, and perhaps let go of the dominant reins for a while. This may send "Sonny" (who, sexually, is the Bottom) out the door, or force him to do some very fast growing-up. Sometimes, simply enough, a confirmed Top decides that the Bottom is having too much fun, and it's time for a turnabout. Or the Top may find that his own basic gay need to submit to the elements within him that are nurtured by another man's power (and to surrender to that power: again going into one of the main elements in the gay mythos) has finally caught up with him—and being constantly dominant has caused him a lot of emotional stress. For whatever reason, role changes can create havoc with some very rigid S & M men. But if the relationship is growing and no longer confined within a strict S & M pattern, it can enlarge the situation.

On the other hand, since you are dealing with fairly hard-set roles, any S & M relationship can become a bit confining. Since S & M as a "lifestyle" (as opposed to a sex style or bar style) may be too limiting to some men, many men who are confirmed in their S & M sexual lives still prefer to have lovers who are not: they will confine S & M to the bars, side affairs, etc., and have romantic "vanilla" sex at home.

Another interesting, and not uncommon, situation is for two Tops to marry—to be romantically attracted to the immense sense of control and command in one another—and then have a relationship which is dependent on bringing in a third, a Bottom, for the kind of hot sex that they want. Instead of finding this situation frustrating, both Top men can find that this brings stability to their home life: they know exactly how far they can go with each other. And they know that bringing in "outside" sex, 71 even sex in the form of a man who may stick around for a while, is built into their lives together.

## Networking Relationships

Networking relationships came about in the 1980s when many "guppies" (gay yuppies) met each other through gay business networking situations, fell in love, and then formed a "partnership" based on their shared business or professional lives. To me, this sounded absolutely flaky: that Ralph would fall for James because they were both lawyers, or both belonged to the same gay legal networking organization, and both had the same career, financial, and social goals. In other words, they had common values, even if their values might seem to some of us superficial. However, many gay men in networking arrangements are working so hard at their careers that having someone who understands the demands—and rewards—of a "guppy" lifestyle becomes the structure on which to build a relationship.

Older gay men who have started their relationships (for better or for worse) sexually, are puzzled by the idea of two young men who will never exchange "body fluids" exchanging business cards. Then going out on a date. Talking about all the people they know in common—their "network." Then dating several times again before hitting the sheets. Networking relationships are based on having something in common besides sex, besides the fact that you're both gay (or "queer," in the new parlance). Men in these situations often "professionalize" most of their social/friendship circles, which may include a doctor, a lawyer, a systems consultant, a CPA, a personal trainer, and an investment counselor. (At some point, a "massage specialist," from the backpages of a gay paper, may also be introduced to the circle for some professional sexual release!)

Some networking relationships cast aside the idea that you're physically attracted to one another, so that physical attraction will take a backseat to the draw of dual career advancement and the possibilities of joint higher income and social power. What is important is that you're both rappeling up the slick faces of the career cliffs, you both have similar goals, and often, for younger men, that you both may share the same level of "outness." This means being part of a larger queer networking group.

The networking relationship is often an extension of a previous friends network that younger gay men carry with them from college into professional life. In some ways, this is a new approach to American gay dating, since many older men remember when they were still in the closet to most of their friends. Now, with gay college and youth groups all over the country, this is no longer true. So for younger men, your boyfriend simply becomes another part of your network of friends.

In many ways, the networking relationship is incredibly old-fashioned. It extends the Victorian idea of marrying your peers (and nobody else). Marrying, in other words, "the right sort." The type of man your friends and family might approve of. In this case, "friends and family" may be your actual friends and family, who all know you're out, or it may be your "queer family," consisting of a more committed network of friends of both sexes.

One thing that seems to work in networking relationships is the gay matchmaker, and in larger cities there are gay matchmaking consultants, who use video dating, computers, and other means to match you up. The idea is that you're not simply dating—and—mating for sex (ugh!)—but for money, class, and everything else, as the English say, "that really matters."

The homophobic aspect of networking relationships is that since "being gay" is no longer that important (you didn't fall in love with him because he's queer, God forbid; but because he's at the same rung on the career ladder you are, and you're both seriously thinking about the Berkshires for the summer), gay men of the older variety, who have more of a sense of gay cohesiveness, will be put down. They're the Castro Street clones who never quite got it right, or—even worse—as young men call them, they're the old "70s disco aunties," who seem to stick around like dinosaurs. The line is: because they made *all* their decisions based on sex, attraction, and more sex, *they* ended up with AIDS. In a networking relationship, sex is only one item on the menu and since so much safe-sex is based on masturbation, you can do that in a dark room and still go home to your networking partner, even whisper about it the next day at the office to others in your network, and feel perfectly monogamous.

Polyamorous Relationships

Polyamorous relationships have been described as the "new relationships of the 90s," although in the gay world they've been around forever, as I referred to them in S & M relationships. They were just never quite so formalized by a polysyllabic name. By *polyamorous*, we mean one relationship with more than two people in it. An old-fashioned "threesome" is one way of describing it, although the new way of seeing it may be three men who are totally equal as lovers, who are all in love with each other, and who share everything quite equally. Polyamorous relationships may also be bisexual, which adds another complication to them.

In bisexual situations, you frequently have a man and woman who start out together, the man decides that he is "bi," and then takes on another man who may be either bi or gay. Although this format may start out as perfectly equal, eventually, either the two men go off by themselves or one member of the original straight couple decides that he or she wants something other than a threesome. Bisexual threesomes are wonderful as one-night stands (leading to a plethora of "Personals" ads that call for them), but as an ongoing situation, they quickly become awkward: the built-in power structure (two men, one woman) can make it hell on the woman, although perfect nirvana for her husband or boyfriend. He now finds that he has all the benefits of a "straight" coupled lifestyle (the two of them can 73 continue living in the most conventional "IHOP" suburb without a single eye blinking), with an added "bi" component. For this reason, polyamorous relationships often thrive in conservative, even redneck areas, where no one guesses that "those good ol' folks, the Joneses' friend Mike, who sometimes spends the night with them over *they-uh*," is the boyfriend of both of them. Biker circles have had polyamorous bi relationships in them since the Year One, and even though the good buddies sometimes suck each other's wienies, they never kiss.

Gay polyamorous relationships often come out of agreement relationships, where the agreement has gone as far as it can and both men suddenly realize that they are ready for a real outside love affair but do not want to break up with each other. Although it seems that the agreement relationship is now going to "go open," once it has evolved into a threesome, the new configuration may *not* be open at all. Since a third person is now involved, the question is how to control it. There are health expectations and demands (or "issues," as we say currently) to be dealt with. How to keep the third person *safe*, both on his own and with the other two. And there are emotional problems as well: how to keep the situation equal enough so that it does not become simply one couple and a third man (which often means one member of the original couple) who feels left out, betrayed, and ready to walk.

The answer might seem to be a constant working out of problems, talking out of concerns, worries, and feelings. But the question, as ever, is will this leave all three members or lovers with the privacy necessary for them to feel adult and, when necessary, recharged? Although talking things out among three people can be good, there are times when you don't feel like rehashing the situation and you may not feel like telling Boyfriend Number One and Boyfriend Number Two what's going on with you right then. Again, as in the monogamous relationship, some space for privacy must be allowed. Sometimes this means that two of the men will go off on a weekend together and then come back to the third, who has been allowed either to go off on his own or be with other friends. It is not really normal—or possible—for two people to share *everything* between them (even as much as this is a constant gay expectation and fantasy in relationships), and expecting *three* to do it is one reason polyamorous relationships may have a higher blowup rate.

## Intergenerational Relationships

In many intergenerational relationships a certain format or "patterning" based on age and personality may be followed. This makes these relationships easier for many men, as long as the format is (usually) more, rather than less *strictly* adhered to. Although some intergenerational relationships are Daddy-Son S & M relationships, in which Daddy is dominant and Son is submissive, in others Daddy simply wants to share his experience, his taste, and his life with a younger man, who will give him the attention (and often high voltage energy) that he desires. Often the younger man may in fact dominate the older man, and many older men get into serial relationships with hustlers this way. Although these relationships, too, may seem S & M—in that one man is constantly exerting his will on the other—in fact they are not. They are simply exploitative relationships and usually there is some sort of emotional problem under them. The man who is constantly paying the bills for a younger man should ask himself why he is in this relationship, just as the younger man should question why he's only treading water with his time as well.

Many men find that in "intergenerationals" they are recapturing the energy and outlook of their youths. This makes the difficulties and misunderstandings usually involved in such a relationship worthwhile. Much of these misunderstandings are based on language. Every generation has a language and behavior pattern of its own and is quick to misunderstand or ridicule another's. Although younger men can be exceptionally attractive and energetic, they can also bothered by things that older men have gotten over years earlier, such as a lack of money, the waning of attraction, or time spent by themselves. On the other hand, for older gays issues like "coming out" and "blatancy" (what some older men call "flaunting it") are painful and volatile. Often younger men don't understand this.

Although many older gay men are quick to accuse younger men of ageism, of being prejudiced against older men, few older men confront their own ageism as far as not wanting to date men in their own age group. As a whole, the gay community is opening up age-wise in ways it could not do twenty or thirty years ago, when the refrain was "Nobody wants you when you're old and gay." (It was also difficult for many of us to face the usual, oppressive questions that required leaving permanent "gay adolescence," such as, "Bill, why isn't a nice man like you married? When are you going to settle down and have kids of your own?" The answer was: *inside*, Bill always thought he was a kid.)

Since our community is victim to the same constant commercialization of youth that affects mainstream society, many gay men past forty or fifty find their lives getting narrower and narrower. For this reason, some of them see intergenerational relationships as a way of opening up their lives, of becoming a part of the exciting world of younger men. At least that is what they think they're getting. They forget that the world of younger men can be just as closed (anyone who's spent an hour watching MTV may figure this out) and as narrow as that of older guys. But younger men do have their own high-powered energy and that edge of "hipness" going for them, and this is not something that any of us can completely discount.

## Interracial Relationships

Very few things in gay life cause as much controversy—with the exception of "man/boy love"—as interracial relationships. The underlying motivation for the controversy is that we still live in a racist society and often interracial relationships have a racist agenda of their own: the idea that a person of another race will *fit* a certain stereotype. Even if the stereotype may be "flattering," or seen as "positive" rather than negative, it still means that someone cannot be himself and must live up to pre-set expectations. Steven, a black friend of mine who is a textile designer, had lived most of his life in New York Jewish neighborhoods. He loves blintzes and other specialties of Jewish cuisine. He listens to opera records as well as rhythm and blues, has been dressing in smart chinos and polo shirts all of his life, and he's not going to change. Ralph, another friend, who was white and "solid into blacks," as he put it, turned down a date with Steven because, frankly, "he wasn't black enough." Ralph said to me, "Who's ever heard of a black guy named 'Steven'? If I wanted a 'Steven,' I'd go out and find myself a Jew."

The stereotype is that blacks are more raw, passionate, sexual, and hung than whites; Orientals are softer, more intellectual, and less inclined to feelings; Hispanics are more impulsive and possessive. All of these characteristics may have truth for some members of each group. But if you go after someone of another ethnic group with this in mind, what is really happening?

Another element in interracial relationships, one especially operative in openly racist societies, is "marrying down." When I lived in New Orleans in the early 80s, a city where overt mixing among the races was limited, white men who were considered "trolls" in a white bar could have their pick in the black bars that welcomed whites. (Yes, there were white gay bars where blacks were not welcomed, and black bars where whites were not.) I pointed this out to Leonard, an absolutely gorgeous, young black friend of mine, who said: "Yes, in this city, if you go after black men, you are considered a freak."

In some interracial affairs, there is an element of Master/Slave going on, except that it is now following racial lines and not lines of assigned roles. Some white men feel when doing this that they are simply "picking up the white man's burden." They assume that some black men find being dominated by a white man "romantic and traditional." On the other hand, turning the tables, so that the black man is now dominant, plays out another scenario, "Mandingo black man with white 'mistress'"—who in this case is a white man.

Although it would be easy to say that intergenerational and interracial relationships are often things that "just happen," as in "he just happens to be younger" or "he just happens to be black (or Oriental, or brown)," going after this situation over and over again and expecting a certain pattern to fall into place when it happens, does make both of these situations types of patterned relationships. For some men the pattern is something they really want to follow, because they feel their expectations will be met. There is also an erotic potential, and denying erotic attraction—and its important place in starting relationships—is something I will not do.

But often men use relationship patterns as an excuse to repeat situations that are "patterned" to blow up: "He was too young and confused; he was really straight." "He was of another race; we'll never understand each other." These men go into such relationships with a self-fulfilling prophesy that accelerates quickly. They are attracted to the tension—the differences—between them and the other man. Scenarios are then set up (an expensive trip that a younger man cannot possibly handle; a social evening where one African-American is the only person of color in a room) where these differences can be accentuated. Often this leads to confrontational situations that compensate for a family background that never allowed these men to act upon intense feelings (the resentful older man who was forced to succeed early, so he never had a real youth; the stereotyped "cool" WASP, attracted only to "hot" Latinos; the "neurotic" Jew, drawn to "clinical" reserved Germans, etc.). Men repeating these situations—and recognizing the problems in them—might consider going into therapy of some sort to work out their family dramas, and then see to whom they really are attracted.

Unfortunately, the fact is we do live in a racist and ageist society. The first thought that comes into many guys' minds when they see a much younger man with an older man is that the younger one is either exploiting the older one (he is being kept), or the older man is "really lucky." Neither situation may be the case. In fact, the younger man might have had to convince the older man to become involved with him. The same thinking often takes place with interracial relationships: that a white man is "marrying down" with a black man; or that a black man who goes after whites is a self-hating "snow queen." Neither situation may be true. We are dealing with individuals, and in any relationship it is individuals who cause all the problems—and bring all the happiness.

"Few men are trained in being doormats—it is not part of our role, which is the reason why sugar daddies change lollipops so often."

## CHAPTER 5

# A Good, Decent Fight

If one thing makes it possible to predict the success of a relationship, it is the ability to deal with conflict. This does not mean that loving relationships can not exist without noticeable conflicts. They do, but often they are places where underground fires smolder until they turn into larger conflagrations. In situations where one partner walks out on the other—"out of the clear blue sky"—usually no conflicts were allowed in the relationship. It was part of the ground rules that none would be admitted.

An example of these non-conflict relationships is found among straights with the so-called "trophy wife." The trophy wife is the gorgeous second wife who came in after the *first* wife—you know, the one who had the kids and worked her buns off so Hubby could be successful?—well, the trophy wife replaced her.

So the second wife is supposed to be perfect. She's the one her husband dreamed about while Wife Number One was doing grunt work in his first marriage. The trophy wife is pampered and adored. She and her loving husband do not fight: after all, the first wife was a "bitch"; and she's a trophy. But this gorgeous thing realizes that she will pay for her position by absorbing all the tensions brought home by her hyper-successful hubby, while she's using his Platinum Amexcard to the max. In other words, she will pay for this marriage emotionally, while *he* just pays for it. The first wife nagged, fought, and screamed. Now she's out of the picture. The second wife will not nag, but will definitely spend.

Although this happens in gay relationships with trophy boyfriends, trophy boys rarely stick around. For one thing, few men are trained in being doormats—it is not part of our role—which is the reason why sugar daddies change lollipops so often. It's easy enough to find a boy who'll want to be wined, dined, dated and fucked, but not to find one who'll put up with Daddy Warbucks when he's saying, "Gimme a break, I'm too tired to deal with your b.s. . . . one more complaint and you're out the door!"

Anyway, the door revolves very quickly with these type of daddies.

In most relationships, then, being able to deal with conflict is a key to keeping them going. There are days when the icing starts to wear thin on anyone's cake. In other words, suddenly *he* realizes that you are not all sugar and butter. There is a *real* side of you and it's reacting, quite naturally, to being handled by another person. Suddenly he can see that not everything *he* does is perfect. This is a normal part of any intimate relationship. It is a part of what I refer to as the "finiteness of intimacy." Intimacy, in other words, *does* have boundaries. Contrary to certain movies from the 60s, love *does* mean having to say you're sorry. Intimacy may have elasticity—true, it can be stretched. But not *infinitely*. So the question is: how can he handle your own boundaries of intimacy, and how will *you* handle the way he's handling it?

So, there are days when your fuse is out to here, and he has all the matches. (Or vice versa—sometimes *you* may have the matches.) Explosions follow. Sometimes these are caused by genuine conflicts and sometimes just by the natural *finite* boundaries of intimacy.

In some cases one partner may actually like these explosions and plan for them. The reasons for this are numerous, but many men feel that these scenes are part of the normal negotiating aspects of a relationship: you *have* to go through them in order to come out lovers. They are the trial by fire—the Hollywood scenario—that produces love. And they firmly believe that this is what gay couplehood should be about; so here we have *The Boys in the Band*, *Who's Afraid of Virginia Woolf?* and *A Streetcar Named Desire* (everybody knew that Blanche was a man, *right?*) all rolled into *One Night with Bob*. To these men, queer relationships are supposed to be acted out. The more fireworks in the acting, the better the sex afterwards—and the more "intense" the relationship is.

(Of course the question is: do you want—or need it—this intense?)

In the old days (which are still here for many of us), when bar life and gay life were one and the same, tense boozy nights were followed by hungover, even more tense, mornings. Alcoholic fights were the order of the day. Instead of relaxing people, alcohol simply brought out the underlying depression and anger in many personalities, and gay couples saw themselves as the perfect combatants for cocktail-enflamed battles.

But you are thoroughly modern. You know lots of men who are still acting out the old sagas, but for you and your friends those days are far behind. Who needs these *drama queens*? You are too busy getting through your harried lives. You are enlightened.

Instead, we now we have "issue guys." These are men without the need for emotional explosions. Often, emotionally, they are almost dead shut. But they have a shopping list of "issues" (translation: conflicts) that they have to get "out in the open," before they can "get real."

In other words, we're back to negotiating. But they're the ones who've brought in the contract, with all the bad clauses set up for you to sign.

What these issue guys (all right, call them "issue queens" if you must) do not want to deal with is that many of their "issues," for the most part, don't have resolutions. Sometimes they come from very difficult personality situations—with old family problems (which you are not going to change) lying behind them. Some of these "issues" include commitment (you will never be committed enough), "outness" (you will never be "out" enough), "in-ness" (you will always be out of things that he wants you to be "in" to: his hobbies, musical tastes, political viewpoints, etc.), and an amazing sexual labyrinth you'll have to wind your way through to figure out what he wants, and/or when he does not want it.

So you can keep butting your head against these things, until you don't have a head left. But the idea of "permanently resolving" these issues, so that "we can have a real relationship," becomes merely a smoke screen for the reality that the "issue guy" actually does not want to have a relationship, real or not. And, despite all the work you put yourself through, he will continue to position his excuses—in the form of "issues"—out there in front of you, in order not to.

Although much has been written about conflict resolution and many people make careers out of it (and conversely cannot solve a single conflict at home), the first thing to do in any conflict is to separate the emotions from the immediate problems.

With some men the emotion is the problem, and dealing with this will mean either he should be in therapy (yes, again, there are times when that does work), or his lover, partner, or boyfriend should realize that there is no resolution of a problem here, but only of an emotion. At that point, belittling the feeling behind the problem is the worst thing you can do. That only calls up the childhood cue of emotional needs that were never met but belittled. But for your part, when you start to feel that every bit of your own emotional capital is being spent cleaning up after someone else, I'm afraid something else is going to have to happen.

Either you will walk out or start to deal with the situation from a more distanced point of view. Often this is exactly what your partner does not want. He wants you to get in there and wallow. If you don't, he will see you as cold, ruthless and manipulative. In his own way, these are exactly the things that he is: it is just that he is able to hide his coldness behind a wonderful decoy of fury.

When you start to see that these patterns of conflict are eating your relationship up, it is time for both of you to plan a way to deal with them. In other words, when the weather report calls for storms, plan ahead.

Basically, this means isolating the causes of conflict and working through each cause separately. For many men this is difficult, because they see problems in "strings," with one problem either leading to others or being "symbolic" of huge "continents" of problems, i.e., their partner's entire personality. In conflict resolution, it's important to lay aside sym- 81 bols and deal with real problems, and it's also important to take as many things *off* the table as possible. *Don't lay your entire relationship on the line every time a conflict arises.*

In the beginning, when you are not sure how much energy you want to invest in a new person, laying everything on the line becomes a reflex action for many men. If he's the wrong one, you want to get it over with here and now! You don't want to go through the pain once more of getting involved with Mr. Wrong. So you keep a lookout for any sign that the relationship is not worth keeping (instead of looking for signs—for instance, that he really cares about you—that show you that it's actually working).

Ralph and Henry met four months ago. Things were working out well, until Henry got bogged down at work, just as an important date was coming up for Ralph.

Ralph: "The reason you forgot my birthday is clear: you never think about anyone! Sometimes I think this is just a symbol of everything you feel about me—I'm forgettable!"

Henry: "I didn't forget your birthday. It's just that I couldn't get you the sort of present I really wanted to get you."

Ralph: "Who cares? If you really cared, that would not have been an issue."

Henry: "I do love you, but I couldn't get away from work to shop. Why don't we go out for dinner, have a nice time, and talk about the kind of present you'd like?"

In this exchange, Ralph may be giving more importance to his birthday than he has actually invested in his relationship with Henry. Like a sex date that didn't quite work out—that wasn't a "fantasy that caught fire"—Ralph sees his birthday as something else that has fizzled. Henry, in this case, is able to get around this, but next time he might not be so lucky. If Ralph keeps putting everything on the table at once, he may end up eating alone—or changing partners there very often.

As a ground rule, when you are working to "resolve" problems (another word for trying to settle a fight in an adult way) put an end to the name calling, door slamming, etc. If the two of you can't do it together, you may have to do it with someone else. It may be a good time for you, individually, to get support from your own friendship network, if only to vent some of your own feelings. This means finding a friend who can allow you to talk, without putting his own "two cents" on the line as well. Sometimes this can be an older man who's been in a relationship himself for a long time and who knows that these tension storms have a way of blowing over—or blowing themselves so out of proportion that they wreck two men.

If this does happen, and you see yourself at the end of your rope, you can try couples counseling. The good thing about counseling is that someone impartial is working for you both. The bad thing is that your counselor may have no investment himself in your staying together. You may be in a part of your life when "finding yourself" is paramount, and then wake up two years later to find yourself *alone*—and out of a relationship whose value you suddenly realize.

Sometimes these conflict and tension "storms," like weather storms, have physical origins. If you're worn down from exhaustion, illness, travel, tension at work, the tension of putting up with a homophobic world (the two of you may live where any show of emotion between you is problematic; you want to hug him and the need to do so is thwarted: the need becomes wrapped in an anger that may be pointed at a homophobic world, but becomes directed at your lover instead), conflict storms can result. Sometimes what is needed is actual physical contact. Not sex. Sex may cloud the problem, although sex can come about naturally from closeness. But a real physical closeness. Half an hour of hugs. Of genuine touching. Of back rubbing. Of sitting together and holding each other.

This does not mean, however, that hugs can do everything. Sometimes what is necessary is simply deciding the boundaries of a situation. You and your lover may need to work these out together, although occasionally your friends who've been in relationships can help you. The main idea is to realize at what point tension is coming into your lives. A good example is what happens when two men have very unequal work situations.

John works in a stressful office situation. He's a sales coordinator who has to produce sales. The office politics around him are killing: they change once a week. Coming home, the first thing he wants to do is talk them through with Robert, his lover. But Robert works at home as a freelance graphic designer. Often he has not had contact with anyone else all day, except to talk on the phone or through a computer network. Robert is starved for company and in his own way he may be just as tense as John. But where John's tension comes from working with other people, Robert's comes from working *without* them. Robert has no one off whom to bounce his feelings and ideas. Although this type of working situation may appeal to him—he has no morning commute; he is his own boss, and has had to develop self-discipline—the loneliness of working at home starts to grate on him.

When John arrives at the door, he is roaring to let it all hang out: the gossip of the office, the problems, the whole "nine yards" of his day. Then suddenly Robert realizes he has nothing to talk about. He shuts down as John opens up. What Robert really wants is to share some quiet moment with John, to ease himself back into a company situation. But John reads this as feeling ignored. "You're not interested at all in my day—or my career, are you? The only thing that matters to you is *your* work!"

Here we have a great setting for an explosion. In a "classically" hetero situation, the wife had been trained to absorb this kind of tension. Her mother might have told her that the correct thing to do was to be waiting at the door with the evening paper, a martini, and the kids out of sight. This classical situation has of course disappeared, along with the two-dollar lunch. Now wives have careers like their husbands, and often they can handle dual tensions as well as gay couples. Still, women, *by role*, have been trained to absorb tension from men, whereas for another man to do it is a new role for him.

To get over this, in a gay setting, you will have to rope off a certain amount of space for both you and your lover when he comes home from work. Allow him time to settle down. You may decide that a few times a week it's time for you both to go out, or for you to be with others—either together, with mutual friends or separately, with friends of your own. Here again, we have a place where unlike "modern" straight couples, who must mean everything to each other, you each can have other, important outside friends. You will both need a certain amount of space for you to allow your relationship to expand—to absorb the tensions between you. Sometimes holding, hugging, and talking about things work; but at other moments just allowing yourself a time to "decompress" can make the difference in your life.

## So Why Have a Lover at All?

This brings up a question: why go through having a lover at all? When Bessie Delany, one of the Delany sisters whose life story was made into a Broadway play, *Having Our Say*, was asked how did she and her sister both live to be past a hundred, she answered, "We never married. We never had husbands to worry us to an early grave!"

For women who have been conditioned to absorb the tensions of men, this formula is true. Women who never marry live longer than women who do. Women who outlive their husbands usually outlive them by many more years than men who outlive their wives. But for gay men who are able to surmount the homophobic conditions around them—and who're in the relationships they want to be in—being married is immensely healthy, both physically and emotionally. Because of our ability to empathize with each other, we take better care of each other than heterosexual couples do, and we can actually switch off the role of caretaker so that both partners have it. We are also not thrown back into the commercial "gay meat market" for company, a situation which many gay men see as synonymous with being gay. In other words, they view their own identity and sexuality in regard to how well they did the night before at the baths, the bars, or in various cruising (or, now, "networking") situations.

For these men, being single is often a constant source of sorrow.

Relationships always seem to be just out of their reach. They usually end up with a relationship "shopping list" that only gets larger as they get older—there is so much neglect to be made up for, so much lost time. The man who succeeds in it has to be "very special." The idea that there may be another man waiting who has a lot to give—real generosity, feelings, history, and comfort to share—escapes them. Instead, like the "issues man," there are vast areas to be fought out, worked through, and maneuvered around.

But for other men, singleness has come about through a choice. The choice is to develop a real intimacy with oneself, a feeling of your own self-growth and happiness. In other words, *singleness is not loneliness.* These men have intense relationships, but they are not committed to being mated. The relationships may be with women, with their families, or even with boyfriends who realize and appreciate the boundaries involved. They are not interested in a man who will be there for them all the time. The idea is ridiculous to them. Sometimes they came from very suffocating families and are delighted to be out of them. One man I knew, who came from a conservative New England family with eight kids, said that the happiest day of his life was getting a room of his own. He had to have his own apartment to do it. "I don't want a roommate or a live-in boyfriend. I want to be able to mess up and clean up when I want. And when I'm feeling sick, the last thing I want is company!"

Although the AIDS crisis has left many men literally dying to get into a relationship, it has also left many men much more alone. They have seen their friends die and many relationships fall apart from the tensions of this period. Part of "growing up" under AIDS has been an enforced desire for monogamy—it is now written into the "contract" that many gay men currently seek and this has raised the level of tension. Many gay couples, especially those who have opted to live more "private" lives in the suburbs away from a community, want no part of other gay men, especially single ones. They are strangling themselves in this arrangement—just as many heterosexual couples are—and for many single men, this is not a cheering model.

Often the few times you see these gay married men out is in a "networking" setting—with gay business and professional peers—a situation which has become as cold and unsupportive as that of many straight working counterparts. You might also run into them in very closed social situations (an occasional house party, for instance) with other gay marrieds who have become so identified with one another that they resemble—to use a line from Terrance McNally—"gay bookends." So for some men, being single has become an enriching choice. It has allowed them the freedom to swim with a more open community of men, to choose their own intimacies without having to screen them through a lover, and to travel when and where they want.

This does not mean, though, that their own survival is a piece of cake. And many of the same problems that affect men in couples will affect them, but without the support of a very significant other to share or relieve these problems.

"There may be someone who walks into your life and rings every bell you've got. The next day you know that you are head-over-heels in love with him. It will make walking through a blind alley in Beirut during their last civil war look comfortable. But there you are: suddenly he has appeared and a week later you are making plans for the rest of your life."

## CHAPTER 6

# Gay Love and Gay Marriages

No matter what pattern your relationship takes, more gay men are getting married now than ever before. Why they are doing this has little to do, strangely enough, with AIDS. *It has to do with the freedom many of us have taken on to be open about ourselves.* Marriage is a part of this freedom. Although heterosexual marriage is basically a political union that involves recognition from the state, a license, and perhaps a name change, a gay "marriage" (and we are dealing with marriage, here, in one of its most intense, complex forms), is still an exercise in courage, faith, romantic conviction, and commitment. It is also becoming a very legally entangling situation as men live together, buy property together, raise children together, travel together, get older together, and finally die together.

This is not to say that straights don't have the same problems with courage, faith, romantic conviction, and commitment. They do. But their very being together is generally not a red flag that something "out of the ordinary" is going on. For the most part, they do not have to feel intimidated walking down the street together in a strange neighborhood into which they have recently moved, or nervous about walking into a bank hoping to start joint checking and savings accounts. Although much has been written about gay ghettos and how bad they've been for gay men (a judgment I very much disagree with), there is something empowering about being in an environment where you can concentrate on getting to know and love someone without having a stream of homophobic signals, both covert *and* overt, sent to you.

In the old days (what we now call "pre-Stonewall") merely living together was an act of defiance for many men. It is difficult for younger men to understand the amount of hatred—and the energy behind it—directed at us. Although the sight of two men together might be enough of a cue to start whispers and looks, the sight of four or five men was enough to cause a riot. I remember in the mid-60s walking into a restaurant in Manhattan with three other men—we were two couples—and being told that there were "no seats available," in a half-empty room. This was on the Upper East Side, not in a small town in Georgia (where probably no one would have cared, if all the men had been white). On the Upper East Side four "single" men had to mean "queers." Strangely enough, once you got over a certain number, a degree of "normalcy" was re-established. In Dayton, Ohio, a group of eight gay men I knew used to go out for dinner once a week. I asked them if they had any problems in restaurants. "No," I was told. "The waitresses think we're a bowling team!"

Because being a couple makes you in many ways a "sitting target" for homophobia, many gay couples develop a closeness between themselves and an openness about their being a *gay* couple that single gay men do not have. You will brave little openness with your family and straight friends if all the men in your life are either bar acquaintances or tricks (holy or not!). But if there is someone you feel close enough to share your life with, you are not going to keep on passing him off as your "roommate," or someone who just *happens* to have been around for the last ten years. If you do and your friends and family believe you, then—very bluntly—they are behaving as foolishly as you are, and you are wasting a large amount of energy as well as the opportunity to share an important part of yourself with people you care about.

In some families or social circles, not believing someone is gay is considered "good taste." It is giving him "the benefit of the doubt." It is also digging a deep and wide trench between them and you. In truth, they know and you *know*. One day they will bury you in this trench, with you going to your grave thinking that "no one knew."

It is important for gay couples to establish a friendship network with people who support them as individuals and as a couple. This means that your cynical friend from your bachelor days, the one who could not keep a guy around long enough to split a pint of Haagen Dasz with him, and who is just *positive* that "these things never work out," may have to be the first to go after you move in with Mr. Right.

This weaning yourself away from some of your past friends can make married life difficult. Sometimes you need to allow yourself room for it to happen. This means room (meaning a time and a private space) for you to enjoy your new partner, and also some other room for you to be with old friends: to let them know that he is now becoming important to you, and his being there is not an "issue" for them. If he does become an "issue" (and here we are, back to the old "issue" boys and girls again) what you will see probably is some clearing away of a number of older friends. Sometimes after they find their own relationships, they may come back. But younger men will probably find that youth is a time of "trying on" friends, and even the most "intimate" youthful friendships have a way of dissolving over time as deeper involvements and love relationships come in.

## When Does the 'Date' Become Your 'Mate'?

It seems that at the "beginning" of every relationship, you come to a certain turning point in the road when both of you have to decide if this one is really "it." I put *beginning* in quotes because the actual beginning of a relationship may have nothing to do with its chronological beginning. You may have known Harvey for years as someone who was always there at parties, beach houses, etc., before you realized—just as he did—that you had actually fallen in love with him. On the other hand, there may be someone who walks into your life and rings every bell you've got. The next day you know that you are head-over-heels in love with him—and you are probably in the most vulnerable and dangerous spot you'll ever be in in your life. It will make walking through a blind alley in Beirut during their last civil war look comfortable. But there you are: suddenly he has appeared and a week later you are making plans for the rest of your life.

The weirdest, oddest, most confusing thing is that *sometimes* these situations actually work, and this man who does ring all of your bells *is* supposed to be there. No matter how much your friends warn you, no matter how frightening it is to trust someone you know so little about (or do you?), he is the right one.

Strangely enough, gay men often go through this phenomenon. Perhaps it is that we've spent so much time alone, and we have spent so much time figuring ourselves out, that when it does happen—when *he* does appear—we do know it. This may go along with the gay motif of "recognition," so important to our collective mythologies. Just as we are somehow able to recognize each other as gays (the old "gaydar"), we are also able to recognize that person into whom we are going to place literally our *entire* emotional collateral.

Putting your whole emotional *collateral* (a wonderfully financial expression) in someone is what falling in love is. Basically what you are saying is: "I'm giving myself over to you. You now have the responsibility of making me happy, because I will not be happy without you." This is a tremendous responsibility to give to anyone. When we are kids and full of high energy (sexual and otherwise) and high expectations, we do this fairly often. Kids are always falling in love; and (just as quickly) out of love.

When they don't fall out of love—and the fall from love is horribly painful, because they don't have the experience to put it into perspective—then the consequences can be fatal. Teen suicide, especially gay teen suicide, can be a result. (I am not saying that gay teens kill themselves often from unrequited love, but being hurt by someone whom you feel you can only secretly care about can be even more devastating: hence the added danger for gay teens.)

Rejection is difficult enough for someone who has had a full life     89 already and some experience with rejection itself; i.e., that you can live past it. But for a younger man these lightning-fast charges of emotion can be deadly. It is for this reason that although your heart (and gonads) are telling you FAST, FAST, FAST, your head should be telling you SLOW, SLOW, SLOW.

None of this answers the question, though, at what point should you be ready to commit to another man? At what point should you be ready to "marry"? Straights do have it over us in that they can get engaged—an idea which currently, for the most part, means you fuck with a diamond solitaire on. But before they make the leap of making everything "legal," they have had some experience with each other. Since today even being illegal can become as complicated as being "legal" (with kids, joint homes, and bank accounts), the idea of an official engagement does not carry the sense that it once had.

For gay men, an "engagement" may mean that the couple keep separate apartments with clothes in each one, that they travel together and split expenses equally, and that their friends now start calling them at two numbers. The real marriage may mean that you move in together, or that you start announcing to your friends that you are a couple and that any invitation for one will have to mean an invitation for two. It can also mean that you will start to pool finances in a way that you did not do as two singles. As a rule of thumb, though, I think that the marriage really starts when both men firmly believe that they can be responsible for each other. They are no longer simply casual acquaintances and their relationship has progressed even beyond being friends—that is, people you are close to, but who can come and go in your life.

This brings up a very important point in any gay emotional couple situation: the importance of your partner and where he stands in your life. For some men, if it is a *question* of their mates versus their families and past friends, their mates are simply *out*. This is a controversial and tricky point, but they will not disrupt their family life, the place that they have established for themselves in the community (both the gay one and/or the straight one), or their own life for a partner.

Part of this rests with their attitude towards their own gayness—the constant sense of apology that they have accumulated around it—and the rest with their sense of themselves. They will always be the "bachelor brother," the "unmarried son," or "the regular guy." For some men, these images are so ingrained that they cannot outgrow them: the image has been shellacked over them, and even though they can barely move under it, they have not developed a perspective that will allow them to see it. At some time in their lives, they may gain it and when this happens, they will start to have real *adult* gay relationships. But until it happens, the term itself—*real adult gay relationships*—is completely contradictory to them.

For other men, this relationship with a "significant" man is what they are all about. Sometimes perhaps even too much so. The result is that they can only see themselves in terms of coupleness, especially if they are not married and being part of a couple is a constant fantasy to them. Or, if they do marry, like their mothers (or fathers) before them, they may find themselves the constant victims of an abusive relationship, that they stay in for "the sake of the marriage."

However, at the beginning of this marriage, realizing the sheer joy of being coupled—when you've wanted it so much—is part of the tremendous release and happiness and freedom of gay married life. I say *freedom* because for the first time many gay men (like many straight men as well) are free to release *the full power of their own romantic imaginations.* They have realized completely what was one of their deepest intentions. These newly coupled men have fantasized a man *in* their lives for, perhaps, most of their lives; and now, finally, *he* is there. His presence has for them a religious significance, and not being able to contend with this—to cynically cast it aside—is for many men, who are forever on the outside of relationships, a part of their own corrosive, internalized homophobia. They cannot see the depth and love involved here.

So you now have this man who means everything to you. You have gone through what I describe as "the ritual of recognition" that is at the heart of so much gay mythology (it is, truly, finding that perfect foot that fits the magic glass slipper—and the heart that seems to speak directly to you). You are now "twinned" to the person who fulfills what seemed to have been an immeasurable incompleteness. I describe it is as like diving to the bottom of the deepest lake in the world, to come up with something you have sought for so long: that most beautiful pearl that lies right there before you. You can't believe your luck in having it there: and now you're picking it up.

Look, it's *there* in your hand. (*Wow! I never thought I'd get it.*)

(But <u>wait</u>: does that mean that—somewhere in your life—you won't try this dive again?

Or that there are no other pearls in the world?

Or that this pearl you now have will be *the* pearl to satisfy you? After all, you don't know how long life is—and how small even the biggest pearls really are.

Well, the answer to these big questions is mostly, but not always, negative—but . . . anyway, read on—)

What you *do* realize is that the pearl is there. And you *can* survive the dive.

What's important for gay men seeking happiness with other men to understand is that the intensity of this happiness, or the degree of satisfaction from it, does not depend on the sexual intensity of it or the degree of sexual satisfaction from it, both of which may be there at a certain point (such as the beginning), but both of which can be misleading. So: if they are not there *one hundred percent* don't discount the relationship and your own feelings towards the man you're involved with. Being able to see sex as a part of a relationship, but not *all* of it, is very important, especially at the beginning.

Nor—let's get this right out, too—does it depend upon keeping your relationship within a pattern of monogamy. So if you fall off that wagon, as I said before, you can still keep much of the loveliness and warmth of this relationship going. And, as I have said before, it should not depend upon how "right" you seem for each other to your friends, or how many hobbies you have in common. But it will depend upon satisfying a group of needs you both have, as well as establishing a common "core" group of values. I will talk later about these important psychic needs which are embedded in the gay mythos.

But it's important to understand this shared sense of *values*, because it is something that often gets lost. Although we popularly think of sex as being the "ultimate" in communications (like it's sung of in pop songs, and—unfortunately—much of the gay press), this sense of sharing values is more important. First, because in sharing values you are revealing a great deal of yourself, and, second, the "hard" evidence of values remains after sexual relations themselves become secondary. This is because values relay much of the inner emotional material that gay men pass between themselves in a close relationship.

"Values" is basically another word for how you see and approach life. Basically, values are not opinions, but some deeper stratum on which opinions are laid and which float (hopefully, with some stability) over an emotional core. If compassion is a value that two men hold in common, it will keep them together. But if one feels that other human beings are beneath his contempt, then this core of shared values is not there. Although values may be difficult to express, they usually make themselves known through life changes, crises, and problems. A good example are men who are "opportunity" oriented, whose basic value is to take advantage of any change that comes their way. These men (and women) can change political stripe five times in a lifetime, and still come out as the same grasping, "opportunistic" people.

Although it's easy to see values in certain political messages (I have known men who were rock-ribbed conservatives who mated perfectly, until one lost his job and suddenly his "values" shifted), our usual idea of politics (especially in this Age of Publicity, when two political parties can use the same word and mean two opposite things) rarely comes into this. What does come in is something much deeper. Often this comes down to the "character," where we keep our values; or, plainly enough, to the basic *substance* that a person is, or allows himself to become.

But this system of values will become communalized between two men and become part of the deeper, "specialized" (meaning: personal and specific) relationship that two lovers have. Often it can hardly be articulated, but it is there at work to keep them together. Around this system of values should be a good support of respect. Respect means that you allow someone the privacy to be himself and you support this privacy. *When you tear this privacy down in a humiliating way, you are tearing down the complete structure of the relationship.* Some very dysfunctional relationships actually work well in the midst of constant character demolition. This is a role model some men have had since childhood—they had the abrasive, castrating mother who was never listened to; the abusive, ignoring father who was never around; or vice versa—and since this was the major early relationship of their lives, they figure that this is how relationships work.

Sometimes all of this violence is done in the name of "honesty," or making sure "there's never a dull minute." I knew one gay couple who had seen *Who's Afraid of Virginia Woolf?* seven or eight times too many, and when guests came by they would replay whole scenes from Edward Albee's classic play about a couple wallowing in its disappointments and violence. They quickly lost most of their friends. After two years of misery, they broke up. To them mutual respect and a core of values were foreign terms. But it also seemed that this was the model to them upon which gay relationships should be based: simple, honest self-loathing. I hope that this is a model you will quickly throw in the garbage, and keep there.

## Ropes, Dollars, and Chains

Getting back to the idea of power—and how it's distributed, remember?—brings up a real "8-ball" in most relationships, gay and straight: money. Now that sex has come out of the closet, money, it seems, has gone back in. Money and how to deal with it puts a real strain on gay relationships, since it is often the means of control that one partner uses on another. Control patterns with money often work in the following ways:

Eric, an older executive, has a great deal more money than Mark, a younger would-be singer. Since Eric has made it plain from the start that he will not be "exploited" in a "sugar daddy" position, he insists that both of them pay their "fair" share for everything, which he believes is "fifty-fifty." Eventually, Mark is made to feel more and more left out of things, and he also begins to doubt the value of his own future as a singer. He goes through a crisis of confidence in himself, until the relationship breaks up.

Both Howard, a middle-management businessman, and Allen, a college teacher, make the same amount of money. But Howard is so distrustful of Allen that he keeps a tab on every nickel that their relationship involves. This means both the money spent by either of them, or the money that they spend together. Often, he tells Allen that, since he's "a businessman," he knows more about money than Allen does, even though Allen has lived on his own successfully. Allen, after losing several money arguments, starts to feel powerless, even with his own money.

Bill, an underemployed but for the most part sweet-natured printer, has a hard time holding on to work. But from the onset of their relationship, he has refused ever to take money from more job-stable Frank, who has worked in the same corporation for years. Frank has money to spare and, rather than see Bill do without things, he is generous offering it. But Bill, with less money, only makes Frank feel guilty for everything he has or can do. He uses his *independence* as a weapon against Frank, until Frank, tired of living a lifestyle of self-denial that he has worked hard to avoid, leaves.

John, a successful accountant who has made all his money himself, constantly tries to one-up David, a social worker who inherited some money of his own. He buys David presents that David cannot possibly reciprocate and buys himself things that David cannot duplicate, and then brings this up to him. David, who, despite his inheritance, is not so money-oriented, starts to feel like a failure and worthless.

Ralph, an advertising executive, has insisted from the onset that he and Pete, a chef in a small restaurant, pool their resources. They put both of their paychecks into one bank account, which delights Pete, since he makes less money than Ralph. But Ralph has made it plain that he has other sources of income, and these are going into a special retirement account that Pete cannot touch. Even though he has more access to money than he's ever had, Pete starts to feel really broke—he has no money of his own that he can control—and if he leaves the relationship, his lover will still have access to funds that are only Ralph's.

After Harry, an office clerk, lost his job, Rick, a lawyer, began to support him. In exchange for his support, Harry did some office work for Rick and also assumed all of the work around the house. In the beginning, this seemed like a good idea. But Rick insisted that Harry only take money from their joint account and since he was now "out of work," that he give up his own bank account. Although it was better than being out on the street, Harry began to feel completely broke and dependent.

Although these money-power arrangements can take many different patterns, one idea is necessary to cut through all the problems, anger, and sorrow that they spread: *the importance of your relationship must rise above money arrangements.* Let me put this in no uncertain, black-and-white terms. No matter what the distribution of wealth is in your couple, in no way is one man the boss, the arbiter of power, bank, sugar daddy, etc. And in no way is the other man the "boy," maid, servant, employee, etc. As dicey as our economy is, as hard-put as some couples are to stay afloat, the bottom line is that you can—if worse comes to worst—survive on your own. You can replace his money with your own. You can also go out and find somebody else to do all of the little jobs around the house that he does—but you cannot replace *him*.

Men in relationships are not interchangeable. No two dynamics between two men will ever be the same as those between two others. Each relationship is a special situation, and it should rise above the financial straits that you find yourself in. This idea must be kept in mind constantly in gay relationships, because the odds for you being in a problematic financial situation with one another are high. For example, since Americans for professional reasons now change locations every five years on the average, at some point either he or you will have to move for job reasons. If this happens, you will have a choice of either breaking up, or ending up in a strange city without a job while he has one, or accepting the professional consequences of not moving.

AIDS and other health problems have also brought their own affects to financial patterns. Sometimes both partners end up becoming bankrupted by illness. Other times only one partner will be severely affected, leaving the other partner in the awkward position of trying to maintain himself professionally while he has to take up the slack.

This does not mean that your boyfriend now has an open season to sponge off you. Or that if you are working twelve hours a day to bring money into the house and he's doing nothing at all, you can't object. But using money as a way of gaining power in a relationship is the best single way to destroy it. Strangely enough, *two* aspects of our lives are actually on your side to *keep* finances from destroying your relationship:

First—the role of men, traditionally, allows them to support someone else. This is not so totally outside our role that doing so goes against either our grain or society's. Thus, at a restaurant, for instance, for one man to pick up the check for another is still considered quite "normal"; for a woman to do this may yet cause problems. I bring this up because some men still have this idea that for them to support another person financially is coming out of left field. "If I wanted to support someone, I'd get married!" Well, you *are* married—and in this particular marriage, at some point, the man you're with may require support. This does not mean that it will happen forever (although, face it, it might), but when the chips are down, you should be ready to pick them up.

Oddly enough, some relationships can only happen because one man is *willing* to be supported by another. This frequently happens with men who are in very high-pressure job situations. They need their own form of support to keep going. They need to know that someone will always be there; that they and their work will be the first priority in a relationship. If two men are in equally high-pressure situations, the pressure between the two of them can kill the relationship. But if one can accept being on a lower professional track, or being financially supported—so that he can move, for instance, when it's necessary to move, or change his own plans when called upon—he can give a larger amount of emotional and physical presence to his more high-pressure, professionally successful partner.    95

Many gays unfortunately do not understand the dynamics of this. They keep looking for other ultra-successful men as "peers" to mate with. They may see themselves as automatic "date bait," and cannot understand why the glamour of their high-profile, pressure-cooker careers burns off so quickly. These matings frequently do not last, since there is no one in the relationship to absorb the pressure from two very stressful professional lives. Very wealthy straight men know, however, that being the wife of a successful man takes certain skills—and very happily they pay for them. It is for this reason that a small group of attractive, smart trophy wives end up marrying—over and over again—from a pool of very wealthy men.

The other aspect of the two that I mentioned is the simplicity with which financial pattern problems can be solved as long as the *emotional problems* that go with them can be put into place. Most of the time, just as with sexual problems in a relationship, finances can be solved with an equitable arrangement regarding money—one that is done simply and clearly—and one also allowing privacy within this arrangement.

First, equitably, if two men have a real difference in their incomes, then all basic bill-splitting should be done in proportion to their incomes, *not* on a fifty-fifty basis that actually penalizes both of them (and often the penalties are greater than the benefits). For instance, in the case of Eric and Mark, the executive and the singer, if Mark makes only half of what Eric makes, then they should work out what proportion of their income will go for bills and work from there. It may be impossible for them to work "50-50," and Eric will end up paying a higher dollar amount, for instance, of his income for rent or maintenance. But he will continue to have more left in real dollars, and the relationship can continue, which should be the highest priority.

And Mark should be encouraged to have his own money, so that he is not left to feel financially "stranded," no matter what. This should go for all men in these relationships. It is important for all parties to have money that is their own; that they do not have to account for; that, like their own private sexual time (something I will get to later), they can maintain with dignity.

What is difficult, though, with the dollar problems are the emotional ones that go with them. Although Freud said about his own oral smoking fixations, "Sometimes a cigar is just a cigar," often in financial patterns you are repeating other patterns that go back to the first relationship you saw in your life: Mommy and Daddy. A Daddy who splurged presents on Mommy after he came home drunk, then while sober made Mommy account for every nickel. ("You *think* money grows on trees???") A Mommy who used her own extravagance as a way of humiliating Daddy. ("I'm used to living like this and you can't stop me!") Or a professional couple who were always in competition with each other. These patterns can be repeated in your own relationships. Just as we find ourselves talking over and over again in the language that our parents used on us ("I'll never do anything for you again!" "You can't be trusted for a moment!" "You've been nothing to me but a disappointment!"), we also find ourselves talking with our wallets the same way.

Some therapists will say that the only way to stop this is to go into therapy and then *work it out*. But another (and much cheaper) way is to realize that you can change—regardless. And that this "voice" you hear behind you, the one that tells you that "he's only after you for your money," "he'll never be responsible," etc., is only that—that residue from the problems with your first relationship (your parents), and it has nothing to do with what is actually going on.

---

## The Kept Man

---

Here is a good time to talk about that gay fantasy so many younger men dream about: being kept. You don't, by the way, have to be younger to be kept—there are older kept men, who got that way, usually by being successful *younger* kept men. I make a distinction here between being "kept" and being "supported." Kept men are *kept* almost entirely for sexual purposes. Men are "supported" as a way of maintaining a relationship that may have little or nothing to do with sex, but with other emotional investments. When the sex stops, the "kept" relationship also either stops—often on a dime—or grows into a "support" relationship, which means that the original "contract" between the kept and his keeper has deepened, and both men can see each other as real human beings, rather than as pet and handler.

In the old days, kept men (or "boys"—kept men, like ballet dancers, were referred to as *boys*) were expected to either look or be "straight." They were discreet, "straight-appearing" lads who had to keep up the image of not being queer (or, in the parlance of the another generation, they could not be "swishes"). For one thing, the men who kept them were often in the closet, married, and fearful; and, for another, as the French proverb goes, "When milk is so cheap, why buy the cow?" Why *pay* for gay sex with a man who is easily taken to be . . . gay? Often kept men were successful hustlers who, like their female counterparts, ended up with a "john" who agreed to sponsor them—foot all their bills, set them up in style, etc.

Today, much of this (but not all of it—there are still very closeted men who keep "straight" boys) has changed. For one thing, there are a huge number of guppies who are barely older than the gorgeous young things they take a shine to. They are more than able to pay their way, and are not trying to pass off these lads as their "nephews." (I had a lovely young friend, once, in San Francisco, who had been the "nephew" of about six completely unrelated men in succession in Pacific Heights.) Younger men are keeping men because their own careers are twenty-four-a-day situa- 97 tions, and, as the winners in our shopping mall culture, they realize that they can get what they pay for—as long as they are willing to pay for it.

There are still older sugar daddies out there who find keeping one boy for some time more practical than resorting to hustlers, escorts, etc. But the transactions of meeting boys and men, of being seen with them, and taking money from them is much more open. There are bars, resorts, and social events where this activity openly takes place. (High-end AIDS events have become good hunting grounds for "sponsors.") Men with money go to them in person, look over the offerings, and then make their *intentions* known very clearly. In the old days, these men might have resorted to a pimp or agent, who took a cut of the whole affair and whose job would also include clearing the boy out, once Daddy Warbucks got tired of him.

What has not changed is that this is still basically a "rent" situation, and when the sex sours, the rent stops. Really successful kept men know that massaging a man's ego as well as his sex organs can enhance the relationship. The bitchy, petulant, kept "teen" (or perennial teen) remains that way for about six months. So if you are in the market for a rich man's kisses, remember that besides getting "Uncle" hot and bothered, it is also important—after his hard day of slogging through the Gold Market—to keep him cooled down and feeling good about both himself and you.

Also: start a bank account. Never allow him to get you into debt (then you start to wonder who's keeping whom?). And if he sets you up in an apartment, don't move in unless the lease is in your name. Also, as I said before, think of this "free ride" as merely treading water—so do something valuable with the time. Enroll in school; work on your design portfolio; get to know *his* broker. And even though you might be treading water on Park Avenue, Lake Shore Drive, or in Beverly Hills, try to put something else into the relationship besides just the Sex = Money routine. Who knows? You might even start to like each other.

> ## A Timetable for a Gay Marriage

Several books that have come out about male same-sex relationships have developed the idea of a "schema," that is a diagrammatic approach or timetable, for gay marriages. In some ways this is important, because gay marriages, at least at this point, do not work as predictably as straight ones (which have been studied more than the Talmud and the Koran put together, and are still not very predictable).

But gay men like the idea that there might be some predictable points in their relationships. We want to feel that, just like anyone else, there is some stabilizing predictability in our lives. For instance, in hetero marriage, you start out with an idea: "You and I—man and woman—*belong* together." This will be followed by some degree of social/sexual exploration (known as "dating"), which will be coupled with immense pressure from friends, family, and society to get the marriage on the road and happening.

All of this is supposed to end up in a long, happy, *authentic* marriage. A marriage that has a true, fairy-tale simplicity. In which, as the computer people say, everything is WYSIWYG: "What you see is what you get."

Americans, as a group, have a phobic reaction to a more "European" model of marriage, one based more on companionability and social responsibility than on K-Mart greeting card sentiments. We *expect* that young marrieds *will* live happily ever after. They'll have no secrets from each other. And the two of them will meet every single need they have for intimacy, companionship, privacy, and excitement. (And, if these adult needs cannot be met by only the two of them, then these needs will just *disappear*.)

Going back to this older European idea, marriage was something you entered into to have children, to make a home, and to keep up a social structure. Among the middle and upper middle classes, within five or ten years of marriage (unless earlier), a married man might take a mistress (that is, if he had not kept her on the side the entire time). When her husband took a mistress, his wife usually turned her head. At that point, she could either take a lover or develop her own interests: travel, friendships, or her education. The possibility that her husband's "mistress" might be another man was also there. It was never talked about, but to keep her home together every smart woman learned to know the signs that her husband's interest in women was minimal. Sometimes she even liked this.

You may ask what does this have to do with your own gay marriage and a timetable for it? The answer is that as you hit certain realities in your relationship, learning flexibility as well as how to communicate is important. And it is important to see that our American fantasy of the "authentic" (WYSIWYG) heterosexual marriage can destroy yours.

To begin with, there are certain *stages* that your marriage will go through. While you are going through them, you may still be adhering to your own fantasy of an "authentic" (meaning "completely open, giving, satisfying") relationship. These are high demands, but basically they mean that you expect your lover to give you everything you have been wanting (or perhaps even, to a certain degree, getting) from a spectrum of friends. These demands include that he understand you completely. That he sympathize with you always. And that he be unstintingly open to you with his feelings, finances, and sexuality.

In short, that he will give you *everything* that for the most part your parents could not.

Other demands may be that he never look at another man. That if he *does* look at another man, he will immediately tell you. That you will both be honest with each other about everything, even if you (or he) are not ready for honesty at the moment. That he will surrender his friends for you. And that all other feelings he has had for past lovers, friends, boyfriends, etc., will come to a crashing end as soon as you become serious about each other.

Also, that his tastes will start to conform to yours. And that, from the very beginning, he will understand the very *language* you use. As you can imagine, it is a tall order, and yet it is basically what most men seek as the "authentic" relationship in which they expect to invest themselves. From this list of hard demands, which many gay men put on a relationship, and the need for an "authentic" marriage, one which satisfies all their expectations openly and (often) immediately, you can see that we are traveling in very difficult waters here, which could put any relationship on the rocks.

Going back to the timetable idea, you can expect that it may take the first two or three years for both of you even to *start* speaking the same language. You say this is impossible: you're both speaking English. But the very words you use have been shaped by your lives. Words that may cause him to become furious, may mean nothing to you. Just as in diplomacy the words in a treaty can mean different things to both parties, the words either of you use can mean different things to the two of you.

What is to you "just joshing" can make him furious. The deepest, most private words to you, may seem silly to him. So it may take a couple of years, then, for both of you to know what your words mean—their lightness, their seriousness, their histories—and how to use them. John, a friend of mine, had a lover named Ernie, who had grown up isolated on a farm in Kansas. He was thin, pale, shy and bashful. His parents were sure he was *stupid*. They used the word around him often, and every time he heard it—both from them and later on in his life—the word "stupid" lacerated him. It cut right through. It took John a year to understand the depth of hurt in that word, and even more time for both John and Ernie to defuse it finally.

Other immediately recognizable problems in a relationship are sex, followed by emotional commitments and finances. Since so many gay men use sex as the main track on which they lay down their relationships, their degree of emotional commitment will be laid down with it. While the sex is hot and heavy, the commitment is there. As sex starts to cool down—an almost inevitable part of any relationship, for reasons I'll go into later—emotional commitment becomes unraveled as well. This is really the complete *opposite* of what should be happening, and yet the sexual basis of so many relationships dictates this. Money patterns are also laid down along the track of the sex/commitment line, which means that as sex cools down, money problems heat up.

Often, then, by the third year, relationships become stale. They have gone through the gay version of the "seven-year itch," and even scratching it with extra fingers (such as new approaches to sex, outside affairs, attempts at counseling, etc.) does not help.

How, then, do you work your way through a ten-year relationship and beyond? Following a schematic approach, some therapists might say, "The first three years you are basically getting to know each other; after this comes three years of nesting, during which time you may decide to pool resources (time to open that joint bank account!); then comes, seven years later, buying a house together; and finally—after the relationship has been tested as much as it can and has still survived—some degree of opening up the relationship to outside interests, yours and his. Possibly, *then*, at that point, outside affairs can be honestly explored.

This is all well and good, except that people don't work this way. Some excellent relationships start out immediately with financial sharing and much emotional openness. Both men want this and realize they are committed enough at that time to their togetherness to do this. Other men may start out with some sexual and emotional closeness, but find that power-sharing problems are eating them alive. Others may start out with a great deal of sexual adventurism, and then finally settle down exclusively with each other.

What is necessary is that men allow themselves to go through various plateaus of communication (either by themselves or with the help of others) that allow them to work with (and through) their problems. They can do this as long as they see their relationship as something that is flexible, growing, and important. And also one that allows the two men in it to feel, as individuals, productive and happy. Also, realistically, they should see these plateaus as being based on each other: what they can bring to the relationship and what kind of work they can do to keep it going. (In other words, not based on what their friends are doing; or—in some cases—on what an eager therapist may say must be done.)

What I am saying here is that men do go through stages in their relationships, but these stages are rarely "schematic." They rarely work on a timetable. They are organic situations of communication and growth. What is important is that they learn to recognize these situations and learn to work with them.

For many men, going back into the closet years "before Stonewall" (when few people outside of an immediate circle of friends *knew*), most gay relationships were seen as something that had to be kept in the background or closet. All gay men could do was hope that any investments they had in being together would keep them that way, because society as a whole was doing everything possible to tear them apart. This went for both straight society and gay society, which had a self-hating agenda ("Show me a happy homosexual and I'll show you a gay corpse," says a character in Mart Crowley's hit play, *The Boys in the Band*.)

At this point, though, gay relationships have become much more alive entities. They are "out there." This does not mean that your relationship should get out of hand and become more important than the two men in it—who will stay together no matter what. But the relationship as a living thing, rather than just a schematic one, should contain a real part of your energy. It can become an extension of the deepest parts of the two men who are engaged in it. What develops then is not the idealized "schema," the "authentic" marriage that is open for comment by all your friends and relatives, but *an adult working together of two men*, who are trying to nourish the passion of their commitment to each other, as well as the necessity for their own individual privacies.

In contemporary heterosexual marriage—where both members of a couple are either working way too hard and/or stranded, alone, out in the suburbs—this idea of separate privacies seems like an impossibility. Children move against it, and gay men who are trying to raise children often find that the first thing that goes out the window (along with a good night's sleep) is their own sense of privacy. When you have children, you are no longer a private person; you are a Daddy. You also have this constant need to produce the "authentic" marriage—in a gay version—that is always open for inspection, like a restaurant kitchen.

But gay marriages, by the very fact that so much of the "marriage" is not or will not be recognized, have much more room in them for individual privacies, for individual friends, for outside affairs which may actually help a gay relationship (but which normally destroy straight marriages), and for *real* identification with each other. This is something that rarely if ever exists in straight marriage: for a husband to identify with his wife is almost impossible. But for one gay lover *not* to identify with the other is rare.

This identification with one another can open up gay marriages to allow tremendous excitement. Suddenly, you are a part of someone else and he is a part of you. You love him so much that you cannot imagine your life without him—and this romantic imagination carries the relationship past so much of the oppression and problems gay men face. You realize there is a part of him which is the *you* you want to be (imagine a husband feeling that way about his wife and you realize why supposedly "straight" men leave their wives for other men). You find that you will do anything to create this magic thing, this couple created from the two of you.

This marriage is the very flowering of your feelings.

You want it to be everything.

The problem, now, is how to protect yourself within this wondrous, lovely, but often demanding "Frankenstein" monster that you both have made and adore. But the first question you may ask is, if relationships–or marriages—are so wonderful, why do we need to protect ourselves within them?

## Protecting Yourself and the Relationship

The answer to that is that if the two men within the relationship are not protected, singly and together, the relationship will not survive. Or, it will become simply a holding tank for two bitter and distant men. Part of your own protection will be allowing and encouraging yourself to grow, even if the pattern into which your relationship has settled discourages it. This pattern may be that the relationship has become sexless, which means that you will have to become responsible for your own sex life—don't expect him to give you permission to have one—and also responsible, if that is what you want, for initiating sex back into your relationship.

For some men this is unnerving and requires a strengthening of their own sense of self-worth. In re-initiating sex into your relationship, there is always the question, "What if"—for whatever reason—"he rejects this?" Is he rejecting *me* or rejecting simply reopening our relationship to sex? Part of your own self-protection should be the realization that he is not rejecting you, but he is simply not able at this point to deal with sexual intimacy *on top of all the other forms of intimacy in a close relationship*. (Despite the gay fantasy that this never happens in hetero relationships, it does. The result, heterosexually, can be a cold, sexless marriage—what the French call a *marriage blanc*—and since any concept of an outside affair may be unapproachable, one partner will simply walk out.)

Sometimes the way to get over the "sex gulf" that widens between two men is to feel strong enough within yourself to allow him to move away from you, get out on his own, and then come back to you—for sex. The fact that you are strong enough to allow a certain frankness, delicacy, and openness towards him and his sexual needs is very appealing. It shows that you are not judging or condemning him. Neither are you tearing down or demeaning his feelings and needs—and this often works as a great invitation for him to bring these needs and feelings back to you.

Other ways of protecting yourself can include: seeking out friends on your own. Seeking out more of a life, such as outside interests of your own, which you can choose to share with your lover. And not losing sight of your own career or life goals, while at the same time keeping them flexible enough to include him.

Often within a relationship, some men feel so unprotected that they *capitulate* everything that is theirs, with the feeling that this is the necessary "price" they will have to pay. Please realize that this is only an excuse: the relationship cannot be there as a whipping boy for your own lack of purpose; it should, to work, strengthen it. But if you find that every night you are doing what he wants to do, instead of what you *need* to do, something is really wrong and you are not protecting what is a very important part of yourself in the relationship.

If you allow this to go on for very long, you will find that the relationship will either fall apart or you will be dragged down in it. Obvious examples of this are men who develop co-dependent alcohol and drug problems: they are literally clinging to each other on a raft of substance abuse. But we also have men whose own sense of individuality and self-worth are swamped in the wake of a much stronger, more successful, and unconsciously demanding partner. Unlike the "trophy" wife who goes into a relationship with an older, successful man with her eyes—and pocketbook—wide open, these men become the "mousy" wives of a couple. They use their partners' personalities and successes as excuses to keep them from having careers and lives that are satisfying, and on a track that they feel they are in control of.

Instead, they are always on someone else's track.

To keep this from happening to you, it is important to retract (or "retrack") at times from your relationship. Not to empathize so much with your lover's needs. To realize that you have needs of your own. They can include the need to go back to school, to stay home and do work that may not bring in an income but that is vitally important to you, and to assert what you feel is the importance of your own identity. You are not simply "Jack's lover who is always with him," but your own person. This situation is operative when a gay couple moves to another city, where one of them already has a job and the other finds himself adrift.

In straight situations, these moves can be buffered by kids, who quickly bring in their own friends and their parents: again, the strange heterosexual custom of making friends through your kids, but this can work in the cold suburban settings in which many Americans now find themselves. Although many cities have active gay communities, just being part of a couple in a strange location can place you outside them. Few communities have planned activities for new men, especially if the men are older and are not part of a gay sports, cultural, or sexual network.

It is important for both men, therefore, to start developing lives of their own in a new setting as quickly as possible. If Dennis already has a job and Will, his lover, does not, it means that Will should work just as hard at getting a life in a new setting as Dennis has. Even if he cannot find a job immediately, he should develop around himself the life support that is necessary for him to feel involved and productive.

Some men will do this by compulsively, secretly cruising on the outside, while at home they are actually giving no time to themselves. They are not protecting and strengthening themselves in any way, but simply trying to dilute the problem with sex. Going back to Dennis and Will, it is important for Will to put together a space for himself in a new setting. Some men do this by setting up a home office, by looking into adult courses that can get them out the house—so they are not barricaded inside all day—or simply allowing themselves time to look inward and see how the move has affected them. Whereas Dennis may be angry that Will is not "fixing up the house," or beating the bushes to get a new job, Will's need to work on himself in a vulnerable situation reflects both partners' needs to strengthen themselves to keep their marriage working. At this point, you no longer have the American dream of the WYSIWYG marriage—which falls apart as soon as it stops being "authentically" shallow—but something that is much deeper and much more satisfying, certainly, to both men in it.

"Anti-gay violence hits most gay men in the most elemental way.
It returns us to that place where the wrong word at the wrong time
could destroy us: could make us *question* our own value
(and our values). Question our existence. Our right to live."

CHAPTER 7

# Surviving Anti-Gay Violence

I had wanted to begin this chapter on a certain *cold* level: with statistics and a clinicalism, a detachment, that would separate me from it. The statistics are there: yes, anti-gay violence in many areas of the country—especially, but not always, areas with large, "out" populations of gay men and lesbians—is the largest growing area of bias violence in America. At a time in which crime statistics as a whole are going *down* dramatically, anti-gay violence is going in the opposite direction. In New York, it comprises the largest number of hate crimes against men by strangers. In certain rural areas, especially in small towns in Texas, Louisiana, and Mississippi, where rabidly anti-gay fundamentalist preachers spew out fire and brimstone at "prayer meetings" several times a week, late Friday nights—after weekly high school football games–have become the traditional nights for going out and "gettin' queers." In other areas, anti-gay violence has become associated with far Right militia groups or as part of an ongoing racist agenda, queers being notorious "nigger lovers," as well.

I wanted to talk about this clearly—without emotion—and yet I find myself almost incapable of this. Because anti-gay violence hits me–as it hits most gay men—in the most elemental way. It hurls us back to that place where we were the picked-on outsiders ("sissies") in kindergarten or primary school, and then junior high and into high school and beyond. Anti-gay violence returns us to that place where the wrong word at the wrong time can destroy us: can make us *question* our own value (and our own basic values). Question our existence. Question our right to live. Our right *not* to kill ourselves, which for many of us appears to be the only route out of a crossfire of violence, both from within and from without. This is a ongoing battle that we are fiercely fighting, sometimes without even lifting a hand against a *visible* enemy.

What I'm saying here is that anti-gay violence brings forth a fight on its own. To survive. But even if you don't fight back—physically or in any way—the battle for your survival is in front of you. It is a constant fight, but too often we defeat ourselves by *normalizing* this conflict and its aftermath. Because while sparring against the rage and anger that people in victimized situations normally encounter within themselves, we find ourselves *not* winning the fight but going on to "adjust" our lives. We acclimate ourselves to this bitter, unresolved, internalized anger. We accept our defeat. This is an adjustment that millions of hurt gay men have had to make for years—and that we should no longer accept. This leads not only to the obvious physical harm done to us by violence, but also to its often far more *damaging* consequence: to being swept under by an *undertow of depression* that comes from an acceptance of our own "deserved" victimization.

I say *deserved*, because the "logic" for years here has been, "Yes, I *am* gay and they did pick up on this and by letting them know it . . . I deserve this."

This last feeling is often reinforced by the police and other law enforcement officials, whose attitude is that you as a "deviant," either by *flaunting* your lifestyle (in other words: *not* hiding yourself one hundred percent) or by associating with other "undesirables" (the pick-up who turns out to be a robber, for instance), have placed yourself in jeopardy.

Several years ago a conservative New York police commissioner said about repealing New York's state sodomy laws that he did "not feel homosexuality was a victimless crime." "Homosexuals victimize themselves. They pick each other up and bring home undesirables. The undesirables beat them up and murder them—so a crime is there and they have just invited it. As long as this is the case, I will do everything I can to keep the sodomy laws on the books." The idea that any citizen does not deserve to be victimized escaped him. What this bit of stupidity does is place gay men—even in "sophisticated" New York—in a victim's role they should not be in.

Going back to the first thing I said, though—that I wanted to feel detached about anti-gay violence—I cannot. Having been the target of anti-gay violence in Savannah as far back as I can remember (I recall at the age of six being taunted by the word "sissy"), I am hurled back into the physical reactions of being hurt and victimized. The feelings of powerlessness. Strangled anger. Adrenaline leaving my body so that my arms felt empty and weak. Feeling blank and frightened and yet almost "sleepy" at the same time, as if I wanted to die right there.

Anything, just to get me out of it.

Although anti-gay violence cuts across all class lines, your reaction to it may stem from your own class training. Boys who are socialized to be part of the middle or upper-middle classes, to be part of the (largely white or white identified) mainstream of American life, often find themselves the most defenseless confronting anti-gay violence. They have been trained to be a functioning part of the *regular* world, a world that does not question its own values. Suddenly, at an early age, other boys are accusing them of being "queer." They are being shoved into the outcast margins of their own culture, out of the "normal" morality of their class.

Although every group establishes its own "code of morality" (with being gay often assigned a place outside it), it is these "good" boys who find themselves with no image of themselves capable of withstanding anti-gay violence. Working-class boys (or those from less stable backgrounds: the expression "working class" holds little contemporary value, as America has obliterated the distinction of a functioning working class; at present the *working class* is only a few paychecks ahead of the non-working underclass) are often raised, to begin with, in a tougher atmosphere. They may be more used to fighting for their own space and capable of understanding power and how it works. This can prepare them to protect themselves; this protection may be physical and/or psychological.

Just as gay men in prison learn that they can hook up to another, stronger man as a protector, working-class gay kids frequently form their own networks. These can take the form of cliques that contain other queer kids, some of whom may be "out" due to hustling. Or they may discover the friendship of seasoned street queens (who in Latino neighborhoods often keep turfs of their own) or an adult, such as an uncle or a family friend, whose queerness is unhidable. Among suburban middle-class kids, this rarely happens. So middle-class "good" boys characteristically find themselves stranded (and alone) when any question of their "straightness" comes up.

All of this seems out of sync with the times. There are now gay characters on television, bisexual rock stars, and some openly gay pop stars like Elton John, K.D. Lang, or Ellen DeGeneres. But the world of teenhood, a world most of us remember vividly, does not move in quantum leaps. Kids still want one thing more than anything else: to belong to a group of their peers.

It is for this reason that "straight" teens often seek out and hunt down gay men. When this happens in small towns or by gangs of city kids—ending in homophobic violence—what is happening is that the kids are no longer acting of their individual accord, but are taking part in a larger *ritual of hate and belonging*. The Nazis used similar rituals fifty years ago to get children to persecute Jews. Many neo-Nazi, neo-fascist, and white supremacist groups also actively recruit kids in the same way: promising them that by going after gays, blacks, immigrants, etc., they will solidify their places in the group. Conversely, many black and Latino fundamentalist churches have now become bastions of social conservativism and "family values" as a way of "solidifying" their communities against outside threats. These church groups have actively worked towards demonizing gay men, people with AIDS, and other outsiders within their own communities, therefore sanctioning violence against them.

Unfortunately, if you've ever been attacked, understanding this may not make your life any easier.

You may be by yourself, or with another man. Suddenly you are surrounded by a group of snarling kids, facing you like a pack of wolves. Early one spring evening in the late 70s, my former lover and I were in a beautiful city park in Wiesbaden, Germany. We had walked through a secluded grove of trees and, thinking we were completely alone in the dark, sat down on a rock. We kissed briefly. A few seconds later we were surrounded by a gang of kids, screaming, throwing bottles, rocks, cans, and sticks at us. We realized that at some point they must have followed us. My lover Tom was terrified; although an American serviceman at the time, he had never experienced anything like this. The kids formed a wall in front of us: we were frozen with fear. Then I took off my belt and started popping it loudly in the air (it seemed to be the only weapon I had— my father had used that to frighten me when I was small). The kids, who were shouting in English and German, must have felt the situation slipping somewhat out of their control. "We have belts, too!" one shouted, but the sticks and bottles stopped. We managed to run out of the park, into a busy boulevard that bordered it. They followed us and we stood in the middle of the street as traffic sped around us.

Safe, but completely unnerved back in our hotel, Tom said that he could not understand "why anyone would want to kill you just because you're gay." He was positive that German kids would never act that way. (This was before the Berlin Wall had come down and neo-Nazism had immediately sprung back up.) From growing up in the deep South, I had a different attitude: that my life has been spent only a couple of steps ahead of anti-gay violence. The major defense most of us feel we have is being able to "blend" in. But as many of us have experienced, this form of violence can pop up at any time.

As I have said, anti-gay violence comes at you in two forms. The violence from outside and the violence you are doing to yourself on the inside. Violence from outside, also, takes various forms, and I would like to talk about them, and about dealing with them.

The first is *overt* anti-gay violence. What we call "street violence," and it usually comes about through sudden, unplanned interactions with strangers. You can be attacked alone in a park, or without warning in a public place, such as in a shopping mall or its parking lot. It can happen if you are spotted leaving a gay bar, or when you are in a "gay place," a place that gay men have allotted to themselves within any given area. Gay areas often give us a sense of security, but many gay men realize that if someone is going out to hunt us, the best place to look is a "gay" place. Especially on the outskirts of one, such as parking areas adjacent to gay bars. The feeling in homophobic circles is simple: gay men must be allowed no safe places. Therefore, attacks are known to take place even within gay bars, and gangs will go into them with the feeling that they have a "right" to damage others in their own spaces.

In a March, 1996, piece in *The New York Times* about a steady escalation of anti-gay activities, Matt Foreman, then executive director of the New York Gay and Lesbian Anti-Violence Project, said, "People come to where they know gay and lesbian people are to beat them up, which is very different than any other form of bias crime. I can't imagine a group of white kids from New Jersey going to 125th Street to find African-Americans and beat them up."

What homophobes (whether members of an attacking gang, a lone psychotic "loony," or bigoted police officers) desire is that you will internally question your own rights at the same time that they are attacking you. In other words: you will make them very happy by pushing yourself into a "defenseless territory." You do this by "confessing" your own inappropriateness, thereby *opening* yourself to the attack.

In other words: you cooperate with your attackers by questioning your right to be there.

This is not the time to bargain with yourself and try to rationalize what's going on. ("I shouldn't be here. No wonder I've been attacked. No one told me to go to this bar: this is all *my* fault!")

The reality is that an attack does not have to take place in what might seem like a "disreputable" location. You don't have to be in a bar or cruising area to be attacked. It can happen in a city park (as happened to us years ago in Germany) or on a beach, in a store or shopping mall—or inside your own neighborhood or home. (If you feel that your right to property overrides their bigotry, forget it: your property will not protect you. In 1994, 15% of all anti-gay attacks reported to the New York Anti-Violence Project were caused by landlords, tenants, neighbors, and other assailants close to home.) So don't try to "disappear" by rationalizing your situation and placing yourself, for the second time, in the victim's role; first as the actual victim of the violence, and secondly by cooperating with the perpetrators by placing yourself "at fault."

### Your Right to Be There

The first thing you must establish, then, if you find yourself under attack, is your *own* right to be there. Many men find themselves *imploding* upon themselves, literally caving in physically and psychologically. This caving-in may be a part of a primal, natural defense mechanism: your psyche is making itself smaller. You want to escape–meaning, "disappear." But the truth is that you are under attack. Both you–and the attack—are not going to disappear. It is *you* they are attacking. They are not after someone else. They are not after someone who looks like you, who looks "queenier" than you do ("I'm wearing the same clothes they are: jeans and a flannel shirt. How can they mean *me*?"). They are after *you*.

It is at this point that you have to make a decision–and a very fast one which can actually save your life–to come back into the arena of violence, instead of trying to disappear psychologically.

A perfect example of this took place in January of 1992 when Henry Marquez was murdered in the parking lot of Pal Joey's, a gay bar in North Bellmore, Long Island, by Angelo Esposito, a local thug who, with a friend, had been running patrons down with his car for an hour and a half before he struck Marquez and killed him. Esposito—who some people felt was a "closet case"—had been in the bar before and had had a history of menacing patrons either in the bar or outside in the parking lot. He had made a game out of this—a hate ritual, as I have called it—and the bar patrons, who, for the most part, were also very closeted, Italian-Americans from the area, went along with this, hoping that if they just "disappeared" at the moment of threat, the danger would "go away."

On the night that Esposito attacked Henry Marquez, no patrons of the bar would call the police, for fear of exposure. On one hand, there was the argument that Long Island has no gay rights law to protect residents from losing their jobs or housing, and North Bellmore, which is only about sixty miles from Manhattan, could just as well have been a small, isolated village anywhere. *The ugly fact was that Marquez's death actually took about an hour to accomplish.*

During this hour any number of things could have been done to intercede between Esposito and the patrons of Pal Joey's, but nothing was done either by Pal Joey's management, other patrons, or the police. Esposito ended up ramming Marquez's car onto a nearby parkway and then smashing the car into a barrier, where Marquez was killed. During this hour, it might have been possible for Marquez, who worked as a federal customs inspector, to have saved himself. But like the patrons of the bar, who from within watched Marquez's car being rammed in the parking lot and would not call the police (or come out to aid him in any way), Marquez's first intention was to no longer be there. It was simply to try to *blend* his way out of it.

"It was lucky for us that two of the witnesses were not gay," said Sgt. William Cocks, of the Nassau County homicide unit, commenting on the fact that no one from Pal Joey's would come forward to testify. Angelo Esposito was later apprehended and charged with manslaughter, not murder. At a trial that was monitored by the New York Gay and Lesbian Anti-Violence Project, Esposito was given the maximum manslaughter sentence, but only after the Project focused a great deal of media attention on the case, something that, for the most part, the gay community on Long Island did not favor. According to a *New York Times* report, one of Marquez's friends said, "If Henry had survived this, I don't think he'd be thrilled to be the center of this controversy. If he had survived, he probably wouldn't have reported it [to the police]."

It is this desire to disappear psychologically that permits much of the violence that is done to us. Many times we rationalize this as wanting to "get on with our lives," but the reality of violence is that it will not allow this. The aftermath of violence is often more painful psychologically than it is physically. One result is that suicide attempts by gay men go up tremendously after anti-gay violence, much more so than after other shocks, such as losing someone to AIDS. Even though AIDS is often couched in the same language of homophobia ("Gays deserve this; this is God's vengeance on you," etc.), anti-gay violence really makes you want to *disappear*, and the most complete method of this is suicide.

## Assessing the Situation of an Anti-Gay Attack

The first step in dealing with anti-gay violence is that you not allow yourself to become the *passive* victim. By passively allowing it to happen, you are permitting the real sickness of violence to kill you in a quicker, even more horrifying way, than AIDS can. Therefore, the first step you have to take in the midst of overt anti-gay violence is to affirm that you will *not* be passive.

If you feel that you are in a cornered, about-to-be-attacked situation, begin immediately to *assess* it and *push out* of yourself. A normal reaction for many gay men is to want to disappear inside, to go into a *denial* state that says: "This is not happening"; certainly not to them, or to anyone who has a relationship to them. A common physical reaction is to hunch over, to make yourself physically smaller. Or even to look over your shoulder, thinking that you'll be able to spot the actual victim of the attack, someone who is not you.

Often victimized men go into an internalized shock situation, literally caving-in inside. It is important to stop this process.

The first thing you want to do then is really *see* what is going on. Open your eyes. Wide. Exaggerate the process of doing this. Look at and start to identify your surroundings. You are being followed. Perhaps cornered. Someone is shouting at you and saying things that you don't want to hear. Don't ask yourself questions, but begin the pushing-out process immediately. Asking questions ("Why are they doing this to me? Are they really following me—maybe they're following that guy ahead of me? Why are they bothering me?") will slow you down and keep you from assessing what's going on. What you do *not* want to do is slow down and start that process of going into yourself that can deliver you directly into the hands of your attackers.

At this point, sometimes the opposite of the "implosion" or psychological cave-in takes place, but in its own right it is just as dangerous. This comes from men who have been taught to "take their punishment." "Take it like a man." Or "just grin and bear it." Some men actually believe that they can "good sport" their way out of this—"If they keep hitting me and I don't cry, they'll leave me alone."

Another defense comes from gay men who feel that in order to establish themselves as not being sissies they will have to stand their ground: alone. This is a test of manhood, and running away is impossible.

Sometimes these men become so frozen with fear that leaving the situation is no longer an option for them. Other times, they go into a "good sport" stance and feel that if they just "stand their ground," and even laugh off what is happening, everything will turn out okay.

The chances are, it will not.

Therefore, in your assessment of the situation, the first defense you should recognize–and use—is physically to get the hell out. You must assess the situation as real. You are really being attacked. Your life is at stake. And you have nothing to win in this fight, except getting out alive.

So, you want to get out of the "freeze or fight" mode. Do not freeze, but don't be prepared to fight *immediately*. Remember, you have every right to be where you are, and no one has the right to hurt you, *in any way*. (I will get on to this *in any way* statement later, as it also includes verbal abuse.)

Widney Brown, an attorney who has her own self-defense school and who for several years counseled attack victims for the New York Gay and Lesbian Anti-Violence Project, sees attack strategies in this order:

"First, see if you can escape.

"Second, if you feel that you are trapped [they grab a friend or your lover and you can't leave], then assess the situation farther. Watch for weapons. Count how many people are attacking you. If possible, right then, split their focus—make their eyes go to another direction, which may cause them to drop their hold on you or your friend for just that second that allows you to escape."

A good focus splitter is: "HEY, WE'RE OVER HERE!" "THE COPS ARE BACK THERE!" Don't be afraid to raise your voice and keep it raised. Your voice may be the only *usable* weapon you have with you at the moment. So use it! Attackers love the idea that you will silently allow them to harm you. The idea that you have been humiliated into silence—the classic victim's stance—is especially gratifying to them. Your voice identifies you as a human being, which is very upsetting to them. This is especially true when men are attacked. Women and girls will often scream, but young boys are usually trained not to raise their voices, not to sound "shrill," not to complain or call out. (Silence is another part of middle-class training.)

Raising your voice makes them realize that you are aware how serious this is and the perpetrators will not be able to "good sport" you into injury or death. It means that you will not "bargain" your way out of the situation. ("If I just keep my mouth shut, they will leave me alone.") Indeed, if you do keep your mouth shut, there will be no voice marker at all to tell others what is being done to you.

You will become, simply, another silent victim.

(Again, men who have shunned violence all their lives are here faced with an experience situation: how experienced are they with dealing with a violent confrontation? I have seen street drag queens get up and face an attacker with the jagged neck of a broken beer bottle and I have seen "normal" gay men who were three times as big absolutely fall apart in the same situation. The reason for this is that the men who can normally "pass," through their own internalized homophobia, are reduced to being cowering, silent kids again, terrified of even the thought of being labeled "sissies." So it is important to *learn to scream*.)

Back to Widney's strategies: "If the situation is *really* serious, and you see that there are weapons involved and you are outnumbered, see if you can negotiate."

The negotiation process is to get yourself out of the victim's passive role—you're not just going to let them beat you up without saying something—and it also, again, makes you into a person, rather than just the "sissy-man-faggot" who (for the most part) young attackers feel is their natural prey.

If the situation involves a gang, Widney suggests using the "Alpha Dog Approach." In dog packs there is one dog who is the lead dog. When the "top dog" backs down from the fight, the fight stops. It will not be taken on by the second dog in command. Gangs usually follow the same psychology. So determine who is the Alpha ( or "top") Dog. Often he will be physically bigger. He will give orders. But he may do less of the talking. Confront him at that moment directly. Focus all your attentions on him, and ignore all the other gang members. This way, the gang confrontation becomes a one-on-one confrontation, and by confronting the "leader of the pack" you become an equal power with him.

The thing to do during this confrontation is for you to start laying down the rules. Tell them, "Man, chill out, okay! Relax! This fight's not worth it. I'm going to walk out of here. You're going to leave me alone! Now!"

You are now putting yourself into the position to give orders. At the same time one of the best actions to follow here, if you're not alone, is to start giving orders to someone you're with. If your lover or a friend is there, even if he is being physically held by other gang members, tell him: "Get out of here! Call the cops!" Again, this splits their focus, and makes the gang believe that your friend may have some power that they are not seeing. Since their focus is now on you giving orders, there is a good chance that they will drop their hold on the other person and let him get away. Make sure he does that—and that they know he is going to get help. If he is indecisive, it will be seen as weakness on your part, and again put you in the victim's position. But make sure that you *order* him to return with help. Have him agree to this, to make sure that he is backing you up—and that there will be *more* witnesses.

Once you have established that you are now giving orders and negotiating, the situation may calm down somewhat and change. Do not lower your voice, but keep yourself breathing as regularly as possible. As victims start to go into their inward-implosion-shock reaction (which is a normal reaction to violence), their breathing becomes choked and their energy level dies. So simply talking loudly can keep your breathing going and keep you focused—and alive.

As this negotiating is going on, keep on looking for an escape route. Make your attackers realize that you are now looking around yourself. Their eyes will follow yours. This will make them nervous because you may be either waiting for (or aware of) help, or of the presence of witnesses who can suddenly appear on the scene. Again: don't freeze. But start to move about so that if the situation stays out of hand, you will be in control of the setting. This should mean moving the attack out of the dark—and once you have moved out of the dark, they may simply split and leave you alone. It can mean going over to someplace where you hear other voices. Or making sure that there is not a wall in front of you, but behind you. You do not want someone sneaking up on your back.

As you can imagine in an attack situation, you are in one of the tensest places you'll ever be. What you want to do is make sure that your adrenaline is moving and working—and that that stunned feeling of powerlessness, which hits most victims right off the bat—is kept at bay. The fact that you've taken on an active role and are not curling over into yourself helps. Also, if you are with other gay men who are also being victimized, giving them orders directs your own attentions outward, which redirects some of your own tension. This also puts other people into an active mode, so don't be afraid to keep repeating orders like, "Get out of here! Go to the corner! There's a phone there! Call 911! Get help! The other guys [meaning other friends] are over there!"

In another way, you are also taking some of your attackers out of the passive follow-the-leader mentality they're stuck in, and younger kids (who may be in this only from peer pressure) can see that there is an alternative: you are giving orders for your friends to leave, and so can they. You are putting another thought into their heads, that they don't have to stay there and hurt someone else. What's important is that you are not reverting to that old childhood ploy, so characteristic of oppressed gay men, of "nursing" yourself. Of turning inward—looking for that emotional thumb to suck—doing this can get you hurt, or killed.

> You're Cornered.

Despite everything that you've done, things have escalated and there is nothing to do now except engage in some form of counterattack.

Widney suggests here that: "You push out even *more!*"

Look around you: make sure you are in the lightest, most busy area you can get into. Make as much noise as you can, again to split attention and draw attention to yourself. This may mean jumping on top of the roof of a car, or picking up a rock and breaking the windshield of one (which, if you're lucky, can cause a car alarm to go off), or picking up a garbage can (which actually worked once for me when I was attacked by a gang of kids in the Yorkville section of Manhattan) and throwing its contents directly at your attackers. What you have to realize is that your attackers' adrenaline is also limited. After a certain amount of time, if you've given them enough resistance and they feel there is any chance of witnesses or help for you coming, they will leave. They may immediately start looking for another victim, but they will see that you are not the easy pickings they thought you were.

If you are pushed to the ground, don't give up. Often it's easier to fight from the ground, where you cannot be pushed down again, than it is to try to get up, and then be pushed down repeatedly, causing you more injuries. What you can do from the ground is kick at the knees (a very vulnerable point) of your attackers and spin on your back. Also, if there is a wall behind you and you are on the ground, you are in a better position than being on your feet and being pushed into a darker area, where you can be exposed to attack on all sides.

It is vital during any attack that you don't allow yourself to feel hopeless. You *are* fighting back. It is also important to keep your voice going—that you keep telling them to "GET OUT! LEAVE ME ALONE! GO AWAY!"

Weapons? If you are carrying a weapon on you and you use it, realize that any weapon you use can be grabbed from you and used against you. I personally believe in using Mace or pepper gas, if simply for the fact that you may not feel completely helpless with a Mace canister in your pocket. In some localities Mace is against the law. This means that if you are attacked with a knife and you use Mace on your attacker—which may save your life—you can be arrested along with your attacker. But I feel that the chances of this happening are far outweighed by the feeling that you have some easily accessible defense with you. Also, although it is possible to be maced by your own Mace, if you do drop it or it is taken out of your hands, being maced may be the least of your problems. And if your attacker has to jump to pick up your Mace, that can give you a "focus-splitter" that will allow you to get the hell out.

Other available weapons: your feet–no matter what you are wearing. Kick like hell, especially at vulnerable places like the groin, shins, or the knees of your attackers. Elbows can be jammed into a stomach, a chest, or a neck. A backpack can be flung directly into a face. Don't feel that you have to go by "good sporting rules" here. You did not ask for this attack. So let it be known that you'll do anything necessary for your survival or the survival of those close to you. However, don't try to escalate the violence yourself with things like jagged glass or knives. These really can get out of hand and propel you towards serious injury or death.

## Calling the Police and/or Getting Help

No matter what happens during the attack or confrontation, the next thing to do is get help. Any help you can find. This may mean running into a lighted area, going to a bodega, a filling station, a convenience store, or banging on someone's house door. Doing anything that can get you aid. Often the smartest thing you can do is bring this into the middle of a street. Stop traffic if you have to. At this point, you are not in the least bit constrained to use words "correctly." You don't have to cough out, "I think these young men are trying to homophobically attack me." You can use whatever comes to mind to get yourself attention, such as, "They've just tried to mug me!" or "I want to report a crime!" In many situations, the public or the police may be a lot easier for you to deal with as the victim of a would-be mugging than a would-be gay bashing. (In similar fashion, for years, before police departments became more sensitized to violence against women, women were told not to report a rape, but to report a robbery. The cops would respond to a robbery instantly; for a rape, the woman first had to prove that she was "innocent" and did not invite the approaches of a man.)

If you are in a situation where the police are not going to be coming around—you are completely alone—then run out into the most exposed place you can. There you can attract attention and at least have witnesses. If you see people around you who you think can help, call out a name—any name. The chances are they will turn, and then you can say, "I thought you were Mark—listen, please help me!"

Under no circumstances should you allow your attackers to push you into a car, even if it's your *own* car that you can no longer defend. If this is part of their plan, leave the car immediately. You may feel that it's less embarrassing to be seated in a car and out of view than it is to be exposed this way on the street. But once you are shoved into a strange car, or your attackers have pushed their way into your car, you are really out of control. They are now totally in charge. Being in a car—any car—you may feel more protected from the embarrassment of a street attack, but it is better to be outside, even on the street, on your own two feet and in control, than to be *discreetly* dead.

When I was in a my late teens and found myself under attack by a group of teenagers in a small town in California, I ran out into the middle of a highway and started stopping cars. Finally, a police car stopped, literally saving my life. (The cops, by the way, knew these same kids, who had spotted me hitchhiking. After slowing their car down and using some very impolite words with me, the kids piled out to cream me. I outran them for several blocks and then ended up on the white line of a highway–at about ten o' clock at night. I got into the police cruiser, and they gave me a lift out of town.)

If the police do arrive at the scene, you do not want to be without some identification, so keep some on you at all times. At this point, especially if you've told the police that you were mugged—as opposed to being the victim of a bias attack—they will ask for a description of your attackers. Again, you will have to keep your focus pushed out and ready. This is not the time to allow yourself to be "absent" from the scene. Your first instinct may be that *finally* you can allow yourself to crumple. *You can't.* Focus yourself. Remember facts about your attackers. Their age, height, weight, race, what they were wearing, mannerisms, etc.

Reporting homophobic violence to the police is a sticky problem. For some men, this may mean coming out in a small community. For others, it can mean joining another one, the gay community, for the first time. Since many straight men, who may be slightly built or crossdressers, are also victimized by homophobic violence (or violence against what their attackers believe is a stereotype of gay men), they find themselves in a no-man's-land of not getting support either from the gay community or the police and the straight one. Often these men will have to be tried as victims and then proved "innocent" (translation: not gay) before anything will be done for them.

Gary David Comstock, in his book *Violence Against Lesbians and Gay Men*, has asserted that the police are the third most common perpetrators of violence against gay men. This makes many of us question going to the police to report an attack, especially in areas where the homophobia of the police has been well documented. In New York City, for instance, at the time I was writing this book, 12% of anti-gay attacks have been attributed to the cops. In other instances, homosexuality is used as a convenient kind of "witchcraft" environment to neutralize any wrongdoings the police are capable of. A good example: the white New York cops who brutalized Abner Louima, a black man, by repeatedly shoving a toilet plunger up his rectum, claimed that Louima had previously been in a "gay bar where he had been having sex." The police therefore will use their role as the community's "normativizing" element—that is, to enforce the "norms" that they are now dictating—to cover their own tracks.

However, unless bias attacks are reported, the police will see this as an invitation to do nothing about anti-gay violence, and to doubt automatically the bias nature of any isolated attacks that come to their attention.

Here are some strategies that gay men can use in dealing with law enforcement—after an attack—if the police were not present at the attack scene and you have to appear later, in person, at a police station.

- If you are in a larger city that has either a victims' support agency or a lesbian and gay anti-violence agency (which several larger cities have), go to the police with a representative from one of these groups. Do not go alone. Every police district has a different protocol that they follow. If you are not familiar with this protocol, you will not be able to follow what is being done—if anything—for you.

- If you are in a smaller community, get a respected "neutral" person whom the local police can recognize and who can "legitimize" your case. Don't bring in a local gay leader, unless he or she has had some experience dealing with the police. A gay lawyer may be helpful, but a clergyperson, someone in business, or a banker, can help. Going in with your lover or a friend who is gay can weaken your cause: it reaffirms the cops' homophobia that you aren't strong enough to go in by yourself. (In some localities, the cops have been known to rough up or verbally abuse two gay men who've come in.) A very good ploy to use, especially in the South, is to come in with a woman. She may be able to get away with things that you can't: such as telling the truth.

There are certain things that optimally you would like to get out of the police. These are minimal and basically say that local law enforcement is taking your attack seriously:

- The police should take down your report in your presence.
- They should render aid to you, if you are still in need of physical assistance. In some situations, the cops will refuse to give you any assistance, because they're afraid of AIDS. There is nothing about you that will cause them to get AIDS, but if the White House police have worn rubber yellow gloves in front of AIDS demonstrators, don't expect every cop in many localities to be enlightened about the spread of HIV.
- They should investigate the bias nature of the crime: that you were attacked because you are gay. Many police personnel refuse to do this, just as for years they have refused to investigate bias crimes against women and other groups.
- The bias nature of the attack should be documented in the report.
- Then, most importantly, they should *arrest* the perpetrators of the attack. Actually arresting them means warrants should be taken out and all the procedures of a legal arrest should be followed. It means that the district attorney's office should become involved and that the police and the D.A. should work together.
- Since many political machines are working here, the chances of the cops or the D.A. fouling things up are high. And, unfortunately, at every turn of the road there are chances that you, the victim, will be "tried" by the police, who'd love for the case to turn from being a bias attack into a simpler "self-defense" situation (in which you were—for whatever reason—attacked and then tried to defend yourself, or—even better—*you* attacked a group of "innocent" youth). The horrifying anti-gay homicide of Julio Rivera in Jackson Heights (a section of Queens, New York), in July of 1990, was claimed by the police to be "just another drug deal that didn't work" until the New York Anti-Violence Project got involved. Here again, the same straight community that produced Rivera's killers also produced the

NYPD in Queens. There was a protect-our-own-turf mentality fighting justice as long as possible.

- Finally, the police should go to court with you. This may necessitate you getting a lawyer of your own, but it is possible to get back your legal fees from your attackers if the judge seeks real justice for you.

## After the Attack

After the attack, you do not want to be alone. The first reaction you will probably go through is intense anger, followed by depression. In certain ways, these are normal, almost "medicating" psychological reactions. The anger is a natural response to the adrenaline rush; the depression is a formation after the anger. Depression is your psyche saying that it wants to bury all of this. It wants to forget. It wants to place all of this deeper, as the computer people say, within your "files." But, unfortunately, the deeper it goes, the more systematically it can poison you. One of the first feelings most men have after an attack is that they don't want to talk about it. It evokes too much shame and pain. You may not want to tell your friends, your lover, or anyone close to you. In replaying the scene and the emotions involved with it, you are bringing yourself back to other primal scenes of childhood bullying and abuse. Parts of your psyche that you never want to resurface will come back. Men who want to consider themselves professional, successful, and in control, will do anything to avoid replaying these childhood feelings.

Suddenly they are there in front of you.

The best thing then is to talk—as soon as possible—to someone who has had experience with these situations. The best people for this are with gay and lesbian anti-violence groups, and there may be one in your city. Even if you have to call long distance to get to one, it is important for you to be able to talk. Also, gay and lesbian switchboards can help, as well as social service agencies that deal with victims' assistance. In some cities, the police department may have an office that deals with this; in other cities, you may have to seek out a counselor who has had some experience and some insight into dealing with anti-gay violence. What you do not want is someone who will make you "explain" why you were in a certain situation, or prove your "innocence," etc. Blaming the victim has been for too long "Part Two" of homophobic violence. You don't have to prove your "innocence." As Widney Brown says: "No one has the right to mess with you."

If you have been physically brutalized by the attack, then you can apply for victims' compensation. To do this, you will have to work with your local district attorney's office or a victims' compensation board. Many major cities have them. The compensation board or your own health insurance company can then provide for further counseling fees. (Although some men are additionally upset by the prospect of using job-sponsored health plans to cover this: it can mean coming out at work, 119 which can, in turn, mean facing more psychological stress.)

It would be easy to say that after a certain amount of counseling, you will be "back to normal." It would be more *normal* to say you will not. You will feel much more vulnerable, and "wiser and sadder" than you were before.

If you are younger, the attack may take on a much greater weight for you, especially if it has happened only a short time after your coming out. A natural feeling is: "Now I'm gay and everybody knows it!"

Unfortunately–although this may not be much consolation to you— you could have been attacked before you came out. Many gay men think of anti-gay violence in terms of being attacked by strangers who perceive them as being gay (for instance, being followed to your car somewhere near a gay bar; being seen with other gay men and then attacked, alone, after leaving them, etc.). They feel that their attackers have a roaming form of "gaydar" that picks them out. But the truth is that many heterosexual men have been attacked for the same reason, giving rise to a generalized atmosphere of fear in many vicinities.

Several years ago, in the middle of a cold winter day in Queens, two Russian cab drivers were dragged from a parked car and beaten up on a busy street. Teenagers saw them in the car, where, being Russian and from a culture where men are more physically affectionate with each other, the two men were sitting close together and talking in what seemed to be a whisper. One of the men was hospitalized and the other barely got away with his life; both of them were completely puzzled as to why they had been attacked this way. Both were married and had wives and children at home. The kids admitted that they thought the men were "faggots" and they had no right to be "displaying themselves" openly in a parked car.

Another example of anti-gay violence that has hit America are attacks against women who may be seen as too butch (and therefore may be lesbians) or who appear, in fact, to be boyish enough to be seen from a distance as gay men—and therefore prime for attack. Another group of victims of anti-gay violence who may not even think of themselves as gay are transgendered people, men and woman who either physically become the opposite sex or live as them. These people challenge society's rigid assumptions about sex roles, although in fact many of them are quite conservative sexually and do not take on either gay or lesbian identities. They think of themselves as heterosexuals born in the wrong gender, but they will end up being targeted for anti-gay violence in the same way gay men are.

But regardless of whether you feel you are "older and wiser" from the attack, or still alarmed by anything that reminds you of it (such as being in a parking lot, walking back from a bar, etc.), the most important thing is that you allow yourself to break out of the depression that comes from it. This depression can literally harden around you, damaging your immune system and your ability to live and work. Even men who've learned to scream during the attack can find this scream later imprisoned inside them. Don't let this happen to you. If you do, then the gay bashers have bashed you again, and in an even more harmful way.

## Other Forms of Anti-Gay Attacks

Aside from confrontational street violence, less overt attacks can mean being verbally abused, either at work or where you live, by people who are acquainted with you in some way. Again, no one has the right to attack you. Even if these abuses are *only verbal*, they are a form of violence done to you. These sorts of attacks frequently follow coming out, especially if you've come out in a manner that you did not plan and suddenly "rumors are flying." (Despite the successful Kevin Kline comedy, In & Out, that was made on this plot line, being forced out of the closet is not always an event for humor, love, and conciliation.)

Such harassment at work can be a part of a systematic plan to sabotage your career, despite the fact that your job performance has nothing to do with your sexuality. This harassment, therefore, should not just be "laughed off."

Unfortunately, some companies have specific "morals clauses" in their employment contracts. Trying to fight this is difficult, unless you live in a state that has anti-discrimination laws covering lesbians and gay men. However, to your advantage, usually these companies do not appreciate the embarrassment of being exposed *openly* as homophobic. As with most bigotry, homophobia thrives in secrecy. These companies consider homosexuality at best distasteful, and the farther they can get away from it, the happier they are. Usually, you will not be harassed within your workplace unless your gayness becomes public in some way. This means that simply being the victim of an office rumor mill will, for the most part, not cause you to lose your job.

A good example of this type of homophobic bigotry occurred for years at the newspaper *The Christian Science Monitor*, which would not allow openly gay men and lesbians to work in editorial positions. As long as you were discreet about your "sexual preference," they would not delve into your "private life," and they chose to keep things this way until they found themselves in the extremely embarrassing situation of actually having to fire valuable employees who were gay—and no longer content to be secretive about it. The *Monitor*'s feeling was that this was your *private* life: as long as it remained *private*, they would do you no harm. But once you were in any way "out," they would be "forced" to fire you.

I hope that no one reading this will sympathize with employers who feel that a man's *personal* life—that is, the one he leads at home—must stay a shameful secret to the entire outside world. But many traditional religious organizations–and companies claiming to have "religious" missions as they turn a profit—have done this to gay men. Years ago, they did the same thing to Jews, who could not be "openly" Jewish; who could not, for instance, wear a yarmulke to work and who were harassed for taking off Jewish holidays, even if they made up the time. Since most forms of anti-Semitism and overt racism have been confronted and pushed out the closet, anti-gay feelings are the last socially acceptable forms of bigotry to remain in it.

What this calls for, then, is confronting companies that have stated anti-gay policies, but for many men this action, no matter how necessary and important, is out of the question. They cannot and will not be this open about their own adult gay feelings.

In circumstances like this, the best course if you feel that life is being made hell for you is to go to your company personnel or human resources department. Don't go to your boss, except as a last resort. Human resource people usually feel that this is in their department. They can arrange a meeting between themselves and whomever is bothering you.

Often what the company will want is that news of your homosexuality be kept as much in the closet, and *out of the open*, as possible. So one bargaining chip you can use with personnel or human resources is to vaguely threaten that your personal life can become *less* personal unless things change. If this has no effect, and you still feel that you are being discriminated against or persecuted at work, then your next move may be to get in touch with a lawyer, who can accompany you to your next meeting. I say don't get your boss involved because, for the most part, your boss is more interested in covering his own skin than in saving yours. However, there are many different variables here, and your boss may be the person who brought you into the company and who has the most amount of respect and feelings for you. As with any violence situation, covert or overt, accurate assessment is important.

In this dispute, it is important to keep your own fears from twisting up the issues. The bottom line is that you will not be abused *in any form*: verbal or otherwise. If the stakes escalate, your company may try to threaten *you* with exposure. If you have invested a great deal of your life in covering up your gayness, this may seem to you like the end of the world—or certainly a lot of your life in it. But be aware that blackmail is against the law, and you can nail them right back for that.

Most anti-gay violence at work, though, does not get to this point. Where it does reach is that distinct feeling that your working environment has changed. It is now hostile. Or, a new work environment has a hostility that either you did not anticipate, or that is very different from your old job. In some ways this is good. It's healthy. What it is saying is that you have not *internalized*—"normalized"—homophobia. You have not *seen* (as so many gay men from previous generations have) that it is "normal" for people to hate gay men and treat them in an emotionally violent way. This emotional violence can take many forms:

- Overt name calling and offensive language.
- The use of homophobic language around you, and about you specifi-

cally, such as "I can't talk now, the *faggot*'s in the room."

- Coldness and abruptness around you, so that you feel isolated and alone.
- Hate mail, often unsigned.
- And, finally, vandalism done to property (your tires slashed; your working area rifled through or damaged).
- And worse: physical confrontations, which may be joked away, but which you should not take humorously in any form.

As with confrontational street violence, the initial reaction many gay men have at work is to go inside themselves. To want to cut themselves off from the pain of what's going on, and afterwards try to "take care" of themselves.

This "taking care" of themselves can mean either reverting to old internalized homophobic attitudes ("Of course they hate me; they laugh at me. I'm a queer and I should expect it") or nursing the pain, instead of trying to relieve it ("I'm going to be a good little boy and just behave myself. I'm going to treat myself right, even if nobody else does").

The result of this is a classic reaction to work-based homophobia: to engage in forms of behavior that are not healthy. These include overeating (feeding the "inner child"); stepping up drinking, especially social drinking in gay bars; working twice or three times as hard—in order to "earn respect"—until your health is threatened. And, finally, "acting out" sexually, even at work. Therefore, the office "queer" suddenly finds himself propositioning guys in the men's room. He realizes that if he is going to be the pariah, he's going to act it.

As in the case of overt street violence, the emotional violence done to you at work should cause you to start refocusing your attention outward. Make things very plain to people: "I don't want things like that said around me." "I *am* aware of what you are doing." "I will not tolerate being abused like this."

Back this up by making a note or memo of every incidence of harassment or insult directed at you. This will have two uses: first, if you do have to go to court, you will have a complete record of what went on. Second, it directs your focus outward concretely. You are no longer simply being victimized and feeling sorry for yourself. By making it clear that you will not tolerate *any* type of abuse towards you, you are putting bigots on notice that the ball is no longer in their court. Sometimes the abuse will stop cold. You have put a boundary around them. Obviously, you are not going to be "buddies." They will not be able to "good sport" you into more abuse.

But more often the situation will diminish when the bigots realize you are there and you *are* going to stay. They are not going to force you out. Often in the case of being the "new" guy in the work area, your gayness is not as important as your newness. You took someone else's place, and you will be made to suffer for that. So simply staying there until you are no longer *new*—which may take three or four months—and your predecessor is somewhat forgotten, may work for you. At that point, people may warm up to you, and then it will be up to you to decide how much you want to "normalize" the situation, to pretend that nothing happened.

In the case of physical harassment or vandalism, this is a direct attack on you. It should not be minimized in any way. Attacks of this sort are as vicious and potentially dangerous as street violence. Document every aspect of these attacks—when they happened, how, and the name of perpetrators and witnesses. Take this documentation to your personnel office and tell them you will go to the police with it, if nothing is done. If you feel that earlier forms of violence have led to physical confrontations, then include these in your documentation.

An important step in fighting work-based violence is the opposite of the "going inward" reaction that gay men take under duress: go outward. Seek alliances with co-workers who may want to be your friends. Every work situation has its in-crowd and out-crowd (and even their in-crowds within their *out-crowds*). The point is that not everyone there is out to get you. The sooner you establish that you are interested in friendships, the quicker it will seem that you really have nothing to hide. This always scorches homophobes, who thrive in a closeted, shame-ridden atmosphere.

Often your most obvious allies will be people who are a part of other "minority" groups. (I say "minority" because the minorities are often the "majority" in many work areas; it is the perception of being a minority and of having less power that is important.) But don't expect automatic sympathy from any group. Even people who appear to be the least likely to cause you pain may decide that you are going to be a great smoke screen for their own problems. This also goes for other gay men, who, closeted or otherwise, may shy away from you if a homophobic reaction to you threatens them. In fact, the "leader" of this reaction may be an ultra-closeted gay man himself. I refer to these "Roy Cohn" gays as *kappos*, a German term for Jews who collaborated with the Nazis and who were often employed in the concentration camps to pick which Jews would die and when. The fact that your abuser secretly is gay—and who may even come "out" to you at some point—is not going to help you. "Kappo" queers can be as dangerous to you as anyone else.

One last note: work-based anti-gay violence, abuse, and bigotry is extremely destructive, especially now when so many men derive huge amounts of their identity from their jobs, their work performance, and from socializing within their workplaces. These trends have become endemic to the 90s, when "doing your own thing" means having a successful career. Therefore, it may be important to "psych out" where you work as much as possible—even before you work there. Try to find out your future company's attitude towards gays and other minorities. What is its feeling about domestic partnerships, fatherhood leave, HIV coverage and rights, and other things that can affect you as a gay man?

And your boss or supervisor, what sort of person is he or she? In the long run, your boss may be your best ally, depending upon his/her feelings towards you. Within the system of "corporate feudalism" that now comprises most work life, there are often safe pockets within certain departments where you can find allies, such as the legal department, creative departments, or human resources. Although I say as a "rule" that it is better to go to personnel or human resources, the best rule is to take anti-gay violence at work seriously and, as with street violence, to assess your situation very well.

(One aside from our very commercialized environment: many big, "straight" corporations are now actively scouting the gay market. Sometimes this can help you. But other times you may be in the confusing position of working for a company that, while advertising for us, has no anti-discrimination policies on its books, offers no domestic partnership benefits, and that may cover up your sidelining or firing behind a very well "documented" smoke screen of "incompetency." At these companies, being a "team player" is all-important. So they may decide that as a gay man you are simply no longer a "qualified" part of their team.)

Many men dismiss homophobic violence closer to home—hoping that it will just go away—until it gets completely out of hand. They may come home and find that their property has been vandalized, their pets brutalized, or their homes burned to the ground. All of this may start out with simple name-calling or phone harassment. It is important then to document and report to your local police every incidence of harassment. Document it by writing down the time and date when it happened, exactly what happened, and at least a description of who did it if you do not have the person's name. If you make enough police reports, you can get an order of protection from your police department, which means that if this order is violated, you can have the violator prosecuted. All telephone harassment should be reported to your phone company; you can also install a caller I.D. system to your phone and supply the phone company with the telephone number of your harasser.

*Inviting Violence Home*

What about the violence that we "invite" home? For many gay men, this is among the more frightening aspects of being *out* in the gay world. Suddenly a pickup attacks you. Not only do you have to defend yourself at home, but the feeling that you are no longer safe in your own house is terrifying. Someone now knows where you live and can come back. How do you deal with threats like this, and still keep an open attitude towards people—and towards strangers?

One of the first things you should understand is that being gay does 125 not *automatically* invite violence towards you. There are numerous ways you can open yourself up to problems and, whether you are a woman, a straight man, or a gay one, the possibility for violence may be there. Women who have known men for months suddenly find themselves the victims of date rape. Any heterosexual pickup can lead to extortion or robbery. What has made gays appear to be more inclined to victimization is that frequently, as outsiders ourselves, we are more trusting of strangers; the police regularly ignore, demonize, or ridicule our problems; and the fear of openness many of us have (as in the Henry Marquez case) skews the statistics against us.

Also, as with any minority group, rumors among us are rife. So that no matter how many good encounters you've had, word of a bad encounter spreads like wildfire. In some ways, this is good: it means that there is a network warning us about possible problems. On the other hand, it makes us more paranoid and keeps even the oldest rumors percolating in the community.

An example: to many gay men, the "gay serial killer" syndrome is now rampant. After the bizarre and ugly cases of Jeffrey Dahmer and Andrew Cunanan, there is a killer sitting on every bar stool. There have been maniacs stalking various parts of the population since Jack the Ripper went after Victorian prostitutes, but every third gay man is now sure that he spotted Cunanan a week before he killed himself, and the next Andrew is waiting for him out there. In truth, things are much more open for us and safer than they were fifty years ago, when gay men were arrested *en masse*, blackmailed constantly, and murdered often. But there is always a lot for us to consider and to try to make wise choices from.

### Assessing Situations

Learning to assess situations is a prime way to keep yourself from becoming the victim of "invited" violence. You see someone in a bar who seems to be drunk, drugged, or out of control. He is hitting on everyone in the bar, until he scores. This can be a good tip-off that if you invite him home with you, or get into a car with him, you are being set up. Don't isolate yourself with any person who appears to be out of control: he may be drunk one moment and violent the next. The appearance of being drunk—"Boy am I sloshed; I wanna have sex with you right now!"—sets you up for letting your guard down. After all, you're sure that he has let his down, so now it's your turn. Question what is happening. When you go outside with him, you may have the surprise of your life—and if it doesn't happen outside the bar, it can in your home.

*Never allow yourself to leave a bar or cruising area with anyone you feel uncomfortable with.* If drunks normally make you wary or suspicious, this is not the time to experiment with them.

126     Don't be afraid to ask a bartender or any regular customers if they

have seen a patron before. "I never been *here* before in my whole life" may be the oldest line since Methuselah. Don't allow yourself to be pressured into leaving with anyone. ("If you don't want me, I betcha somebody else does!") And don't try to do social work with your cruising ("You're the only one here who understands me!"). A paradox of the "hit-on-and-run" violence that is frequently associated with gay bars is that *good hustlers hate violence*. So if you feel that you are being hustled—by a hustler, as opposed to just some "street traffic" who wants to hit you up with his sob story—check him out first. Usually bartenders can spot hustlers from fifty paces. If the hustler is a regular in a bar and wants to stay in business there, he will not want to dirty up his act by roughing you up.

If you are open for hustling, then make sure you get this out in the open as soon as possible. This is a professional transaction, so make sure you know *all* the terms: how much it will cost, for how long, and where. If you are in a hustler bar or a bar that allows hustling (many bars do not), let the bartender know that you are interested in someone and tip him for any help or information he can give you. On the other hand—and even better—use an established "escort" service. These services want your business over and over again, and will back up the "professionals" they send you. You will generally have to pay more for them than for street trade, but it's worth it.

Once you have crossed hustling out of the picture, this does not mean that you are no longer in a vulnerable position. Try to maintain some sort of support network around you, such as friends at a bar or in a cruising area whom you can share your plans with—"I'm going home with him; let me call you later." And then, call. I refer to these men as "cruising partners," and they can be very important to you, especially if you live in a suburban or secluded area and the chances of your getting help otherwise are nil. As a rule, do not get into a car with strangers. Either follow him home or allow him to follow you. Once you are in someone else's car, or he is in yours, you are very vulnerable. If you do go in someone else's car, try to remember its make, model, or its license plate number. Again, be aware of what's going on.

In your own home, plan some escape route. This may mean using a bedroom window that you can easily unlock from inside, having a phone in the garage, or the use of a fire ladder. As with street violence, any weapon can be used against you, but in a home situation there are weapons all over the place (knives, heavy tools), so you are that much more vulnerable.

Just as going home with a man who is out of control is asking for it, being out of control yourself makes you an excellent target. So even if you were sober as a judge when you met him, don't think that just being back on your own carpet allows you to say: "Hey, let's kick back and have a couple of drinks to break the ice?" You could end up robbed, bound, gagged, and drugged the next morning. Even if you're into bondage, this 127 is not *exactly* the finish you expected.

Watch what you drink, and how the drinking progresses. While you're on your third scotch, he may be taking his to the bathroom to water them down. He can also find a way to drug your glass once he's found some way to divert your attention. And if he's brought his own drugs, such as pot, be very careful. He may "smoke you under the table" and then tie you up. Many men who have gay self-esteem problems think drinking, drugs, and sex go together like Curly, Larry, and Moe. The first two loosen them up for the third. They also open them up for anti-gay violence.

- One of the myths many of us had for years is that anti-gay violence is only perpetrated upon us by "straights" or non-gays. Not true, as the serial killer Jeffrey Dahmer and the "spree" killer Andrew Cunanan dramatically proved. Whether both killers could be categorized as gay, closeted, or simply pathologically self-hating, gay sex was not the issue for them—they went looking for this.
- Many men have the idea that a potentially violent partner does not *really* want to have sex with them. Again, not true. You may have great sex and then end up hospitalized or murdered. So don't feel that the completion of a sex act means that you are now on safe ground; i.e., your partner is "gay" and sympathetic to you.

What will help is knowing more about your partner, so try to find out things like where he lives or works as soon as you can. Expect that he will want to know the same things about you. As I have said before, recognition is important to us. Often we have developed an ability to recognize self-love, self-hate, acceptance and denial early on in other men. Don't denigrate these feelings: most potentially violent situations—and the men in them—telegraph their contempt for you amazingly quickly. Once you pick up on this attitude of contempt ("I'm just here to get my rocks off. Don't you think fags are funny?"); one word of advice: LEAVE.

Some other ways to help you deal with invited guests and the problems that may come with them include:

- Have a neighbor or friend whom you feel safe about calling in the middle of the night if necessary. Check in with each other often.
- Burglar-proof your home as much as possible: lock up your valuables and pay attention if he suddenly starts to ask about the location of them. ("Say, where do you keep your cameras and computers?")
- If you live out of the city, install outside lighting around your house. The fact that your house is dark and secluded is an added invitation to rob it—and it will certainly tempt him to come back, even if "nothing" happened the first time.

Make sure that your house is easily locatable for the police, emergency medical help, or the fire department. This means lighting your house number or your mailbox. Keep a light in your parking area, so that if he does come back you'll know this as soon as he drives up.

If you feel threatened, do not be afraid to say "No" at any time. Don't feel that you have to get out of any situation *gracefully* with a ready or clever excuse. If you feel threatened, simply say, "I don't think I'm into this right now. It would be better if you (or I) left." Contrary to the feelings of many gay men outside major gay centers, the more reclusive and closeted you are at home, the more vulnerable you can be to invited violence. Having other gay friends, a sense of support, and being a part of a community can save your life.

Although it seems that much gay violence involves strangers, there is also the violence that happens between lovers, that can come from your family, and even from other friends. Your feelings about all of this should be simple: although being gay is a part of your life and identity, it does not automatically open you to violence. *It is not the price you will have to pay for your life.* It is not simply, as some homophobes say, "a natural part of gay life."

For centuries gay men felt that their calling was to be a shield *against* the violence that tragically seemed to be part of human life. Characteristically, we were the monks, poets, doctors, and nurses, rather than rigid knights and hostile warriors. For this reason, we were kinder to strangers, warmer to new ideas, and more caring towards people in vulnerable circumstances. The real victims in homophobic attacks are our feelings towards opening ourselves up to these things, and the civilizing effect this has had on human culture. The final word about all of this seems to be: stay focused, have compassion for yourself and for others, and don't allow anyone to take away from you your right—and obligation—to be yourself.

"Many gay men . . . are stuck between child*lessness* and child*ishness*.
It is a complete dead-end that has become for them
what the 'gay world' is all about."

## CHAPTER 8

# Beginning the Gay Work:
# The Search for the Male Companion

In a proceeding chapter, I talked about intimate needs and your lover's role in satisfying them. In this chapter I will talk also about these needs and how they are a part of what I call "the gay work." This work stands silently aside from all the competitive, draining situations in which often we find ourselves (rejection games; status climbing; the pursuit of "enemy-friends"; pill, steroid, and drug popping; etc.). The "work" is a very important part of our survival. More than a decade ago, when I first said that there was such a thing as "gay work," one of my friends started doing this up-and-down head motion, like he was ravishing a banana. In other words, the only "work" for gay men was sucking cock. I realized, then, that he was not quite ready for the idea.

Now it seems that many of us are ready—but are also having a difficult time articulating what the gay work is. Writers like Larry Kramer and Michelangelo Signorili are calling for a gay culture that goes beyond sex and body centeredness, something that gay philosophers and mystics have been talking about for several thousand years. But people still question that there might be *serious* work for gay men to do; and that this work can help us in the most difficult times. In times of intense homophobia (on the outside) and personal crises (on the inside). It can also help us in our own aging process, and bring us together with other men—both gay and straight–in a truly real way.

The "gay work," then, is a relationship that we need. We need it as much as we need lovers, partners, or friends. It is very much a part of our relationships with ourselves, and a foundation we need to combat internalized and externalized homophobia.

My realization of *the* gay work, though, came from my feeling that no matter how far we've come along the road to gender "parity," there is still such a thing as *women's work* and *men's work*. The crux of women's "work" is to recognize the importance of women, something that women in patriarchal structures like the Catholic Church or the military, to name only two examples, have to struggle with every day. The crux of men's "work" should be (but rarely is) to realize and implement that men, also, have a value of their *own*.

Our value is not simply predicated on how much money we make, or how well we have been able to integrate ourselves into the corporate and professional world. That has become part of the oppression that heteros place on themselves. Making money is now the equivalent of bringing back meat to the larder. The more money, the bigger and tastier the "meat." Sometimes the "meat" gets translated to mean toys (My Lexus can still beat your Caddy). But you have to drag the meat home before you can trade it at the adult F. A. O. Schwarz.

Also, the value of men is not determined by how often we beat each other up. Nor by how much pain and physical abuse we can take before running home to Mommy to cry. Or by how many women we get to fuck. The value of men is simply that *men are valuable in themselves*. So far, this seems to be a completely gay (okay, *queer*, in the original reading of the word) concept.

For thousands of years, queers were the *only* men who saw men for being beautiful in themselves. This idea became downright unpatriotic. It totally threatened the predatory nature of heterosexual society. If you see men as beautiful, how can you send them out to war, to become "cannon fodder"—another digit in the statistics of war? If you see men as beautiful, how can you enslave or destroy them?

Yet looking upon another man as beautiful, not necessarily as an object but simply as a living, feeling, breathing creature—seeing him with pathos and empathy—is considered . . . absolutely revolting.

As the kids would say: *it sucks*. And they are probably right. Kindness and warmth *suck*, in the same way that infants suck and men suck when they find themselves getting sexually turned on. And that is the tragedy of it: that men are still not given respect for being valuable in their own right. Generations of gay men have witnessed aspects of this tragedy; and many of us—whether we want to or not—have been swept into being a part of this tragedy, too.

So if we have the work of men and we have the work of women, what is the "gay work"?

What is the work that you as a gay man will do, the inner work, that will keep you on an even keel in life?

First, though, we have to understand that work *is* necessary. It is an absolute fact of life. Gay men without this sense of work *are* useless. We are simply spinning our wheels deeper into the same rut. We are thrown back into the stand-up-and-stare bars, the commercial sex clubs that advertise everything and give nothing, the adolescent "club" circuits that attempt to give younger men a sense of belonging while existing solely to take their money. We see this little meaningless dance performed constantly (and for most of us with no alternative), since few gay men have been able to formulate the idea of gay work and understand its importance in their lives.

But the gay work brings us into another, more immediate level of closeness and directness with each other. It is *tribal*, in that a tribe is a level of society that has direct contact with itself. It passes down through direct contact its beliefs and rituals. This is something that many of us are losing daily as "queerness" becomes a slick magazine, "digitized" experience—and we lose real contact with those wondrous, deeply compassionate queens (or *queans*, as they used to say) who came before us. The gay work is one of the main activities of the gay tribe. (I will talk about others later.) It is another way of placing us in the tribe and connecting us with it, just as any form of meaningful work places you within a functioning culture. But, even deeper, when we are conscious of the gay work, the tribe itself becomes a living entity, because we are working within it.

So, I'm sure you are asking yourself what is the gay work? Where do we go to find it? Do you apply at an employment agency? Maybe "Gay U."?

The answer is more involved—and, strangely enough, simpler. At some point, many of us have glimpsed some part of the gay work. And, often, we have become frightened by the emotional depth behind it. For people who've had to wear a mask in society, this depth presents a real burden. It means having to acknowledge, quite nakedly, our own deepest feelings. First, I will say that much of the gay work is involved with the gay mythos that I have spoken about earlier. So far, in my own thinking I have been able to isolate six basic elements in this mythos that I feel affect gay men, and from which we operate constantly. Those inner needs that I have been referring to, in the sections on gay lovers and couples, stem directly from these six elements, and here I will give some detail to them.

### The Six Elements of the Gay Mythos

These elements are, in the following order: recognition, twinning, submission/surrender, merging, individuation, and sharing.

I find these six elements running continuously through our life cycles as gay men, and also through various points in our sexuality. Our "coming out" is characterized as a peak recognition moment, although it may have little to do with actual homosexual sex. (There are many younger men, now, who recognize themselves as gay, even though they've never had sex with a man.) There is also the "recognition" of another man (which many gay men label as "cruising") as a suitable "twin," the man whose characteristics we feel will complete—even on a fleeting basis—our own.

Past twinning comes either submitting or "surrender" to another man. Submission may be tentative, voluntary, or involuntary (going back to the old question of do we "choose" to be gay), but it is something that our society, with its emphasis on "rugged individualism," finds difficult and frightening. Yet we lean towards submission/surrender regularly in our attractions to power or male poignancy and beauty. For some men surrender to another man's attraction seems longed for, delicious, and romatically desirable; while submission—which is often cloaked in elements of violence, humiliation, sports, defeat—seems frightening and distasteful. Yet there is a large amount of "space" within the submission/surrender aspect of the mythos, in that most men are willing to surrender, but some men really desire a complete submission—they desire at some point to be psychically, spiritually, even physically overwhelmed by a Male figure. Submission may lead these men into a final, blessed acceptance of death or the possibility of an embrace by the Presence of God. So submission, whether tasteful or "distasteful," is often at the center of many gay mythic feelings and rituals, and its longed-for presence in our lives can cut through much of our fear and distance from other men.

Submission/surrender reaches its fullest extent in "merging" (which many heterosexual men find very frightening, leading to deep-seated masculine fears of femininization, of being "pussy-whipped" or "house bound"), when gay partners may actually exchange personality traits. This exchange of traits, through intimacy and empathy, can be extremely supportive and nourishing for us. It usually leads to a deeper feeling and tenderness towards other men. But as with most intimacy situations, there should be boundaries around it. So, coming out of this merging mythos is "individuation," that awakened period that you can describe as coming after climax, when you realize that you are now back on your own: you have reached "into" another man through various sexual/emotional feelings, and now you must reassemble your own personality traits and strengths. You have to, in other words, come back into the real world: deal with your own boundaries, responsibilities, and needs, which have been expanded by the presence of another man.

Finally, there is sharing, which is expressed in much of the gay work, but which also has post-sexual aspects in that you recapitulate these warm experiences by caring, and exchanging tenderness and openness.

These six elements are repeated constantly in our relationships, fantasies, dreams, porn, sexual scenarios, desires, and expectations. I have placed them in this order and feel that, life-wise, that is usually how they operate. But, as with any schema, they can fall out of order. Sometimes, this can be frustrating, such as when a man feels sexually towards other men but has not recognized his own coming out—and is terrified of surrender to another man, or losing his identity in a twinning episode. He may go out with the idea of looking, but become terrified when looked back at. At that point, he may go into what is described as a "homosexual panic." Basically, he cannot allow himself to be integrated into the mythos at all. So these elements can become crossed up, and this can lead to
unhappiness and violence.

I see these six elements working within us, and also behind all of our involvements, which lead back again to the "gay work." To those aspects of gay tribalism that hold us together, whether we are conscious of them (that is, having *recognition*) or not.

### The Male Companion

Uniting these six elements within the gay work (so much so that he becomes the personification of it) is the vast *mystery* of an almost unnameable figure that I call the "Male Companion."

Who is this "Male Companion"?

Why is his existence a "mystery"? And how does *he* figure into our lives? To understand him, we should recognize that the Male Companion exists in that sphere in which the spiritual and the sexual meet and unite. This is a special sphere that many of us as small children could remember, before we were driven out of "Eden" and made to feel ashamed of our bodies, sex organs, and more tender, personal feelings. The Male Companion is the *incarnation* of this sphere. He (or "it," because he transcends gender) is the guardian (as well as the friend) of that deeper, transcendent soul (the loving, working, gay imagination) which allows us to *realize* our feelings and bring them closer to us.

[Please note: I use the word "gay" here because I have no other working one, at this point, for this state of the imagination. A better term might be "same-sexualized," or "personally sexualized." What we're talking about here is a type of sexuality that has not been cut off from you or dictated by others, but which is deeply, personally, held within your psyche and mythos.]

So the "Male Companion," this incarnation of our own deepest self, is the object of a specific quest. Like David Hockney's famous painting of a beautful male swimmer breaststroking under the water's surface towards a fully-clothed man standing at the side of a pool (*Portrait of an Artist— Pool with Two Figures*), the Male Companion lies just below our feelings of want, of being cut off, and of existing alone—below a neediness that is so large in us that we will "drug" ourselves to keep from feeling the magnitude of this need. Our "drug" can be in the form of chemicals, violence, consumerism, religious and political cults, and abusive relationships with ourselves and others. His existence is a key part in a primal consciousness that connects us with the full human past. This need to connect with him is overwhelming, even though the "face" of the Companion changes from culture to culture.

But the specific, immense, nurturing "maleness" of him makes the Male Companion our main conduit to the gay work. I refer to him as the "Companion," rather than in such Judeo-Christian terms as "Our Lord," "King," or "God" because of the important tribal concept of him as our healing, nursing (but very much "commanding") Equal. He is both the 135 "brother" and "Master" with whom we want to *merge* as we go through that element in the gay mythos. He symbolizes the inevitable and, at moments, frightening flow of ourselves, both physically and psychically, into the Great Other.

In the cosmology of many other cultures, he is the seed that older men want to plant in younger boys, in order to make them more masculine, commanding, and wise. Conversely, he can also be the playful, energizing spirit of youth. Sexually, we may see him personified in physical or fetishistic terms (the big phallus, the Hindu lingum, the Top who commands us to make *him* the Bottom, ecstatic bondage, etc.), but these are only avenues of approaching him.

At the moment of perceiving him, he offers himself to us with a complete, disarming generosity, and with an intensity of closeness that can only be experienced in small durations. The overwhelming immensity of this psychic closeness ("intimacy overload") makes us realize at once a concept we have dealt with—the *finiteness of intimacy*—a concept and experience that, unfortunately, escapes many gay men. Because of distant parents, the secrecy in our pasts, and our enforced shame, gay men are often starved for intimacy. They believe that any "authentic" intimate gay relationship must be total. It must be constantly fulfilling and capable of nurturing this bottomless hunger. For this reason, our intimate relationships—which start in the search for the Companion—are often weighted with impossible responsibilities.

Because intimacy between the sexes has traditionally been limited, heterosexuals had few of these fantasies. Although lovers (or partners) of the opposite sex could be intensely—sexually—intimate with each other, it was normal for men to go back to their male friends on a regular basis for more casual companionship, and for women to seek out female friends, who gave them a kind of support and "sisterly" affection that men could not. For thousands of years men had a culture of their own, based on mentorship, companionship (what the Germans call *brudershaft*), social rank and skills. Women had their own culture based on the home, their body needs (a "female world" that men were not allowed to enter), and mutual nurturing. Although these parallel cultures easily led to sexism, they also provided both genders with much of the nurturance they needed, as well as a satisfying relief and refuge from the burdens of heterosexual intimacy. (Amazingly, Catholicism has kept these two cultures somewhat alive today, even in technological societies, through the cults of the Virgin Mary, a mythic descendant of Diana, the virgin goddess beloved by gay men, and of Christ Himself, one of the great Brother/Father/Friend figures, whose parallels can be glimpsed in the beauty and sensitivity of Apollo and the affectionate friendliness of Krishna.)

In dealing with the emotionally charged presence of the Companion, we quickly understand that any "normal" experience of him must be of fairly short duration. As with any intense sexual intimacy, the

Companion's presence is both very satisfying (as an experience of complete self-knowledge) as well as emotionally exhausting.

So it is important to experience his presence again and again. Not on a continuous basis, which becomes, frankly, dangerous (and leads to the kind of unbalanced, religious extremism we see in "Jesus freaks" and other cults), but on a basis of psychically renewing experiences. To do otherwise is to risk your own sense of (and need for) individuation, as well as your sanity: to merge, in short, with something so large that you can become completely lost in it.

The Companion, then, is a same-sexualized approach to the greater experience of knowledge we refer to as "God." This is one reason why, in connecting with him within the demanding environment of an intimate relationship, we often find these relationships closing down sexually. This leads to too much intimacy, too much emotional material being thrown at us. The Companion has become too close to us. We have to push him away, then seek him in someone else.

I know this seems "illogical" and contradictory. (Much of the problem with our Western, therapy-centered approach to relationships is that we want them to be "logical." We want them to follow set, fashionable, "mental health" patterns, instead of coming to terms with the depth and richness of psychic patterns.) If we can find this Companion that we want so much (and find him, especially, within a much sought after, intimate relationship with another man) why shouldn't we want contact with more and more of "him"—both the Companion and the (real) physical man?

But this boundary—this finiteness—of intimacy, which leads to rejecting intimacy at moments, to "closing-in" on intimacy, therefore giving it closure so that we can step out of it, is universal. Like incest taboos, it may be psychically and even biologically hardwired to us. In a nutshell, it says that as we approach the Companion sexually (a very common approach to him), the Companion himself, as our deepest incarnation of spiritual/psychic union, can push sex away.

Although we think of mysteries as being "who-done-its," the Companion's continuing "mystery" is more a question of how will he be perceived. Interacting with this mystery, becoming aware of the Companion's presence, is something that is revealed to us at certain moments. He is that frank incorporation of the greater Male spirit that makes us complete. It is a spirit so large that at moments it dissolves its own gender divisions, and crosses or blurs into the presence of the Holy Androgyne, the Divine Mother/Father/ Herself/ Himself.

I put *mystery* in quotes because the Companion is very much a phantom—an elusive spiritual entity—and, paradoxically, he is also within the reach of each of us. On a more immediate level, he is that emotional tenderness centered on men that goes into the quest for the *true friend* that gay men—no matter how they have termed themselves in the past—have historically sought. He is that creature of amazing innocence and wisdom, experience and freshness, that we seek and at some point want to return to in ourselves.

The *true friend* will understand us, comfort us, and come to us in a way that does not deny our inner selves. In other words, the *friend* will clear away all the homophobic barriers between us and him. He will know us (recognition), and cross over to us (twinning) , and satisfy us (submission into merging). The *true friend* is an *idealization* of the Male Companion. The Companion and the *true friend*, then, are ways of imagining our selves joined to a much larger sphere of knowledge that we think of in terms of the experience of God.

Most of us have, at some point, "woken" up to realize that we *are* searching for something behind our everyday needs. We may search for this inner Companion in compulsive cruising, with that feeling of loneliness and emptiness that many of us never satisfy. We may "wake up" in the midst of this search and see, too plainly, a connection with our deepest unmet needs. At that point, it is common to stop the search and become even more bitter, cynical, and needful. But, hopefully, later, the quest will become more maturely centered within us. This is either after we have found a lover—and started to locate some functions of the Companion within him; or realized, finally, a much greater satisfaction and closeness to our inner selves.

So, in the quest for the Male Companion, one completes oneself. Gay men search for this completion all their lives and find it, for the most part, either in other men, or in more far-flung moments of recognition doing other parts of the gay work. A real tragedy is that many heterosexual men also search for this Male Companion—for this Male completion and centering within themselves—and too often they are forced to try to find him in women (who have their own psychic needs and cannot satisfy those of men). They cannot, in short, achieve this intimacy that they want so very much with another man, with another man.

This leads to one of the most difficult problems we see within society: men who cannot (because of homophobia) be intimate with other men, so they seek either an aggressive and violent intimacy with women or with other "straight" men. Much of what we call "straight porn"—and the culture of rape that it represents—is based on this misplacement. (This "rape" culture says that all women at heart are *cunts*, are *bitches*, and must be punished. By doing this, straight men will join with one another, on a very homophobic, queer-safe level, in a self-righteous, woman-hating "brotherhood.") We see this in war experiences, when men can only support each other, hold and kiss one another—when they are two feet away from death. Or in sports experiences, when only after men have beat the crap out of each other, can they mutually touch.

In our own community much of the violent, internalized homophobia we see lashed out at other queer men—by homosexual killers who seek other gays—is caused by men who can never connect with the Male Companion. They are endlessly empty, and incapable of experiencing within themselves any nurturing sense of kindness and mercy.

(Another violent and bewildering contradiction is that Christ, our most dramatic—and recognizable—incarnation of the Male Companion, is often used as an "excuse" for right-wing Christian homophobic violence. Who is trying to avoid what here is only too obvious.)

To characterize the Male Companion, he is at once totally vulnerable (or, as the pop press would say, "female") and malefully strong. These two forces are entwined within one another in a constant, complementary state. He gives himself to us and we take strength from him, releasing our own need to be vulnerable. We in turn pull him to us and take on the voluptuousness of his own strength. In doing this, we achieve the strength that is necessary for our lives. By incorporating the Male Companion, that is, seeing him as a reality and bringing him into ourselves, we achieve, finally, the complete (and amazingly selfless) *self-love* that evades most men their entire lives.

Finally, in this marriage of the male and female in the Companion himself, gay men are brought closer to the more open, sensitized female world and are distanced from a more predatory, opaque—but necessary—"male" one. Among many Native American tribes, men who might be labeled among us as "gay" were considered to be "go-betweens" between the sexes. They brought back messages from the (male) Sky gods or the (female) Earth gods. They were called, therefore, "two-spirited."

For many of us, this is very frightening: it seems like a renunciation of that basic "maleness" that we fetishize and desire, that very much excites us. This produces a contradictory (some might say "neurotic") dynamic, and many gay men try to resolve this by pulling the more "dumb," wordless, harder world of straight men–an environment they find more predictable and reassuring, even in its violence—closer to them. This power-laden "butch" world mesmerizes, enslaves, and diverts them. So, defensively, we try to embrace the "butch" world, and bring it (even kicking and punching us in the face) into the "gay" one.

Recently, I have begun to see this appropriating of the butch world—which is often characterized by working-class associations (football, country music, sports craziness, redneck attitudes, etc.)—as "flopping," from an old graphics term for reversing an image. Just as gay men in the "olden" days flopped to the left, appropriating female images (drag, opera and pop divas, camp), today they flop to the right, appropriating butcher, working-class ones. For many of us, what this is saying is that, even if we can not get the "All-American" boy, we will try to be one. And even if we were hurt by this stark, "butch" image in our youths, we will bring it closer to our hearts in adulthood as a means of capturing it. Many gay men (and women) find this flopping to the right repugnant; they see it as embracing internalized homophobia, as sucking at the poison that 139 hurts us in order to neutralize it.

But I find another feeling working here. That, by embracing butchness, we still want to nurse the fallen hero. That like Walt Whitman in the Civil War (whom I will talk about soon), we still want to bind and nurse the wounds of (in the old, starkly limited sense, "real") men. We want to grab their action, bloodiness, opacity, insensitivity—and run with it. We want to be needed and a part of their world. But, with the ever-present gay "genius" for finding an authentic self, I believe that we are actually digging though this wall of butchness to find female roots in it. And there, at these roots, we find, once more, the Male Companion.

As I have said, the need for this completion is not limited to gays; it is, in fact, universal. Unfortunately, heterosexual men, especially in our male-phobic society, cannot approach this need. For the most part, they must avoid it completely. *To do otherwise threatens their own very vulnerable sense of maleness, leading to the homophobia and male-phobia we see around us.* Since heterosexual men cannot complete themselves with another man and cannot identify or complete themselves with a woman—the thought of this (of being dependent upon a woman for psychic completion) is both distasteful and terrifying—their only completion now comes from having children.

In having children, they approach a necessary selflessness. In other words, they must relinquish all of their own satisfying, inner spiritual life to their children. The demand to do this is placed upon them both by our secular society and by orthodox religions who see children as "innocents," as angels who, on one hand, heal the sins of their parents and who, on the other hand, must take on so many punishments for them. ("The sins of the fathers will be visited upon the sons.")

Children also keep many men away from an abyss of depression—a complete lack of intimacy and love—that they feel threatens them. The result is that these men often contemplate suicide if separated from their kids. But this newer, contemporary psychic "importance" of children has not made us protect children any more effectively as an unprotected class. When we hear about children being beaten, or left to starve, or left homeless, people grab their own kids to them and want to protect them more against these outside threats, while at the same time quietly forgetting the plight of other children. Various child "predators" (especially gay men involved *in any way* with children) are completely demonized, as services for children get smaller and smaller. An example of this is that the 1996 budget for the Children's Defense Fund, a leading national lobby to protect children, was $15 million. In the same year, the budget for the American Association of Retired Persons (AARP)—which will go mainly to protect Social Security—was set at $449 million, about 30 times that of a fund whose sole interest is a basically unprotected class: kids. So we find ourselves now in the midst of an epidemic of child abuse, neglect, and murder–to a rate of 2,000 to 3,000 kids a year who are murdered, usually by a parent, guardian, or close relative.

The father, then, looks upon his children to be what he is not: sinless. Yet he knows that they will suffer from and bear his sins. This causes modern parents terrible anxiety; they see their offspring as threatening mirrors. Will their children make them proud? Will they reflect their own values? Will they be those "trophy kids," worth all the sweat necessary to educate them? Can they compete in the modern predatory world? Because women are often compelled now to do "Daddy's work," that is, to prove their worth in a competitive society, we see more women destroying their children (as witnessed by the by-no-means isolated case of Susan Smith drowning her two small sons in South Carolina), with a violence once attributed to men at war. When the Male Companion is dismissed, maternal instincts—in their own way gifts of the (Fe)Male Companion—are now perceived as "frills," and not a part of the real self-preservation of our human race.

Part of growing out of childhood is testing the bonds that connect you with your parents. While these bonds are being tested, you must develop your self, not as an extension of your parents, but as your own creation. In the past this was done with an extended family or community circle (the uncle, aunt, grandparent, or teacher who took kids under his/her wing and explained things to them). With much self-creation stopped or stymied, children now stay in constant rebellion with both themselves and the world. They can look at and accept neither. The deeper "mysteries" of life escape them. Instead, kids must negotiate their way, often alone, through a minefield of demanding, set, commercial images towards their own "success." We now accept these images as "normal." Or, even worse, as "cool." We rarely question or look deeper into them.

Unfortunately, the ritual of testing the bonds between children and their parents has become only another one of these set images. It is a template for thousands of sitcoms, TV commercials, and magazine ads. We have the very commercially desirable children who are "smarter" than their parents because they can manipulate the technology better. They are "cooler" than their parents: meaning, they buy the newest thing faster. They pride themselves on leaving aside *all* innocence and empathy, before they have any opportunity to prove their adulthood. They throw their own babies in garbage cans, like unwanted samples from Toys-"R"-Us. They are cold, cynical, hardened children.

Many gay men, after also going through a childhood without innocence (an innocence that was denied them because of an early recognition of their difference), try to reinvent a later childhood for themselves. This allows them to opt out of the difficult waters of the adult world. But it also keeps them from doing the difficult work of gay men, which is important since (most probably) they will not have children themselves to create (or at least further) the sense of completion they need.

This means they are stuck between child*lessness* and child*ishness*. It is a complete dead-end that has become for many gay men what the modern "gay world" is all about.

Once these men truly begin the road towards their own adulthood, difficult and treacherous as it may be, they will find some form of the Male Companion to give them the completion and guidance they need. Even without naming him specifically, experiencing the Companion (as a spiritual entity) fills in the gaps, aloneness, and needs in a gay psyche. In reality, though, as much as gay men may wish to find the Companion in one man, it is impossible for one man to fulfill the enormity of the Companion's place in our lives.

What follows, then, is a dialogue between the gay need for intimacy within a community and a tribe (a need that is primal, and that mainstream society denies) and the need for intimacy with one man, who represents in a more immediate form the Male Companion himself. This man may take on, for a while, the *true friend*'s role, until he comes out of it and becomes—for better or worse—simply another wondrous human being. But in the lovely emotional shimmer behind him, is the Male Companion.

On the way towards the Male Companion, many gay men find themselves most fulfilled in a society of men; even if this society, such as a religious order, the military, or fraternal organizations like the Scouts, does not have an openly homosexual agenda. In fact, it may have an *openly* homophobic one. Some men (who often enough were once part of other same-sex, mainstream societies such as the military) have taken this need and formed leather clubs, fraternal groups, and other organizations which have a sense of hierarchy and structure, but often with a clear message of gay sexuality working through them. This sense of *hierarchy* is important for us, although we have a difficult time acknowledging it.

Despite our needs for and advocacy of liberalism (or even libertarianism), hierarchy, which offers us a psychic chain leading (hopefully) up to the Male Companion, attracts many of us. It is the reason why queer men fit so beautifully into oppressive institutions like the Catholic Church, the military, the FBI, and mainstream or even right-wing politics. These all-male (or extremely male-dominated) groups create in our own psyches a background for finding either the *true friend* or the secret, luminous Male Companion who is above us, Christ-like and caring.

Recently, within this context, we have had the "coming out" of dozens—and probably hundreds—of gay men as "gay conservatives," "gay fundamentalists," "gay Republicans," etc. These were men who felt that they could not come out earlier because it was "impossible" then to be both gay and (for want of another word) *reactionary*. The gay movement was seen to be "left-wing," "progressive," or "liberal." Because these men had been out of contact with the community itself, they could not see that in the past gay men and lesbians were often very conservative, culturally and politically. Being so different in one life area, meant that they needed to be extremely cautious, or conformist, in another.

However, many younger gay men have now incorporated this "coming out" of gay conservatives, and seem to feel that there is more "honesty" within gay conservatism than within the idealism that spawned the gay movement at its every turn. The motto of these much more cynical young people might be: "Real repression is better than fake liberation." I feel that they are using this kind of more "open" thinking to distance themselves from the vulnerability that comes from a real connection with other gay men, and the Companion.

On a more immediate level is the formation of the gay family, or "family of choice," that men often form once they leave home, come out, and develop friendship networks. Many men find their chosen families more responsive and satisfying than their "real" families. They come closer to placing the Male Companion within them. But this has come about because their biological family has become only another set of Christmas card images, and gay families have not, as of yet, been able to do this.

Within gay families (whether of choice or biology, as when two men adopt a child or raise one fathered by one of them) lies the difficult but empowering reality that no set image exists for us yet. Because none exists, we can be more flexible and sensitive towards each other. There is more room for the Companion and a wonderfully satisfying sense of spirituality to come into our lives. We complain that no one knows what we look like; that, generally, we are not pictured in mainstream advertising and the media. But it also means that we do not have to navigate a series of images that may have little to do with us. We don't have to be characters in a sitcom. We don't have to be anorexic models, or look like the "white bread" men in TV commercials. So by not having to work our way through these images, our whole "family" can get closer to the nurturing Male Companion—who has no set face, race, or class—who speaks in our language and is waiting in our hearts.

"Walt Whitman often nursed the psyches of men as well as their physical problems. He wrote extensively in his journals of holding the hands of dying men, of kissing them good-bye as their eyes closed for the last time, and of writing letters for them—acting, therefore, as their scribe, another part of the gay work."

CHAPTER 9

# Creating Our Selves:
# Continuing the Gay Work

Although perceiving—and experiencing—the mystery of the Male Companion is the cornerstone of the gay work, there are other aspects of it as well. I wanted to include them in another chapter to give them the importance they deserve. Here are some other features of this important work that I have identified so far.

- *To act as the remaining key to a lost male function*: recognizing the male as a being of intrinsic beauty. In most animal species, the male must attract the female by his physical beauty, as well as by his movements and attentions to her. In antiquity, male beauty was celebrated openly by other men, who prized it as a special gift from the gods. In our more guarded society, this male function of celebrating the beauty of other males has been for the most part lost. For centuries this key was entrusted only to artists or other individuals who were deemed "suspect" by the Church or the forces in power. Even creating anything purely beautiful questioned the Judeo-Christian taboo against "decadent" beauty for its own sake.

This key was later openly re-introduced to Western culture by such gay writers as Walter Pater and Oscar Wilde, who taught an "aesthetic" philosophy of "Art for art's sake," or beauty for its own sake. This philosophy became associated with the "Aesthetes," a nineteenth century movement of writers, artists, and art lovers who practiced Wilde's philosophy. It also served as a Victorian code word or umbrella term for sexually "ambiguous" men, i.e., homosexuals.

To the Greeks and Romans of classical times, art was ennobling, civilizing, and refreshing. Like the beautiful mosaics and frescoes found in ancient houses, it was a pleasurable part of ordinary life. In the Middle Ages, to survive, art had become enchained to spirituality and official Christianity. Ideas like "Art for art's sake" and the unexpected beauty of "normal" or non-spiritual things (the naked athletic body; pictures of working men, sporting scenes; and scenes from classical or "secular" mythology) became identified as "queer" concepts. Without the role of the gay artist (and critic), the idea of the male body as *inherently beautiful* would not exist in Western culture.

Within the gay work is the task of celebrating the beauty of men. Not simply commercially "hot," centerfold men, but men whose own beauty might be overlooked. This includes younger men, who are very much ignored in mainstream society unless they are rock stars, actors, or models; the "bear" movement, which has uncovered a whole new approach to appreciating the "raw" beauty of men; older men, who because of our homophobically inspired fear of growing up and older, have become pariah in many gay venues; and physically handicapped (or challenged) men, whose combination of vulnerability and strength should inspire within us a direct call from the Companion. Within this gay work is paying attention to other men, and offering them a perception of their intrinsic beauty and worth, as it is mirrored within our own.

- *To provide a normal brake on population.* It is biologically very possible that homosexuality may be "imprinted" on the human gene structure for this purpose. Homosexual activities occur in many animal species, such as whales, dolphins, and the pigmy bonobo chimpanzees, our closest evolutionary "relatives," who engage regularly in homosexual pairing and lovemaking. Bonobo males do not simply hump each other out of claustrophobia or stress (something that biology researchers have stated for years about caged-animal homosexual activities), but seek out each other as a part of their normal socio/bio-patterning.

In Native American (or Amerindian) societies, gay men who were a part of this patterning were referred to by early European settlers as fulfilling the role of *berdache*. These were men who dressed as women and did the women's work of preparing food and keeping house. Their work also included marrying other men, often hunters or braves, who did not want to have children or who were simply homosexually inclined. Berdache men, by European accounts, always took the "passive" part in anal sex, or gave oral sexual service. However, there is no way of telling if this was the actual case, and, as is seen among drag queens today, "fems" on the street often turn into "butches" between the sheets.

Berdacheism has survived in many Indian cultures, and frequently, in the tradition of being "twin-spirited," berdache men are also gifted shamans or spiritualists. In contemporary rural Latin American societies, it is considered normal for a "straight" or macho man to go to a "sissy" or *mariposa*, when his wife is pregnant and does not want to have sex with him again, until the birth of their baby. As masturbation is looked upon as unmasculine, the "sissy" will have sex with him, in the "female" role, and therefore the *macho* feels that his manhood is intact: he has not masturbated nor committed an act which the village will see as adulterous.

This also keeps him from producing bastard children. Many men, paradoxically, keep their wives pregnant in order to do this, since at heart they are homosexually inclined.

Many younger village men also go through a phase where, before having a girlfriend, they will have a *mariposa* boyfriend who will introduce them to sex. They will stay with the boyfriend until they find a girl who is acceptable to their families; they will marry her and then visit the boyfriend from time to time. This pattern is repeated in numerous Arab or Moslem societies where male-female relations are severely restricted and there is almost no premarital sex. In these societies illegitimate children are heavily stigmatized and sex outside marriage is usually characterized as rape. But same-sex premarital sex is commonly accepted and not condemned, as long as it is not publicly talked about.

- *To become the scribe* (or point of consciousness) *of families.* Since we are often a break in the bloodline, it is our job to learn the stories of our families and tell them, and also to tell our own stories. This is a job that heterosexual men, who are traditionally taught not to talk about themselves, often find embarrassing. It is our job, then, to turn attention on the male role, since conventionally that role is to "disappear," except when performing a function such as war, sports, earning a living, etc. (The converse of that is that men, often not so secretly, yearn for an attention that has been denied them: Mothers Day, for instance, delivers the second greatest telephone usage, except for Christmas, on the calendar. Both men and women expect to have a real "telephone" connection with their mothers. But Fathers Day is a complete black-out. Who wants to remember Dad, when the father's role, internalized in our society, is not to talk?)

If, biologically, we may be the witnesses who will go on no further, often we as "single" men are engaged to explain the family to others, or provide a repository of its secrets. In short, many of us keep the scrapbooks and write the family letters. These secrets may include our own gay lives and other "stories" that, despite the family's various rituals of denial (drug or alcohol dependency, physical and sexual abuse, etc.), we do understand.

Since we are often "out on our own," other people find it easier to speak to us. We are not there to push our own kids forward. Biologically, we do not have to keep our spears sharpened. Psychically—believe it or not—we probably have fewer axes to grind. This has given us space for others; we do not have the anxiety of children over our heads. (Despite one of the great gay fantasies that children, as a hedge against the future, are "designed" to take care of you in old age and trouble!)

This has also allowed us to enlarge our role as friends, and to take risks with strangers. Now that strangers (and the "strange" of any stripe) are suspect in society, this has added a heavy burden to gay men, who often have to rush into stupid bureaucratic situations and rescue people. This was the role of the great Irish patriot Roger Casement, who came to the rescue of abused native African workers in the Belgium Congo in the early years of this century; of Raoul Wahlenberg, a "bachelor" Christian who rescued thousands of Jews during World War II; and of the late, closeted Dr. Tom Dooley, who rescued children in Viet Nam in the 60s. We did precisely that in the AIDS crisis, while it took the federal government ten years to figure out what was going on. As "scribes," we had to remember what went on. We had to call attention to it. We could not forget. All of what we call "gay history" will be the "scribings" of ourselves. We cannot expect the mainstream media to say, "Oh, yes: we took all that down."

Another aspect of this secretiveness—both of bearing and keeping secrets (two activities which have branded gay men as "subversives" for centuries)—is that we are also the repositories of "secret languages." In the old days, this language was "camp," something that allowed us to speak in front of straights (and still be undetected) and also to signal to each other. Now, however, that language is often one of male endearment, something that straight men find almost unbearably difficult.

As part of the gay work, we preserve what has become a secret language of tenderness towards other men. Since women now try to speak as toughly as men, in heterosexual relationships this "language of tenderness" towards men may be completely absent. Therefore, straight men rarely find themselves addressed in terms of privacy, warmth, and sensitivity, and many of them yearn for a return to these terms.

Unfortunately, I also find that gay men are losing this important language of endearment, so it is part of our gay work to bring it back. When younger men come to me and complain about how difficult it is to achieve relationships, I ask them how much of this special *language of endearment* do they have? Usually they look at me puzzled. Basically, the language of endearment is a private language between two people, although its codes and signals may come from the general language. In Victorian times lovers often "talked" to each other by exchanging flowers. White lilies were given to virgins of either sex; roses represented the Virgin Mary; carnations were dashing and adventurous; and pansies (from the French word, *pensée*, for thought—hence our word, pensive) denoted having a thoughtful, philosophical nature. (Therefore, pansies often found their way into the buttonholes of gay men!)

Flowers became very much a part of this private language of endearment, even though their meanings were understood by many people. What made them private was who presented them, and when.

Other aspects of this private language are using special words ("darling," "sweetheart," etc.) that you do not use with everyone. (If—like Tallulah Bankhead—you call everyone "Darling," it is no longer endearing.) Actions that become part of this secret language may include: sharing a bath, preparing meals, allowing a quiet time to be together, presenting special presents from the heart (books, photos, etc.), and acting with spontaneous tenderness. The poet Allen Ginsberg used the expression "heart talk" to signify speech of openness and tenderness. Like Whitman, whom Ginsberg claimed to be a direct forebear, he used "heart talk" often with "straight" men, who needed its healing warmth and directness.

Often men used to speak this way together in bed. But lately this simple, sweet language has been lost in the need to jump up, rewind the VCR, and get moving. Another example of losing this language: men who must schedule other men on their business calendars, even after they've met in an intimate or sexual way. After deciding what spare "quality" time they can bestow on a prospective lover, they can't—for the life of them—figure out why new friends, who want something more than to be figured on a business calendar, vanish around them. It is important, then, for gay men to keep this spontaneous language of male tenderness and affection alive, and as part of the gay work make room for it.

Often the "official" *work* of gay men (what we do at the office, or at home with others) is directed at consciousness, in that frequently we work with ideas. This has directed us into philosophy (and the very "gay" concept of the ideal or "platonic," named for the openly homosexual philosopher Plato), as well as the pursuit of "amusement," whose original meaning was a happiness that came "directly from beauty": the joy that is reached through the Muses themselves.

This work is immensely important. We see it in the activities of curators, archivists, decorators, historians, designers, and of course "opera queens," "show queens," etc. They are taking human feelings and directing them into their own personal language of style, music, or art. As Buzz, the musical comedy queen in Terrence McNally's play *Love! Valor! Compassion!*, says, "You may wonder why I fill my head with such trivial-seeming information. First of all, it isn't trivial to me, and second, I can contain the world of the Broadway musical. Get my hands around it, so to speak. Be the master of one little universe." He can also use it as his own language, a language that many other gay men speak.

Conversely, because so much of the gay work deals with consciousness, from our first consciousness of being different ("coming out") and onward, we are also attracted as well to leaving consciousness: to hot, ecstatic sex. To dumb "hunks." They represent to us Eros in a pure, unfettered state. We are drawn in turn to primitivism—there is a history of gay explorers who have gone "native"—and to a primal, childlike sweetness that we associate with an unspoiled, non-homophobic world. So, highly closeted queers invented the Boy Scouts, as well as the art of interior decoration. We are drawn to both extremes.

In this part of the gay work, I am making a distinction between consciousness, which is holding on to thought and directing it, and *creativity*, which is producing what is new, often through states of unconsciousness, or what gestalt philosophers called "leaps."

Creativity is a completely human activity. It is not at all restricted in 149 any way to gay men. But again, it is unfortunate that creativity, which has become (inaccurately) associated with neurosis and childishness, is often associated with gay men. This has come about because gay men often speak openly and proudly of our role as creators, a role that embarrasses heterosexuals unless such creativity is seen as a direct path to money. Stephen King, for instance, is not seen as an influential, prolific writer, but as a "hardworking money machine."

- *To enrich and enlarge the role of men.* Man as mother, nurse, companion, and "sister." This is probably the most controversial and remarkable aspect of what the gay work is. In its simplest form, it repeats the mythos of the man who keeps his maleness and yet discovers his femaleness. He is, in short, embracing the Male Companion, the spiritual figure within him who transcends gender.

The realization of this transcendence often happens in the midst of great turmoil, such as a war or the current AIDS crisis. Only then can men cast off homophobic social restrictions. In the past when this happened, men frequently found themselves feeling safer through gender role-enlargement, instead of going through the "homosexual panic" that we see now. An example were men sent off by themselves for years to distant colonies, where they had to do "women's work." This included sewing, knitting (English soldiers were famous for knitting their own socks), cooking, and happily looking after each other. Many men sought out these all-male adventures and, instead of feeling deprived and put upon, felt more needed and happier. In reality they were placing themselves in these situations in order to do the gay work.

Although we have accepted a lot of the idea of "unisexuality," for a man to expose his own deepest feelings and needs in a "womanly" way is still considered, at best, "iffy." To rationalize what he is going through, the most a (to his mind) suddenly "feminized" man can hope for is that he will have a "crack-up," and be accepted as emotionally unstable. In the past this was a course of action for men who were "caught" in homosexually compromising situations. They disappeared into mental hospitals. This same situation continues today in places like Mormon Utah, where gay men and youths (as well as many lesbians) have been committed to mental facilities by their families for "treatment." Although this is sometimes done punitively, to punish "sex offenders," families of these men still feel that it is far less embarrassing for them to be known in the community as mentally unstable than gay.

In our presently enlightened "mental health" environment, being considered mentally ill or unstable is still better to many people than being identified or recognized as "queer." (Strangely enough, for this reason, retarded men are allowed to hold hands on the street: they "don't know better.") This has resulted in millions of men who are now on antidepressants, rather than face a turn in the road of their lives. What is ahead, simply enough, could be characterized as the specter of the gay work: the need to release the yearning, "male/female" part of themselves, as it seeks to merge with the Male Companion. Men who have "come out" have often told me that it capped years of depression. Despite all of their turmoil and fears, they could finally release this part of themselves.

It is important, then, as a part of our gay work, for us to understand this, and offer solace to men in this situation. To let them know that they are not alone, and that we are a part of the Companion and are there for them.

While doing the gay work in a time of crisis, a man can allow his soul to open up so that his "anima," his nurturing female spirit, is released through an unlocked door of feelings. Then the Male Companion (either in the form of another man's naked generosity and vulnerability—or his own) can manifest himself to him, giving him the psychic aid that he needs. At these moments, when outside pressures have caused many layers of defenses to drop, a vision of the sublime, compassionate Companion arrives.

Sometimes this is in the form of an actual person, whose presence becomes wonderfully recognizable. (The poet Allen Ginsberg referred to this very humanized Companion, in the form of his lover Peter Orlovsky, as "the ambulance driver of my Soul.") Spiritually, the Male Companion may appear in the form of a Christ or God vision. This also happens in times of stress on a mass level, as cults are formed.

Or it may happen politically, when the next *savior* arrives in the person of a Napoleon, Hitler, or some other dictator. Political "saviors," unfortunately, are often enough disturbed and power-hungry. The public does not see this until its infatuation with them has ended. But they are able to manipulate and leach off the needs of whole societies, who are seeking, on a mass level, the Male Companion.

For gay men, these roles of mother, nurse, companion, and "sister" have become recognizable and acceptable to us. With straight men, they are considered embarrassing or comic, as witnessed by dozens of Hollywood or TV "bachelor father" movies. The role of Mother as the center of creation and nurturance is different from the role of Father as the source of physical strength and energy. What is critically important to understand is that men, also, at various times should be in "mothering" roles. For us not to be, for us to abdicate the role of nurturance and warmth to women, also robs this role of power. It turns this important role into that of "the little woman," "the weaker sex."

This is exactly what has happened to women in the last hundred years or so, as straight men have become more and more frightened of "womanliness." Even the adjectives we use for women—such as *ladylike, girlish, frilly*—are for the most part derogatory. Western society has wanted to forget that in nature the female is frequently the more powerful and assertive; the male, more vulnerable and eager to assent.

On the other hand, it is often a part of the gay work of men to support women in positions of power. When a man does this, he is considered less than a man. The label "faggot" or "degenerate" circulates around him. (In the movies or television, he is still portrayed as the simpy male secretary working for a powerful, swaggering woman. A leading recent example: "Josh," the always too "obviously" closeted assistant in the TV sitcom *Veronica's Closet*) He has stepped outside the role of men, which is to control women.

It is important for men to support warm, powerful, goddess-like women, but for a man to do this still makes him suspect in society. Some women need and demand power to fulfill their personalities, and become frustrated human beings without it. These women blossom through using their own power. Often the only men who can understand this are gay. And it is part of our *work* to see this.

The role of "sister," which is different from the role of male friend, means to be tender, supportive, direct, and *truthful*. Men have reached the point of never being truthful with each other. To do so would be to invade their most *masculine* bastions of privacy: to surrender the secrets which stand like ramparts around their own delicate testicles. In other words, exposing weakness is not allowed.

Biological sisters, though, were usually allowed to be truthful with their brothers. In gay society having a "sister" became important. A "sister" said things to you that a lover could not say. When you weren't looking your best; when you'd had too much to drink; when no one had the stomach to tell you that the man you believed was *just perfect* for you was . . . NOT! Sometimes "sisters" though could be castrating (i.e., not respecting a man's psyche), and it is important for a man reaching into his "sister" role to understand that he is not rejecting the male part of himself, but enlarging it. It is also important to distinguish between the "sister" and the "enemy-friend" that I wrote about earlier. The sister, in short, is not a *bitch*.

Another aspect of the "sister" is that of the nurse (or *krankenschwester*, as the Germans say: "sister of the sick"), something that gay men have learned to do well. One of the first role models for gay men as nurses was Walt Whitman, who acted as a "wound dresser" during the Civil War. In this capacity, Whitman often nursed the psyches of men as well as their physical problems. He wrote extensively in his journals of holding the hands of dying men, of kissing them good-bye as their eyes closed for the last time, and of writing letters for them—acting, therefore, as their scribe, another part of the gay work. For Whitman, doing this work during the "Brothers' War," as he called it, was a great privilege. Often gay men feel this way about working with the sick and frail.

However, due to homophobia, any man in a woman's job cannot be perceived as a man unless the job is "masculinized" and upgraded. The first women who worked as army or hospital nurses were often prostitutes, since they saw strange men naked and no "respectable" woman could be allowed to do this. As respectable women did come into nursing, more distance had to be placed between them and the men they nursed, especially in the stressful, very sexualized times of war. A nurse became a woman who had a real job to do—but could only follow male "doctor's orders." Because many men have gone into nursing, and the profession has tried to attract "real" men, instead of compassionate gays, the male nurse has been turned into an administrator or a doctor's aide. Although he will now make more money, the idea of nursing as a profession for compassionate, empathetic men has been "butched" up, and much distance is again placed between wounded men and the "sisters of the sick."

One final remark: I would like *you* to use and bring forth your own glimpses of the Male Companion, your connections with the gay tribe and its work. Think about the gay work you have done and will do. Little of this has been spoken of in the past, and when it was, it was often spoken of homophobically—that gay men reject their "maleness," their *responsibilities as men*, is a fairly common charge.

Many of us will see that the gay work has always been in our minds and experiences. Despite homophobic denigrations, it is important and powerful. It is for the most part only waiting to be "archived," to be brought to consciousness and given the honor that it deserves. What is important is for us to allow the gay work the depth that is necessary for it to take place. This is serious! It cannot and should not be joked off. Often it has to be done alone.

But please, smile while you do it.

"What you want to do . . . is re-establish the nakedness of sex: sex which has been over-clothed in intimacy, in fact, may even be strangling in it."

## CHAPTER 10

# The Mystery of the Death of Gay Desire

The death of gay desire seems to be one of the world's great murder mysteries. I am asked constantly what causes it. You find someone. You settle down. Everything is going hot as a Bessemer converter. Then, after a certain amount of time, the desire between the two of you evaporates.

**Bang**. It's gone.

You keep looking for it, and keep trying to blame someone for losing it. It was there a few months ago. A few years ago, maybe. And now it's gone. But who killed it? And where the hell did it go?

Many gay men want to model their lives after a fantasy of what they believe their parents' marriage was like. They still have a kind of Disney Wonderland, very 1950s, pre-*Playboy* view of this: husbands who did not look at another woman. Mommies who came directly out of black-and-white TV. They want to believe that this fantasy life should be the ideal for them. And when they meet someone, they are sure—just positive—that they are already on the road to this "ideal."

Instead, they come to Dead-Man's Gulch.

There vultures are circling the spot—with a sign that says: "Sorry, Buddy. You just hit the Death of Gay Desire."

What happened? How? *Why*?

You can't quite place it, or understand it. How does it happen that as much as we want it to stay there—forever—our desire in a relationship wobbles? Then it wanes . . . then it fucking disappears. In fact, all the *fucking* disappears.

Many answers have been thrown out to this question. One, of course, is sexual boredom. Many gay men feel we have a monopoly on this—since straight sexual boredom was chest-deep in the closet until just a few years ago. Then, suddenly it seemed like half the smart young women in America—all those budding "Mayflower Madams"—were hiring out      155 their pretty young friends for the new "adult" version of fast-food sex. (Take it out. Drive it in. Then put it on your Amex card.)

Who was screwing all these pay-by-plastic harlots? No one other than the fathers, boyfriends, and husbands of many of the young ladies themselves. In other words, het-sex boredom was getting into the mainstream Big Time. It was no longer something people on the wrong side of the tracks did. It was now in Beverly Hills, in the Social Register, and winking to the Marine guards at the White House.

But gays still feel that heteros just don't stray as much as we do. They don't cool down as fast, and they stay hot-and-bothered working the same sheets year after year.

In *Intimacy Between Men*, a 1991 book that uses mental health models to deal with questions of intimacy between gay men, John H. Driggs and Stephen E. Finn, a social worker and psychologist respectively, say: "It may also be that same-sex relationships are particularly prone to sexual boredom. Intragender empathy allows gay men to understand each other better and to know how to physically pleasure each other. However, a familiar partner of your own sex may begin to feel predictable after years of sex. Heterosexual couples may maintain more sexual excitement because the differences between men and women are mysterious and challenging." Uh-huh. Tell that to Bill Clinton.

Of course, anyone who watches *Melrose Place* knows better, but one of the hallmarks of conventional (or "straight") society (which may not always be that straight or conventional), is that marriage is based upon the idea of closing the wagons in at night. Security. Protection. Us versus *them*. "Forsaking all others." Some of this goes back to the idea I've mentioned before (and certainly before the advent of multiple divorces, remarriages, and step families) of Daddies needing to know *exactly* who the fathers of their kiddies are. Point-blank, they were not going to be using their hard-earned peanuts to support somebody else's brood. Now, of course, that has changed (somewhat), but the basic attitude—whose kid is this, and how can I prove it?—has remained.

Strangely enough, in many "primitive" societies, this is not an issue— or problem. Children are considered a resource and joy for the whole tribe. Extended families allow for extended care for all children, and children who are born outside of recognized pairs are not stigmatized as bastards. If you have stayed awake through most of the preceding part of this book, you have probably seen that I have a viewpoint that some gay men may share, but not all of us. It is essentially that we need each other and the essence of what we call "gay life" is tribal.

This instinct is deep within us, and is probably just as deep within all people, except that gay men have to some degree preserved it. Perhaps this idea goes back to the concept of gays as being "throwbacks" to an earlier, more open form of relating or behavior; before industrial social-
ization had turned people into isolated, competitive, "family" units. By

the end of the twentieth century, these units have come to consist solely of one husband, a wife, two-point-something kids, and—if they're very lucky—a part-time baby-sitter. In olden days, "family" meant that several generations of a family lived under one roof. That gave each member of a "nuclear" cluster (Daddy, Mommy, the kids) someone from the *extended* family with whom to share feelings, frustrations, and problems. These were often aunts and grannies, cousins, and bachelor uncles: in other words, people who might have been you or me.

Now, because of many factors (divorce; career moves, etc.) this situation has changed. There are fewer and fewer people fulfilling an intimate—yet largely safe—role in your life. There are no longer people around to make you feel at home as part of a larger family or clan. To make you feel that you are fitting into a tribe. Most of these folks have been relegated to the role of semi-strangers. You see them once or twice a year. They are voices from an occasional long-distance call. Signatures at the end of Christmas cards or, currently, e-mail on the Internet.

Therefore, even our families seem like strangers; and strangers, as I have pointed out, are not welcomed anymore.

*Strangers*—I hate to say this—*in industrial societies are considered garbage.*

They are housed in faceless motels on the sides of highways. They are given the same status lepers had in the Middle Ages: you are told not to eat, touch, or sit with them. Unless they come with some business deal in hand, they are to be feared.

But, here is the sock in the kisser to all that: it is a basic human need to seek fellowship with strangers. Strangers produce "new blood." They bring in new ideas. Excitement. Styles. Fun and sex. It is, of course, a two-way street. We fear what is strange, on one hand. But, on the other, as any Wes Craven fan knows, we don't want to look away from it, either.

Cities were instituted to allow strangers to meet and talk with each other. From cities have come our ideas of *civilization*. (The civilized were people who were *citizens of cities*.) But we have almost no way of directly meeting strangers now (despite the new, strange games of meeting them anonymously through computer talk), and many gays are following this route of packaging their social and emotional lives very tightly.

Paradoxically, among the various Biblical edicts that the religious Right dictates we should all be adhering to, the kind treatment of strangers was a high priority. The Bible is filled with stories of closeness and compassion to strangers, such as Abraham washing the feet and giving bread to the passing angels who would declare the birth of his son Isaac, and Christ's parable of the Good Samaritan. Levitican law says that widows and strangers were to be left with provisions for their well-being. But now the Pat Robertson brigade wants you to be protected from strangers at all costs.

Unfortunately, as we buy more into the values that the Right wants, *the death of gay desire may be one of its first victims.* Since we don't want to openly discuss meeting strangers for sex—Larry Kramer (and his various minions) has convinced many of us that it is both "immature," unpatriotic, and unhealthy—we keep asking ourselves why is this "death" such a "mystery," and what can we do to keep it from happening?

Despite all the good mental health intentions (and constant directives about the "maturity of committed sexual relationships"), no one seems to be able to hit it at all. No one except the myth makers of the ancient world, who understood desire perfectly, without all the Judeo-Christian barbed wire around it.

To the Greeks and Romans, desire was something that hit you like a lightning bolt: there was no telling where it would land or from which direction. *No one could control it.* As an arrow shot by little Cupid, whose mother, Venus, was Beauty and father, Mars, was War, desire—or Eros— came quickly and dead-on target.

No one was immune to that little bastard's arrows. And no matter how powerful you were—as in Jupiter's infatuation for the boy Ganymede—it was expected that you would act upon your attractions. And also be forgiven for doing so, as you were not in control of them

Desire, especially in the male, was something no one could control. Desire was like the "head" (or glans) of your own cock. Although every penis has a sensitive head, you can never tell *exactly* in which direction that head will point. This has brought us to an age-old conflict that "modern" man is still trying to resolve with his usual sledgehammer finesse: although the essence of the male role is *control* (the old "Captain of your Destiny" routine), one thing that is absolutely <u>necessary</u> for sexual excitement is to lose—even momentarily—*control.*

In fact, orgasm itself requires—and then produces—the release of this control: it is that wondrous momentary release of our whole selves into the universe. The *petite mort*, the "little death" that propels us out of ourselves and into an unknowable void, something that humans seek continually if only for a flash. Although this lemming-like rush to lose control is a basic human need, some men find it so upsetting that they have to *control the need to lose control.*

They do this through religious sublimation, S & M sex, which allows protracted but exquisitely choreographed out-of-control sessions, and *attempts at monogamy.*

How orgasm actually works and the human drive towards it is still mysterious. Only among human beings and a few species of higher apes is orgasm not restricted to procreation. It may be that the human drive to orgasm is a *sublimation* for our own need to kill. This idea was recently formulated by researchers among some of our closer relatives, the previously mentioned pygmy chimpanzees, or bonobos (scientific name: *pan paniscus*), of Zaire. The bonobo is closer, intellectually and genetically, to

human beings than its cousin, the larger, more aggressive "common" chimpanzee (*pan troglodyte*). In fact, the human line can be traced, evolutionarily, directly back to these smaller, reddish chimps. (Perhaps because the bonobos were smaller, they had to work harder and evolve quicker to survive.)

Unlike the common chimps, which are really only slightly larger than their pygmy cousins, the bonobos do not engage in regular vicious tribal warfare. They do not murder their own offspring or engage in cannibalism—two standard practices of common "troglodyte" chimps. Instead, the bonobos have learned to *substitute* sexuality for aggression. They love orgasm and will have one with any chimp they find available. Their unions can be heterosexual, homosexual, bisexual, and polyamorous. Sometimes they involve several partners at a time, resulting in friendly orgy sessions.

This constant, non-procreative sexual activity keeps their numbers down, and, since so much aggression—and war—is tied to overpopulation, they don't need to depopulate themselves. Instead of using aggression and the wild hormonal rushes that follow it to experience being out of control, they experience these feelings through sex.

In many pre-technological, older societies, having these out-of-control experiences was sought after. Part of this may go back to a more "primitive" religious feeling that a large and various group of gods were watching over you. Instead of having one disapproving God, there were many dieties. Some were even smiling. Therefore you could allow yourself the joy of stepping out of yourself and into other magical states of spirituality, ritual, and orgasm. In these societies being out of control—and in an ecstatic state—and then inviting someone else to come in with you as a shaman, priest, or sex partner was an acceptable part of the culture. It was neither feared nor punished, unlike in our present environment, which is filled with conflicting messages of sex-negativity and consumer-oriented sexual voraciousness.

As two men become more involved with each other, they are now controlling one another and reducing the areas of non-control between them, even as newer "stations" of intimacy open up to them due to their closeness. Often these stations, as nice as they are, become, for some men, literal stops along the way to the "Death of Gay Desire." As they start to share more and more things (eating, sleeping, and bathroom schedules, social and work habits, and, of course, the values I have mentioned), desire gets pushed farther and farther off.

This is a conundrum: as you become more sexually involved with a man and want to give more of yourself to him—holding back less–you also start to give him emotional parts of yourself that (can) inhibit sex. You are showing him a great deal of your most secret behavior. He now has keys that open up many of your most private doors. You have "signed" over a lot of your own power to him—your own secrets—and now he can control you in a way that is no longer simply sexual. 159

Although you have given him, freely, as an act of intimacy, a great deal of power over you, this satisfies none of your own *needs* to be spontaneous, sexually shame-free, and out of control.

This scenario often works with men in the beginning stages of a very hot sexual/romantic relationship. They find themselves suddenly, inexplicably, cooling down. There's an iciness between them. Some therapists feel that this happens due to a long hidden "fear of intimacy," something that you've kept in your own closet and that is lurking to keep you from happiness. But this cooling down is not always due to a fear of intimacy itself—since there is already so much intimacy in the relationship. It can happen so fast that two men can't understand why their relationship fizzled when it should have been taking off. What happens, then, is that the men retract. They will reaffirm their own needs for "space." At this point, it is common that either relationships stop or "agreement relationships" take place.

If they are able to get past this cooling-down stage, they can hit the next plateau of being together—such as living together—and this may mean an even more involving intimacy. At this point, as a romantic concept, they want to be able to *believe* they can control everything about their partners, until very little does not "belong" to the two of them together. (They have produced, in fact, a *fiction* about their being together: a script that says everything is working "exactly" as "we want it." In heterosexual society, this script is, for the most part, mandatory. It is enforced by the law, the family, the workplace, etc. It says, "Everything is perfect: this couple is now locked together.")

The two men now know *everything* about each other. They have seen everything. The converse of this—not knowing—is frightening ("I've been living with a stranger!"), but knowing , unfortunately, is boring. It kills desire: it means that one partner wants the other partner to be "perfect," to be always available to him: to be the person that the script—the shared fiction—predicts he is. These areas of control start to produce corresponding inhibitions, since sex itself desires nothing so much as to *fight* control.

Sex wants what is at once open and *forbidden.* It wants the openness of emotion—of riding off into that romantic vista of the two of you together—and the "down-and-dirty" forbiddenness of traversing, of walking across, of tramping over, the taboo. Of conquering fear, and delighting, even childishly, in its conquest.

It is for this reason that men often seek what is most forbidden to them as their greatest fantasy—and would have it as long as the taboo does *not* expose or harm them. Thus researchers have learned that the greatest fantasy many heterosexual men have is to be forced into a homosexual act in which they *must* participate. There is no recourse. It is the male fantasy version of a "willing rape." Scenario: The lights go out in the elevator of his office building and Bob Jones, "clean-cut, wholesome married," with two kids and TV-show wife—who is (to his mind) "at least one-hundred-and-fifty percent straight"—finds that he's been surrounded by a band of four threatening, armed strangers. One of them, an attractive, well-built hunk even in the dark, has pressed closer to him and then quietly unzips Bob's neatly pressed trousers. He takes out Bob's shy but (definitely) ready cock, and, after using a little spit and hand action, is now kneeling over it, giving this married man one of the world's great blow jobs.

Of course poor Bob cannot resist. Several strange hands are at his throat. All he can do is grin and bear it. A moment later, before he can protest, he is pushed to his knees and is doing the same thing in the dark for all four of the hunky strangers, who are directing his face to their throbbing . . . (anyway, you get the point).

The elevator door pops back open. The strangers leave. Lights go back on. And Bob, after one of the great sex moments of his life, has crossed the taboo: without having to pay for it. No one has known what he has done; he will not bear the scarlet "H" for the rest of his life.

(This is one of the most representative fantasies heterosexual men repeat countless times to sex researchers. The other one is being in the same elevator with a posse of aggressive, man-hungry women and being "forced" to do the same thing to them.)

For us, part of every gay desire is crossing the taboo. It is exciting. It *is* the kerosene on the fire. We remember our first time out in "queer waters," when we found ourselves swimming in what felt like a naked current of sex. It was so exciting that we could barely keep from "cumming" on the spot. Desire itself was something that we'd had to keep hidden. Now desire was meeting the availability of sex itself. The real thing. And if anyone reading this book can tell me that he can't remember how that first sex tasted, and felt, and smelled, all at once—then he has just wasted his money. (I remember being so excited that my ears burned and I almost threw up. Moral: there is no roller-coaster ride like a waiting dick.)

Crossing the taboo is still one of the unmentionables of our lives, as we try to mainstream ourselves into being the All-American gayboys-next-door. This has meant that many publicly gay men now have to socialize themselves as "neutered." They have to be the "good queers." The taboo becomes something they cannot negotiate or consider. It destroys their personal lives and means that having an intimate relationship—one that reveals the complete span of their personalities—becomes more difficult; not less.

For other men, engaged in a monogamous relationship, this original, thrilling taboo must be crossed every night in bed with the same man. Simply being there with him must be enough. Or two men may revise their fantasy lives on a regular basis, so that they experience themselves as two "others" in bed. Or they can invest their monogamy itself with such an intense fantasy ("Just you and I on a desert island: surrounded by sharks, cannibals, and your mother!"), that their relationship itself becomes a taboo that they must traverse to get to one another.

Although homophobia is not *per se* a reason for monogamy, many homophobic couples maintain monogamy as a way of cutting down on their contacts with other gay men. Since they have decided they no longer need gay men sexually, they can delete them completely from their lives, and believe that they are living in a strictly "straight world." In this instance, two monogamous men may find their own homophobia—their rejection of other gay men—intensely exciting. It is again the "just-you-and-me-in-the-same-boat-babe" syndrome, but the exclusiveness of the boat is also contributing some sexual heat to it.

I have seen this occur with many homophobic couples, who despise other gay men and yet maintain long-lived, intense, sexually driven relationships. The homophobia of their relationships is often re-enforced by other men who may come on to them (thus bolstering their feelings that *all* other gay men are *only* interested in sex), as well as their own anger and pain at being isolated from (and feeling rejected by) gay tribalism. They are working from an emotional starvation that reacts, in turn, as sexual aggression towards one another. I think that this is a high price to pay to keep sex going, but I think that many heterosexuals also pay this price in the misogyny that many men feel towards all women (except, we are led believe, their wives) and the anger that women often feel towards men, in general, for locking them into these relationships.

So the mystery of the death of gay desire may be solved by going "out of control," but how do you do this with someone *you* are trying to control in a relationship—and who also feels controlled?

For some men this is an impossible bind: it means *unwrapping* the deepest, most taboo parts of their psyches—and I am not sure that I would recommend it, even with the most "professional" help. I would like to make this point, as they say, "in spades," because for a long time grinding out constant sexual satisfaction from the same person has been a goal of most of the "therapeutic community." These have included, besides the usual suspects in psychiatry, psychology, and social work; gay-friendly Catholic priests (who want you to do it, but evidently can't do it themselves), rabbis and other clergy*people*, and armies of your in-laws, ex-laws, etc. In other words, they all want you to succeed in a gay, mainstreamed, monogamist "environment," even though they are not a part of this environment, and they may not be able to do the same thing in their own.

However, they would like *you* to succeed at it.

If we had a dollar for every time gay men are beaten up on for their "promiscuity," the gay movement would be as rich as the Moral Majority. But as Jimmy Swaggart, Jim Bakker, and a host of other shekel-shaking televangelists know, it's a "Do-What-I-Say-Not-What-I-Do" world. And the worst aspect of this hypocrisy is that it is clothed in such psycho-newspeak as "fear of intimacy," which is a real fear, certainly, but it does not take into account the very real human need for novelty and release in a sex life. Therefore, if you are in a relationship and you have experienced the "Death of Gay Desire" (and it does feel like it's as dead as a doornail), then the problem may not be "fear of intimacy," but *just too much of it*. You may, in fact, be choking on the sheer (as the song goes) *loverliness* of all this damn intimacy.

This is something that heteros have known, strangely enough, for a long time—and it was the reason why for centuries men kept other women on the side (and why women, bless their hearts, went the same route if they could get away with it). And why they were smart enough to get away from their wives whenever the opportunity presented itself. At that point women and men lived in two separate worlds and the bridge between them was sex—a happening which the animal kingdom understands beautifully.

For gay men who have experienced an almost morbid lack of authentic intimacy (while at the same time substituting a great deal of pseudo-intimacy in various forms: volunteerism, being the "neutered" uncle, sex-less best friends, etc.), finding another man—as I said in my chapter on "Gay Love and Marriage"—can come as the most wonderful discovery in their lives. It feels like a religious experience, and in many ways it is. Certainly they want to experience everything with him. They want to be a part of *every* part of him. And it is not so much that they fear intimacy, as it is that intimacy takes more of a price from them than they can possibly, with all the other stresses in their lives, psychically afford.

For these men, coming to this "Death of Desire" is like having an indictment handed to them. All the words that they don't want to hear will be leveled against them. Shallow. Flighty. Immature. Fickle. All of these labels are plastered on them, when in reality they have already shared more with another male person than has ever happened in history. At no time have men in what we might call "gay relationships" ever shared as much as we are doing at present. In the past for two men to live together on a full-time basis was an extreme and isolated act. It was dangerous, often illegal, and unless they had the cover of being a Rockefeller with his live-in "nephew," "chauffeur," or "secretary" Bertie, they could barely get away with it.

Yet today men live together, stay together, celebrate a dozen anniversaries together, go into business—eat, sleep, shower, and shit—together. And still can't figure out why they're not lusting after each other like two young pigs in heat, exactly as they did two months after they met.

If you are in this same leaky boat, and have tried everything from couples therapy to an Esalen weekend to sex games to aphrodisiac cooking (and the usual complement of poppers, drugs, threesomes, etc.), it may be time for you to bail out of it for a while. And get to some dry land.

In other words, try an *affair*.

The affair can be friendly, sweet, adorable, or red-hot, but remember to keep limitations on it. You are not out there husband-hunting, and a lot of delicacy must be observed. The affair should give you a certain amount of *emotional* as well as sexual satisfaction, something that "pure" casual sex does not. This emotional satisfaction can enrich your relationship with your mate, who is now, let us say, "at home"—if you allow yourself to be open to this satisfaction and not feel degraded by it. You are not looking upon this other man as an "extended trick," but you are seeing him as a real person who is open to you and the limitations placed on your life.

The affair can often work well with another man who is in the same situation (okay, that *boat*, if you want to extend the metaphor) as you, who is also married but needs another route to his own sexual life. In truth what you want to do with the affair is re-establish the *nakedness* of sex: sex which has been over-clothed in intimacy, in fact, may even be strangling in it. This conflict between sex and intimacy is something that the straight world of "mental health professionals" (the ones who are always trying to close down on-site sex joints) and "maturity = adjustment" does not want to admit. But the truth is that *nakedness* is an important part of the *homo* sexual response.

Part of nakedness comes from that which is unfamiliar, which is startling—and wonderful. For gay men the flip side of nakedness is fetishism (leather, Western wear, rubber, etc.), and, in its own way, fetishism produces the startling, exciting response that nakedness does. What gays are not good at is faking a response, something women have been doing in heterosexual relationships for years, while at the same time straight men are famous for only desiring a certain part of a woman and being disinterested in the rest: leg men, breast men, pussy men, etc. So that, whereas a great deal of heterosexual sex takes place semi-clothed (or in darkness: there are many straight couples who have not seen each other naked for years), gay men retain this important need to get back to real nakedness, to that original bare-assed, hot self, without clothes on.

Now, the nicest thing would be for you to be *open* with your mate about the affair, but sometimes that is not possible. Your mate, after working so hard to establish a "mature" (read "monogamous") relationship, may not be ready for you to go galloping off into "immaturity" again. However, if both of you can be (really) mature (and open) about this, then having the affair can be an emotionally enriching experience for you both (and, not to forget, spare you some of the riskier health aspects of "tricking" around, if you can negotiate safer-sex practices with the man with whom you are having the affair). It can also allow your mate some security in knowing that you're not reaching a point of sexual no-return with him, which will force you to leave. Actually, in situations like this, it's amazing how the original case of Desire *Rigor Mortis* can come back to life. Suddenly your lover appears as a *different* person—warmer, sweeter, more thrilling—because you've been seeing one. Of course there is always the danger that the grass may be greener on the other side—and you'll break up the life you've established for another man. But if this does happen, once *again* you will have to face the danger of hitting that old bugaboo: the "Death of Gay Desire."

For men who may be more mutually realistic about the problem, the idea of openly cruising again (okay, we'll call it just "networking" for sex), either separately or together, may be the solution: the "sex hunt," that primal and vestigial activity that gay men participate in—and that, in a more honest world, should link us together on a basic level—can be opened to include intimate partners as well as fantasy ones.

The fantasy partner, of course, is the Trick who comes in to teach us about a new environment of sex. He will lead us once more out into that orgasmic vista we associate with the flash of existence I refer to as "being out of control." He is the "Holy Trick," and, as I have said in a previous chapter, he is not to be put down or discounted. But why can't we go into the sexual hunt with intimate partners as well? The answer is that it is dangerous. It brings up feelings of jealousy, fear, abandonment, and also breaches in the privacy we need to keep our own psyches intact. But it is possible, and for some men lamenting the end of desire between themselves and a partner, it may be necessary.

Sometimes this can mean simply opening yourself up to your partner, sharing fantasies and feelings with him that you have kept in your own closet for years. The reason why you have kept them there, of course, is *shame*—and sometimes your partner may be a *willing* partner in that shame. In that case, you will have to forgive him for this, and that is no easy task. A part of this shame may be a need on your part to keep a certain image of yourself intact for him: that you are less sexually "compulsive," less active, more responsible: that is, of course, why he did "pick" you—you are sure of this.

Shattering or even changing this image may be difficult for you. It should be countered with another image—as a *larger* person—one who is capable of greater depth than you allowed yourself before. Of course your partner may not feel this way, and in shattering this old image—one that he may have had a real hand in building—he is also changing an image of what your relationship was built on. It may be that a certain iciness-"properness"—you have maintained about yourself attracted him, and by now revealing more of your inner self you are making him do more work than he is capable of. In short, he will have to see you in a different way, and that is not easy.

Another way, which is really wading into choppy waters—talk about going out of control!—is for the two of you to go out *together* and cruise. Some gay couples have been doing this for decades, and it holds them together. If they had to sneak around, they would hate one another. Then, back at home—when you're alone together—you can talk about what the evening brought, explore fantasies ("Remember the cute guy at the end of the bar; what do you think he looks like naked?"), and rekindle the night in bed. Although some men might find this even more inhibiting than the coldness that has crept into their bedroom, for others it brings an honesty and sexiness that has evaporated from their relationship. When you are out there cruising, you can have an agreement either to go off alone with another guy, not pick anyone up but just look, or option men for a three-some—if the third man is interested.

Which opens up the idea of bringing someone else into the relation-ship, either as an ongoing threesome or a series of them. For some men this is a great jumpstarter for libidos and can provide some very-high-octane sex where once the wheels were barely turning. Except that here, instead of being jealous of fantasies, there is someone real to turn on all your insecurities. Many men feel that the future of gay relationships will depend upon polyamorous relationships: now that we want and expect our relationships to last a long time—ten, twenty, thirty years—allowing someone else into them at various points is healthy and smart. In the "old days" when having a gay relationship that lasted three years was an endurance record, a threesome seemed ridiculous—if not "immoral." How could you share your lover with someone else? But now that there is a healthy and organic quality to our relationships—they are stronger and more flexible—why not?

One problem with polyamorous relationships is how to deal with chil-dren in them. Since kids are now a part of the lives of many gay men, this is a sticky point. Kids may find it unsettling that their two daddies now have a third, or that Daddy's boyfriend is no longer enough. Will they (the kids) no longer be enough? So dealing with kids may put a necessary damper on this form of relationship. Another problem can be living arrangements. For a new man to live in a space that once belonged to two others and not feel constantly outvoted is difficult. So, ongoing three-somes often end up looking for a neutral space to start over again. But if none of these problems daunt you, then this option can help a dead-cold relationship.

Although it seems that there are no "cures" for the death of gay desire (if it does truly die), once you understand the mechanisms behind it, it is much easier to deal with. You don't have to blame yourself or blame him or blame the both of you. You don't have to feel that you have to "blow up" the whole relationship—leave it—in order to get sex back into your life again. And you can also understand that sexual desire comes in cycles and waves. Even if you've had a drought for five or ten years, the cycle may change again at some point and there you are, on that brink of being out of control again: poised in front of that infinity of orgasm, with a new adventurer, a new explorer of this fabulous terrain, who might just *happen* to be the one who's been there all along

*"We went from being unmentionable to *sellable*."*

## CHAPTER 11

# Yesterday I Was a Queer; Today I Am a Gay Consumer!

A funny thing happened on the way to Gay Liberation: we became a market. We went from being unmentionable to *sellable*. The nice thing was that we weren't stupid enough to buy this idea wholesale, although many of us (myself included) are a bit amazed how fast it happened. It is indeed part of America's wonderful, unique, democratization process: we're all consumers, and even though our sexual and romantic lives may still be to many people (for the sake of "taste") in the closet, our own taste has been recognized as . . . marketable.

A decade ago, if you had mentioned the "gay market" to most of corporate America, it would have been too embarrassed to laugh. The gay market? You mean bathhouses, sex services, and poodle grooming? Right? Now you mention the gay market and corporate America thinks: well, maybe the laugh's on us; after all, things are tough now, and facts are facts. The gay market translates into ONE THING: a *white*, cohesive, middle class that seems to want to be tapped and at this point is ready for it.

(I emphasize the word *white* because to marketers this is the operative word. For their purposes, we are a uniform, *white* market, and we are seen as perhaps the last segment of this market that has gone untapped.)

Or is it?

The gay marketers themselves, those lusty, trustworthy guys who have all the answers and seem to come up with new projects every week with which to cocktease straight, big-bucks "America, Inc.," have had the answers, of course, for decades. Literally, they will tell us, since the early 70s.

The average income for gay households is . . . $60,000. No, it's actually $72,000. No, wait a second, it's—would-you-believe?—$93,000. Wow. Yeah. No.

Well—actually it's *any* amount of money they want to put on it, since the majority of gay households are just as underground—that is, just as invisible—as ever. The proof of this pudding is that despite the 20-30-60      **167** million gay/lesbian households in America (a number that no one can lay their hands on, no matter how hard they try), gay causes still have an unbearably difficult time limping along. The 1994 Gay Games in New York, for instance, were left with a whopping near million-dollar deficit, even though the event, coupled with Stonewall 25, was the largest public gay event in history and produced millions of dollars in consumer revenue, mostly from tourist dollars. A huge number of gay businesses, especially gay magazines trying to milk the "ever-growing, recession-proof" gay market, go under quickly.

There are many reasons for this: to be openly gay and wealthy is still to be a rare exception. Sure, in any urban setting there are hundreds of "A-Gays": queens with large amounts of inherited wealth, or their social-climbing fellow-travelers, who may not be as well-heeled, but still want to swim in the same icy waters. These men are the backbone of any symphony society, the local opera, ballet, etc. They preside over animal society fundraisers and will raise millions for stray poochies, but don't ask them for money for stray queers.

The only thing that has brought the A-Gays six inches out of the closet has been AIDS. As the A-Gays started dying of the same disease that the Z-Gays were dying of, a few—and we mean very few—old money A-Gays started venturing out. For the most part, the A-Gays align themselves with the "A" everything else. They will not jeopardize one dollar of their money (or one millimeter of social position) for any cause, no matter how close to home. This is not a matter of cowardliness, homophobia, etc. It is simply a matter of dollars-and-cents wisdom. The A-Gays are not interested in being on the "cutting edge" of the arts, politics, society, etc. The place where so many gays feel we should be. Instead, the A-Gays are interested in keeping their well-manicured fingers on the *handle* of Power's cutting edge. And you don't keep your grip on that slippery handle by allowing yourself to slip down to the razor side.

To put it succinctly: they don't want to be the ones to get cut.

So, take away the famous A-Gays. Then take away the Z-*Gays*, who are working-class or out of work (and overstressed and, for the most part, silent)—and what have you got left in the "gay market"?

That's right. It's the "U" Gays. People like you.

These are people who are struggling like hell to stay included in the middle class (whom marketers still read basically as one word: *white*) and who always have the same conflict, that reads simply enough: Is Amex (for instance) just using us as a market or actually recognizing us as real people?

This conflict puts a real kabong on much of the gay marketing idea, since corporations have done very little (if anything) when the doody hits the fan, to go down on the mat for us. In other words, they are not going to start fighting Jesse Helms for you and me. Corporations are traditionally conservative, despite the fact that gays are, traditionally, amazingly loyal as customers. We will follow stars who've recognized us early on, way after they've gone mainstream and conveniently forgotten us. We will buy underwear aimed at us even after the stud models wearing them have said the most stupid homophobic things possible. But we won't swallow everything.

A good example of this is that the Joseph Coors Brewing Company, run by one of the most right-wing (and openly homophobic) families in America, started an intense campaign to prove that they were going to be the good-buddies of the gay community. They took out full-page ads in gay papers, they sponsored activities like the New York Gay Games, they did some test marketing to show they were interested in getting into the "gay market." What they learned from the testing was that being part of the gay market did not jeopardize their standing among other groups like, say, straight college kids. The kids, to their great relief, would not reject Coors Beer if it became known as a "queer beer."

But neither did it help Coors with the gay market, because most urban gay men had already heard how Coors was one of the major backers of anti-gay offensives in Colorado. Coors had backed the Christian Right all over the country, and was patently anti-Choice. So, despite great attempts at positioning themselves within the gay market—and even the fact that this spill off from "Rocky Mountain high" is still sold in many, non-political gay bars, Coors has never become a great gay beer.

The gay market concept reminds me of an old story I remember hearing years ago. During the Middle Ages, the Jewish community in Rome used to come out once a year carrying the Torah for the Pope to bless. Each year, the Pope would come out in all his robes and say the same thing: "Great book! Bad people!"

Corporate America is now doing a wary dance on broken glass around the gay market, because they see that it is there, and that it does satisfy some of the criteria of a "legitimate" market: it is—somewhat—recognizable; it is loyal (in other words, why spend money on people who will switch brand allegiances on a dime—a terrible problem with the "youth market," which switches every thirty seconds); and it is white. That is, upwardly mobile, identifying with the (literate) upper-middle classes. This, of course, is the skeleton in the closet of the gay market: that the gay market is another way of reaching into the white market. But it is a part of the white market that is already—by marketers' standards—wondrously "presold." ("Presold" is a great marketers' term: it means that the targeted market already wants—and is willing to buy—what you have to sell. Now you just have to figure out exactly what among all your goodies to sell them. Then when, and how often.)

This market, in short, already knows *what* it wants.

It wants basically the same things other people want: cars, vacations, homes, booze, food, credit to get it all, etc. And, according to marketers, it wants to be recognized. *Make me* uninvisible *and I will buy you*, the gay market says. "Show me that you actually know what my face looks like." 169

*But, please, don't make me* too *uninvisible.*

That's the other rub. The gay market does not want to be known, simply, as "gay." Unlike other "minorities," we still feel that "gayness" in all its varied aspects (black gays, white gays, female gays, young gays, old gays, Hispanic gays, Jewish gays, atheist gays, athletic gays—okay, you get the idea) *limits* us too much.

To be spotted as gay (in other words, singled out) is a no-no. In an as-close-to-comprehensive report as possible on gay consumers, done in 1993 by the respected market research firm of Yankelvich Monitor in Westport, Conn., gay and lesbian consumers said that what they really wanted was to be "included" as the sales targets of companies that "target all kinds of people."

To be recognized, therefore, as worthy of being labeled a "customer," among other customers, seems to many of us a noble enough intention. This puts us back, somewhat, into the contemporary community of America, whose local temple is the shopping mall and whose main means of communication is the TV commercial. (Or its new "news" version, the *infomercial.*) In short, some of us have actually bought the idea that we can be bought, that by buying us as a group, corporate America is giving us the recognition that will make us "legitimate." We just don't want to be embarrassed by being singled out.

This Yankelvich report, by the way, also stated that the average yearly income for gay men was $37,500 as compared to heterosexual men, who average $39,300. Lesbians did somewhat better (as a comparative class for these purposes), with an income of $34,800, compared with straight single women, who were put at $34,300. However none of these figures deal with working-class people, who rarely respond, or are even asked to respond, to such consumer reports. It also picks on pretty much a self-selected group: those who are open enough to respond to such a survey as being "gay." (Like the famous Kinsey Report and other reports that deal in sexuality as a social phenomenon, what these reports really report on are current attitudes towards sexuality. In Kinsey's time, a lot of men flatly said they were *not* homosexual or even bisexual. Even though they had been having sex with the same sex, they could not be. After all, they were married to *women.*)

But the Yankelvich report does refute the idea that gays have endless "discretionary pockets." Another finding of the report was that gay men do not see themselves as "trendy," despite the slick gay media's constant need to present us this way to advertisers.

What they did find was that we are more used to stress in our lives, and therefore can accommodate changes fairly well. These include adapting to new technologies such as going "on line," and new computer services. Because we are less tied to conventional family structures, gays are also more apt to be self-employed or at least somewhat outside the corporate structures that run America. This, again, keeps us from the big money strata that gay marketers see us in. The unfortunate fact is that very little of our vaunted "creativity" leads to the big bucks that both many gay media people, as well as homophobic gay-baiters, want to attribute to us.

The new thing in gay baiting is to establish "gay inner circles," the Lavender Mafias that are supposed to run "vital" parts of the American economy like . . . fashion and show business. Since what really runs both of these enterprises are conservative banking interests who put up the money behind the shows, queers are for the most part still swabbing the decks—and guess who owns the fleet?

Those gay media figures in fashion and show business who are "out," for whatever reason, usually find that being this way does not conflict businesswise, and, if necessary, they can soft-pedal it when the time comes. In other words, we are not seeing any sort of "major" merger in the gay community of art, fashion, and social change, although there are a few important outposts. I would include among them Ellen DeGeneres, who has shown that it is possible to come out on network television and not be blown off the map (at least not immediately). Ellen's impact has been stunning, but like Tracey Ullman and Sandra Bernhardt, comedians who if they are not "out" are certainly *out there,* commercial television, when pressed, will find suitable ways to marginalize her.

Regardless, though, of the (questionable) success of gay marketing, its real problem is that it satisfies nothing in the gay psyche. But a great number of men and women who are in the process (as most of American society is) of retracting from any threatening form of consciousness still want to be sold on it. They want to see that the blatant homoeroticism that currently sells everything from underwear to plumbing fixtures is making the world more "comfortable" (one of those beloved watchwords left to us from the 80s) for us.

Although I love watching pictures of near-naked men sell anything, I realize that mostly what these images do is hammer us back into a closet of surrounding non-sexuality. In other words, your "wife" is supposed to get turned on to them. Not you. Although the images are undeniably homoerotic—in fact, sometimes they are downright molten—they are placed in front of a society that still wants to be in complete denial about gay sex. So men who get turned on to them are simply considered neutered. They don't exist. Heterosexuality is seen as the big ticket for selling anything, and when this form of sexuality is questioned, or not "completed" (usually as in one man + one or more women), the sale is seen not to be made.

This translates simply enough as: "I have 'straight' sex, therefore I am." One of the constant joke forms on TV is still the ancient "'normal'-guy-who-is-taken-to-be-queer-but-isn't" format. Only when his hetero-ness is confirmed is the sale value of the show, as far as selling it both to the sponsor and the audience, validated. It is only then that we realize we are watching a *real* comedy. Jerry Seinfeld's *nebeshy* buddy, George, played by Jason Alexander, went through this format several times a season. In each episode, the audience got to watch George explode in denial, until the forces of normalcy (better known as "babes-aplenty") would wave back over him, and the comedy end.

Likewise, there are constant sitcom jokes about hetero couples who have been together for as much as two weeks, and (is there something queer hiding in the basement?) still haven't got around to sex: "So, what's *wrong* with your boyfriend? He seems like such a regular guy."

"Gee, I don't know. Maybe he's just forgetful!"

These same shows frequently include gay characters who are embarrassments to gays, who see these characters as either cartoons or castrated. The shows are followed by commercials of male-stripper-type hunks peeling their shirts off, but ostensibly only for women. The hunks themselves are in a closet in which their sexuality is neutered: they are obliviously exercising, doing construction work, or horsing around. Just being "guys." To be otherwise would open them up too deeply for homosexual targeting or interpretations.

All this leads us back to gay men cutting themselves off from their real *gayness*, that is, from their important inner lives as men who *are* gay (and, thankfully, don't just "happen to be that way," another lovely euphemism from the 80s). It also leads us back to straight men who, strangely enough, are doing the same thing: the straights have cut themselves off from their real maleness (something which also cannot be bought, like they can buy an IBM clone). But they seem to have made this bargain with marketing sometime back, in order to get that ticket towards inclusion that they need and want so much.

Since this ticket has been denied gay men all along, one would think that we could now provide our own tickets: that we would make use of being outsiders; and for a very long time we did. But human nature—in a conformist, market-driven society—makes this extremely difficult.

I am not sure that there is any way out of this cycle on a grand and large scale, but only on the scale of individuality. The idea that you are reading a book instead of watching something on TV may be a beginning, even though this little book may get "nowhere" (nowhere, that is, if it is outside a mass market, where all *good* little books are supposed to go) without being driven itself by the marketing/publicity machine. But I believe that gays (or *queers* in the new, queer-positive parlance) have to have their own saints (and gods), and these are not the men who provide us with Calvin Klein underwear or Ralph Lauren overalls.

We have to be pugnacious and combative in entering that place of our own selves, a place that is not always particularly "comfortable" to be. Although our relationships with friends and lovers are great comforts to us, these relationships do not come about as the rewards of marketing. ("You have all the right toys, so you get the right boys!") Sometimes, in fact, you have to be a little kick-ass, a little *out there* and taking no backtalk, to establish the "space" that is yours.

This space is not going to be given to you on TV, or validated by having Coors beer sold *expressly* to you. As an ever-ready queer bandit, I believe in using commercialism to get what I want (and saw some amazingly human touching and spirituality even in commerce-driven events like the New York Gay Games). But I know that commerce and marketing take over quickly. It's easy to lose sight of what you're doing or hoping to do, and I think that recently gay men have done that too often.

One of the things that we really get lost in is our fetishism. A fetish is a material object that stands in for a psychic (as in religious or sexual) part of you. For instance, deep inside you want to serve what you feel to be a "higher," more powerful Source. The idea turns you on, excites you, and moves you both spiritually and sexually: as it has done men for thousands of years. So, what do *you* do? You become a "slave." Instead of wanting to follow your Master across an ocean and then into a forest, you'll just follow him into a backroom and then maybe lick his boots.

(As if this were the *hardest* thing in the world to do.)

The slave has to have a uniform, so who will sell it? Currently, you can get all the slave rags you want mail (male?) order, or even on the Web. The slave wants his toys—all good slaves are supposed to have their toys, right?—so who will provide your manacles and lubricated rubber duckies? There are umpteen gay versions of Toys-"R"-Us, so that won't be a problem, either. What follows then is that the slave—who only has so much time, heart, and energy left—will become a slave to his own uniform and toys; and not to the heartfelt Master he seeks.

A wonderful example of this are the White Parties and Black Parties, which started out, about twenty years ago, as druggy, sexy, communal affairs. Now, the question is: will you get your tickets through Ticketmaster (which seems to have become the final Master in gay life), or pay 40% more at the door? On Christopher Street in New York I heard two men talking about the most recent incarnation of the Black Party: "Are you going?" "No, baby, I'm *blacked* out. The party's become so expensive, so organized and overproduced, why bother? It doesn't feel like it's for me anymore."

Anything that can be externalized, of course, will be sold. Christ had to throw the money-changers who sold sacrifices at the Temple out of it. So it seems like there has always been a big market in selling our fetishes back to us. But, when externalized and sold, our fetishes become "tired" quickly and lose all their psychic functions. All of the energy and magic that we want them to have, dies. Instead, it would be much better if psychically we constructed our fetishes ourselves. The need to serve, for instance, should go further than whips, boots, leather, and hankies. The need to master should go further than standing rigidly in bars.

We have to go deeper with these things, into the fires that forged them, and then bring them back out. We do this, again, through what I    173 have referred to as the gay work. This work is inner and psychically, as well as physically, involving. One aspect that is important about the work is our sense of flowing with it. That sense of "flow" that artists talk about (that time dissolves for them while they are working; that they, in the process of doing their work, become such a part of it that they feel temporarily lost in time) is also a hallmark of the gay work. It is the sense, finally, of being fulfilled by an open, willing surrender to this work.

This sense of "flow"—of releasing ourselves into the larger, psychic channel of the work—is something that cannot be bought and externalized. It is part of the truly humbling (and yet elevating) process of *submission* that is a deep component of the gay mythos. It is at the core of a psychic need, that gay marketing can do so little to satisfy. Mostly what the marketing does, then, is let us know that there is a need which is *not* being fulfilled.

The gay work is an important part of an underground element in the lives of gay men and I would like to keep it that way: uncommercialized. Only this way can we see past the toys and the marketing, and connect with each other and ourselves. If we do not keep this underground element in our lives (an element that is rooted in a tribal consciousness that cannot be externalized), we will simply be playing with the same toys over and over again, and edging closer to nowhere with them. In many ways, I find this more upsetting than being in the closet ever was, as gay men find themselves being *neutered* by gay marketing, instead of being excited by it, a stage that we passed through quickly.

One of the sadder outcomes of all of this is that many gay organizations now must get on the marketing bandwagon or perish. Some of this results in linking themselves with corporate sponsors, as in the case of gay choruses, performance groups, or athletic events; or hiring marketers, in the case of community groups. This puts groups within the "12-second sound bite" category of trying to sell themselves, both to the corporate world and the community. The rationale for this is that we are living in an era of professionalism (and constantly escalating "professional expenses": when the "professionals" get in, expenses go up). You can no longer do a "Hey-kids-let's-put-on-a-Community-Center!" if you want anything to happen.

But another outcome is that the "market" (translation: you and I) that has already been bludgeoned by various forms of gay commercialism, starts to turn itself off to our own causes. "Oh, no, not another AIDS benefit!" "Oh, no—the Community Center wants money again and it's sending out this slick letter to get it!" So we are no longer even a community, but a market. And everything ends up in the trash, including what may be an important stake in your own life.

A friend of mine who spent the last seven years in community involvement told me, "In the gay community it is now dog-eat-dog.

People are tired of being hit up for money. They're tired of having things sold to them. They can't even look at each other." I asked him what he thought was the answer. "I think," he said, "we have to get the big picture right. We get caught up in all the details, and then we stop looking at each other."

I completely agreed with him. It brought me back to my basic premise: *Yesterday I was a queer. Now I am a gay consumer.*

I think I preferred it when I was just a queer.

"We enter the tribe alone and naked, without a previous personal history.
And yet our own history is a part of the history of the tribe.
It is part of the tribe's nature that it can recognize our own past
and see it as a natural continuation of its own."

| CHAPTER 12 |
| --- |

# Contacting the Gay Tribe

In one of my favorite books, *Keep the River on Your Right*, by the gay ethnographic writer Tobias Schneebaum, he writes about his first encounter with a small, hidden tribe of Indians in the jungles of the Peruvian Amazon. He is there completely alone—he has trekked through the deepest jungle to meet the tribe on their own ground. To do this he has got rid of every preconception of himself that will not fit in with them. He is as naked as they are when they meet. The first thing they do is surround him, touch, and explore him. They have never encountered a white man on this level: that of complete openness. They feel his penis and smile, amazed at the redness of his hair and the whiteness of his skin, and that he is as naked as they are.

Our first encounter with the gay tribe also has these qualities: that we are leaving behind everything that will keep us from it. So that, somehow, we will become open to it—even if only for a brief moment. We also become aware that the ground—or environment—on which we meet the tribe is special: it is free and fragile and yet it has a strength of its own. I remember the first gay bars I went into, sneaking into them at the age of seventeen in Georgia and later in San Francisco. My feeling was one of tremendous energy: that all the anxieties that seemed to be gripping me—and us (the hidden, oppressed, covert members of this tribe)—that were also holding us together like so many chains, had suddenly fallen away; and I could now—if only for a moment—be myself.

Of course, I was still frightened: suppose someone should see me? Or I got caught for being underage? Or, stranger yet, if someone came on to me? I still had almost no idea what to do. There are always those questions when you're first out: what to do when the first move is made? How to move? What's the game? The dance?

And yet the music, with all those men swaying and moving to it, seemed different to me from the music of, say, a high school or college dance, which was static. The music in these bars was a part of the men in them: men would talk through the music, sing along with it. Let their bodies move through it in ways they could not on the streets or in "straight" places. Suddenly there we all were: a part of the tribe. We *knew* each other. There were adult men to meet. And kids close to my own age, although we could barely look at each other, we were so frightened of where we were. In a gay bar, with other gay men. But there was an electric movement between eyes, full of desire, curiosity, and nakedness—a nakedness of being there in rooms with other queer men—and the movement flowed with the same forbidden electricity.

The first *gay* bar I went to was in Savannah, Georgia, about an eon before this Southern city, caught in the web of its own past, became hooted for "decadence" and drag-queenerie; when Savannah still had its own, non-Hollywoodized gardens of good and evil. This bar was supposed to be *very* evil: it was in a hidden, "underground" location, up several rickety flights in an old warehouse close to the sleepy Savannah River. The bar's actual address changed several times a year as it was raided. Or the landlord succumbed to pressure from the "authorities" (meaning whatever crooked arm of the local Dixiecratic party was in office). It was 1965. I was seventeen.

With an older friend from high school—drunk one night, he had come out to me, but I was still shy, still unsure about declaring myself even as *sexual*—I walked up the dark stairs, shivering with nervousness. In the dim light at a landing, a doorman let us in. He knew my friend and didn't ask any other questions and the first sounds—waves of laughter; steady music—ran through me. I was nervous and yet strangely relaxed. Although I had not admitted it yet, this was my tribe. More so than any other one I would know. There was an amateur drag show (almost an obligation in the South), and I still remember the songs (especially some choruses from *The Boyfriend*) and the innocent fun of it—not boys wigged and painted up like drag queens, but just cute young guys dressing as girls; like in a school play.

My friend went to the bar and bought me a drink. I had several others, and I got slightly "tight," which helped everything. Although I had been having sex with men, I'd never done it with a friend, and I went home with him that night. Then it seemed like another initiation had begun: we became two completely different people in bed from what we were in "real" life. It was very much like *magic*. But the next morning, I was still nervous. I was on spring break from my freshman year at the University of Georgia, in Athens, an aggressively "Ag-Frat-Jock" school. (Translation for the non-Dixie inclined: *Ag*—Georgia was the world's capital of professional poultry studies; *Frat*—good ol' boy clubs, with Confederate flags flapping over the verandas of then, all-white fraternity houses; and *Jock*—great, steaming shitloads of beat-'em-senseless Southern football.)

178    Georgia, like any good Dixie school, had a gay underground, buried

under sixteen tons of repression. You had to drive to Atlanta, seventy miles away, to flick off even a pound of it. But there I was, seventeen, in my own hometown, Savannah. Sneaking out of his house the next morning, as the city's moist, coastal warmth rose back up into the air, I felt that every eye in the world could see me. I'd become as transparent to the world as I'd been transparent to him in bed: he could finally see all the way down to my real self. In his bedroom, we'd stopped being friends. We had become very much something else: members of the gay tribe, exploring the rituals of sex in a Southern environment so morbidly tight-assed that it could explode violently at any moment.

Later I would contact the gay tribe in a number of places. In polished corporate washrooms, a man would look at me and I'd know. Or in the middle of a religious service. Eyes would meet. Yes. Or at a "straight" party, in a bedroom, with the door closed and noise booming outside. Unexplainable. Real. It wasn't simply *cruisiness*; it was that, with no explanation, you were suddenly outside of what people were expecting of you *inside*. And you could now pull those secret insides out: you were in contact with them. With the very tribalism inside you. It was part of that energizing—and erotic—element of gay "recognition."

But I had experienced this going on throughout my life. Even before I "came out," an expression that hardly begins to define the vastness of this "going forth." Of coming out into a *greater* light of yourself.

Unfortunately, we see this too often in only sexual terms. We think of "coming out" as the first time you have sex with a man, or acknowledge your own gay sexual dimension (now called "sexual identity"). But, in fact, what you are doing is "coming into" a disquieting, deeper relationship with yourself. It is a relationship that keeps on going; it does not just stop. Neither is it simply reactivated by a series of sexual experiences.

I remember (like an ancient snapshot from the past), as a small child in tiny short pants with masses of blond curly hair, adult men stooping down and transferring something to me: that recognition, tender, unexpected, that my busy parents could rarely give. A moment of attention that comes by having a male stranger speak your name.

The earliest recollection I have of this was of being caught in a sudden downpour one summer afternoon; I might have been three or four. My nurse, a young black woman in a white uniform, was taking me out for a walk in my stroller, and she brought me for shelter under the high portico of a building in the middle of one of Savannah's beautiful squares, edged with azaleas and towering palms. We were safe there from the rain, and a stranger appeared. He bent down towards me and asked me my name.

At first I was too shy to speak, but my nurse told me to speak up. "Perry is a nice name," he told me. Then he took out a roll of butterscotch candies from his pocket and gave me one.

This lovely, early bestowal of attention, caught significantly in that warm afternoon light, would remain with me forever. It would stay mixed with the tribal element of my deepest gay nature. Perhaps this was the first time I had recognized my name coming from a stranger and not Mommy or Daddy. But that a man had bowed to my level and had given me a butterscotch candy (before I could be warned not to take it) remained lucidly in my mind. I remember him still (yes, I know it's possible that the memory became linked to adult fantasy): he was young and handsome, with dark hair and striking blue eyes, which might have been what he looked like; or, in truth, perhaps had not.

### An Arranged Marriage

We enter the tribe alone and naked, without previous personal history. And yet our own history is a part of the history of the tribe. It is part of the tribe's nature that it can recognize our private, gay past—a past which seems as personal and private to us as our secret dreams and fantasies—and see it as a continuation of its own. Therefore, even going into a commercialized situation, like a gay bath or sauna, into a dark area where another man takes us exactly as we are and we explore each other without words in the most physical way, completes a tribal ritual beginning with recognition, following briefly with twinning, surrender, coming back out into individuation, and then, if we are lucky, sharing. Even though we are bound together by only the fleeting sparks of desire, this is still one of the connecting forces between us, bringing to mind the basic rite of an arranged marriage, in which two individuals who do not know each other are united through the intercession of a strong outside influence.

Usually with arranged marriages, the goals are children and keeping the tribe intact. Once children are conceived, husband and wife can go back to a privacy of their own. They may, in fact, decide privately to avoid each other, as long as the public aspect of the marriage is respected. At the baths, once sex has been consummated, you may go back into the privacy of your own world. Sometimes this privacy is so strong that it cannot be broken by sexual acquaintanceship, but frequently sex itself will penetrate barriers in ways that nothing else can. The "ice" between strangers has been broken in a way that will not happen at—say—a Las Vegas convention.

In certain ways, it is unfortunate that raw sex itself—needy, impulsive, and direct—is creating this closeness in a gay tribal context. Sex should be an extension of tribal closeness, and participation in the gay work should be the main engine of intimacy. For thousands of years, when gay sex was more sublimated, this was so. Otherwise, sex operated in tandem with other aspects of the work, such as the Greek concept of sex being a bonding element between younger men and their older male mentors.

But sex, in this ritualized environment of sexual "recognition"—which the baths become—is immediate; and satisfying. So even men who go into the ritual with the focus only on "anonymous" sex come out, in a way, *bonded*: they have found a partner, even though this "arranged marriage" has not been arranged by outside society. In fact, it may be difficult for these men to explain how they met, if it ever comes to that. But a marriage, in the sense of a ceremony of two strangers coming together under intense intimacy, has been arranged, by the forces of the tribe itself.

The relationship between gay tribalism and a religious impulse has been understood by gay men for years. It is often a component of the gay attraction to hierarchy that culminates in the charged environment of the Male Companion. An openly gay minister I met ten years ago, who was ordained in a branch of the Metropolitan Community Church, told me that in the midst of Christian ritual, he would suddenly become totally *turned on* to the men around him; not necessarily to individual men, but to the *totality* of the men. He was now immersing himself in them—in the united physical presence of their spirit—with Christianity as a medium. With Christ in that immediate, lightning-rod role of the Companion, he had experienced a connection with the tribe.

In very repressed nineteenth-century England, religion was often the only means of public expression gay men had. This was especially true of proper young men from the "professional classes," whose sexuality was cut off from them as part of a class upbringing. Stable boys, street kids, and working-class men were more sexually open. On a pejorative level, it was spoken about them that they were "closer to the gutter."

In more primitive times, the "gutter" was where products associated with unwanted, butchered animal guts—or of human "dirty" parts (such as the rectum; the cock)—were left to be washed away. There were no sewers, but it was directly connected to the town or settlement's river. The lower classes sometimes bathed in it. So the gutter, like sex, was about churning, sweeping movement. Since sexual enjoyment was for the most part questionable—and best engaged in on the run—returning to the gutter or the stables (filled with animal sexuality), was both disturbing and thrilling to properly brought up Englishmen.

The gutter, therefore, as a symbol, became a stream connecting the upper and lower classes. It was also a symbol of the return to the raw, sexy "hunt," since "gutters" were also men who gutted game animals. The brutal, masculine image of these men—often in bloody aprons—had a naked power that figures in the art and literature of this period. Religiosity, too, was filled with churning, "gut"-level emotions and, frequently, a charged, hyper-religiosity ran through Victorian homoerotic behavior and writing.

In the throes of religious ecstasy, you might cast off your clothes and go naked into God's woods and fields to worship (in the midst of a *raging* storm that mirrored your own state of mind) with another male devotee. The pages of Gerard Manley Hopkins, Alfred Lord Tennyson, Henry Cardinal Newman, and the Uranian writer Edward Carpenter, who started out as an ordained Oxford dean, were filled with these twinnings of 181 religious/ecstatic and sexual feelings.

In a wonderful evocation of the Male Companion theme, Edward Carpenter wrote about a young man who was so smitten with "a man twice his own age, captain of a sailing vessel — a large man, well acquainted with world" [the image of a good ship's captain is a common religious one] that in a moment of complete emotional surrender, the youth "hurried after him, and when they came to a quiet spot, ran up and seized him by the hand, and hardly knowing what he was doing fell on his knees on the pavement and held him."

Men could pull a rainbow of these feelings around themselves, and feel tribalized and free within it. Along with religious feelings often came a shared aesthetic that became emotionally consuming and liberating. Thus for many gay men, opera, with its exoticism and open call to feelings, became a key to the gay tribe. Opera became a language gay men could use with each other, and often opera houses themselves became free spaces in which the tribe might meet for gossip, recognition, and plain old cruising.

Learning to use social repressions as a *defense* against outsiders also became a means for the tribe to find a refuge for itself. Therefore, gay men in religious settings could actually use homophobia as a shield against intrusion: by not wanting even to open up a dialogue concerning homosexuality–keeping it completely hushed and secret—the tribe used the closet as a way of becoming more insulated against outsiders. But, within their various closets, the tribe developed secret codes, languages, and archival methods (such as monks keeping alive Greek myths) as a means of revealing themselves only to other queer men.

## The Opposite of the Holy Trick: *The True Friend*

Every tribe has a quest which unifies it and reveals much of its desires. For two thousand years Jews prayed for Jerusalem to be returned to them. Christians still wait for the return of Christ. Moslems believe they must make a pilgrimage, physically and psychologically, to Mecca. In a similar way, one of the most important themes for men in the gay tribe has been the quest for the *true friend*. The true friend prefigures the Male Companion: finding this true friend has been both a quest and a rite of recognition for many gay men. Realizing his closeness and goodness— a "love that transcends that of woman," as it was often characterized— became part of an earlier "coming out" ritual for many of us. This has been (and is still) especially true for younger men who first realize their homosexuality in the form of a school crush—whose intensity is literally unfathomable to them—on a friend. While recognizing this crush, they begin to refigure their own feelings, and the process we now call "coming out" often begins.

The *true friend* transcends the tradition-bound roles of mate or wife;

and our love of him exceeds even the love of family. The friend's presence restores us back to our selves; he is the transcendent (or, again, Christlike) figure for whom we feel a depth of connection beyond sex. In the past, he was often seen as pure, or as radiating light. In the Arthurian legends, he was Sir Galahad, the son of Sir Lancelot, who was described in Thomas Mallory's *Morte d'Arthur* as "the clean virgin above all knights." Galahad was every knight's desired friend. His purity allowed him to drink from Christ's chalice, and after drinking and eating of Christ's true Body, he soon died, still a virgin.

In similar ways, we may find ourselves not even physically attracted to the *true friend*, once we have discovered him. Or we may be so enveloped in the power of our love for him that this attraction can never be satisfied *physically*. One thing is certain: the friend has no profound sexual expertise. Our feelings for him will not call for this; he is the opposite of the Holy Trick. But once we have allowed him to enter our lives and have realized the importance of his presence—as well as our feelings for him—certain boundaries are inevitably set into place by the aura that he brings with him. Like the lover who leads us to the Male Companion, the true friend also does this, but on an even more profound and mystifying basis, because sex has been excluded and only the complete romantic isolation of maleness and friendship has remained. Therefore, being with the true friend even for small moments of time is satisfying, offering us a cleansing relief from the gay world's cynical hardcore, from its commercialized sexuality and from what has become the deadend, soulless body culture around us.

Much of the true friend's attraction comes from his actions: from his freshness, sincerity, and unselfishness. Honoring these attitudes can lead us to developing other deeper, intimate relationships with less idealized gay men, some of which can or may be sexual.

As was often spoken of Jesus, the *true friend* is, in fact, the "lover of our souls."

The *true friend*, as our guide within the gay tribe, will lead us towards that illumination in God which we might call a real "coming out." In the early 70s, gay men, reaching back into this tradition of bonding through religious/sexual affinities, formed fairy circles. The fairies, or to use the older form, *faeries*, wanted an alternative to what they felt was the deadness of the gay bar life. They wanted to release their own feminine, wild natures at a time when they felt that most of gay life was becoming mainstreamed: gay men as "clones" were wearing the working uniforms (Levi's, work boots, etc.) of oppressive, working-class straights; S & M patterning based on dominance/submission was seeking, they felt, to align the gay subculture to a repressive straight one.

Although the fairies, like other gay spiritual groups that have come after them, tried to release this lovely (and often repressed) part of their nature, they also asserted a dogmatism that for many men was a turn-off. 183

The fairies were frequently anti-sexual. Sex was negatively grouped with other parts of our repression. It was part of the cruising bar world, where muscles and clothes determined success. Although fairy men went back to nature, they rejected men who could not go in that direction, who could not give up their "straight jobs," but who often hungered for the same spiritual connections that the fairies were seeking.

I have noticed that in much gay spiritualist writing and feelings, when the spiritual level rises, so does the dogma level of exclusion. In this way, a real connection with the tribe, which is the grounding for gay spiritualism, will be blocked for men who are excluded by some "negative issue" in their nature, such as sexual compulsiveness. Sadly, these men will be made to feel out of touch with the tribe, when they are the ones who need it the most.

Sometimes in the midst of sex (either with several men or one), you will look at a man and capture within him the *true identity* of the two of you: in his individuality you will suddenly see your own. You will allow him to penetrate the vast anonymity of sex (an anonymity brought on by sweeping waves of passion) and become real to you: become complete and intimate. Conversely, within monogamous sex, you may see your lover as *all men*, as the spirit of every man you have ever wanted—or had sex with—and then as the man, your *own* man, who has finally returned to you in the "sexual moment," with your own needs fulfilled and your wounded spirit healed.

He has become for you at once *father, mother, true friend*, and, at last, your own Self, which he is showing to you. When this happens, you are pulling off the veil that surrounds the gay tribe. You are penetrating through its deep forests and touching it. You are obtaining the emotional sustenance that can nourish you through the ups and downs, disappointments, and hurts that are a part of being intimately involved with another person.

Just as finding the *true friend* codifies the quest of the tribe, locating the tribe itself—within the jungles of the gay world's commercialism and the deserts of our mainstream culture's emotional deprivation—is part of the tribe's spiritual work. However, these moments of recognition, by the very intensity of their nature, *cannot* remain with you forever. Just as I have written about the limits of intimacy, there is also a limit to contact with the gay tribe. Contact with the tribe will be an ongoing part of a gay identity. *It may be the strongest aspect of a gay personality, and the most misunderstood.*

For years do-gooding religious figures and "mental health professionals" have warned us about the "dangers" of the tribe. They have seen the tribe's existence as a component of gay promiscuity (the "good" gays who stay at home isolated, versus the "bad" queers who "go out") and the rootlessness and lack of stability in gay life, which they attribute wrongfully to the tribe, instead of to the compulsive commercialization and alienation of the "gay world."

It is not true that promiscuity *equals* a connection with the gay tribe, although many men do become involved in aimless, endless promiscuity because they will never be (or allow themselves to be) in contact with it. Their sexuality will never be satisfying. Neither do connections with the tribe have to be sexual. But most connections with it become sexual in nature because the tribe opens up a *totality* of feelings that cannot deny sex. What is important is that the need to connect with this tribe is universal with us, and the denial of it is dangerous to gay men. I believe that our very mental health depends on it.

Why this is so and why we are the way we are is a mystery that we are piecing together slowly. Much of this has been roadblocked by conservatives who are threatened by the idea of a tribe that is a *subversive* element. Strangely enough, the far Right believes—without any understanding of it—in the gay tribe. They are able to see that same-sexualized men *per se* are a subversive and unaccountable element that they would like to eradicate. To them we are like carbon monoxide: unknowable, invisible but *deadly*. The one way they can distance us is to keep pointing out negative "markers" that identify us. So a whole army of "neutered" conservative political and religious leaders lash out against our "feminineness," "weakness," or "elitism." These are signposts, they are sure, to the gay tribe. Pointing them out, demonizing each sign as it pops up, will keep young men away from us.

Often this backfires, since pop culture has embraced and been able to sell many "gay" characteristics, such as the idea of the outsider, the James Dean loner whose existence poses a mystery and a question—and who has a spontaneous sexual and inner life that will always be threatening to anyone who denies having either.

One suggestion that comes to mind regarding the existence of a gay tribe, or a collective gay consciousness, is that it may be a throwback to a more primitive state in human consciousness. Gays, in other words, have escaped "normal" human conditioning. Since we have placed ourselves, often enough, outside male-female patterns and constrictions, our imaginations can range farther "out there," both back into primitivism and through many different mythologies that we can appropriate as our own. This theory would seem ridiculous to queens whose dreams take them nightly to Bloomingdale's. But even within that part of the gay world, there is an element wanting release (and not just from the rules of throwing a cocktail party!) into the forests of the tribe.

Thus we have gay archetypal fantasies of rape (Ganymede, the irresistible, submissive boy being carried off by Jupiter, the personification of power/dominance); of prison/war fantasies (enacted by strangers brought together under duress); or secret twins (two men, who do not know each other, suddenly find that they have something elemental in   **185** common). In all of these fantasies, elements of the gay mythos are important: that each man *recognizes* a special relationship with another, that he gives in to *twinning* or *submission* desires. In the rape fantasy, a man finds himself powerless to control his most forbidden impulses towards domination; in prison/war, it is recognizing that all "rules are off," and now the players can give vent to their own repressed, *natural* feelings. In the secret twins fantasy, an unexpected closeness—cutting through homophobic distance—is revealed between two men.

In all of these archetypes, we have the basic elements of the gay mythos that I have dealt with earlier: recognition, twinning, submission/surrender, merging, individuation, and finally, a sense of climactic sharing, which can mean sharing sexuality itself ("coming out," or revealing one's feelings to a friend and then having sex with him). Or sharing "intimate information," which can be physical (as in sex) or spiritual (sharing hopes, prayers, meditations), and which can extend into a mentoring or helping relationship.

Or—past all of this—simply by sharing a meal or a moment of rare, healing closeness.

Although in heterosexual fantasies, the only thing immediately recognizable is desire, it is almost impossible for a man to identify with a woman and still desire her. He may recognize her specialness, or attractiveness, but he will never want to become her (and lose his own masculine power).

But in gay fantasies, recognizing a commonness with the desired is often at the center of desire; so much so that both men realize in a way that they are now involved in desiring *themselves*. They are strengthening their own innate maleness by desiring each other. In some primitive societies this actually encourages homosexual participation: it is recognized that men ritually "suck off" another man's maleness in his semen, thus augmenting their own. The fellator is therefore made *more* masculine by actually stripping another man of his "seed." This encourages reciprocal, "69" activity. (It can also produce an identity problem: whose "strength" belongs to whom? In some tribal societies, this requires either a recourse to violence—as monogamy problems come in—or changing homosexual partners often so that strong "seed" is circulated.)

The more rigid or conservative elements of society find this aspect of gay tribalism disturbing. For one man to discover a desire for himself in his feelings for another male means that he can now isolate his own sexuality: it is no longer tied to procreation and the continuation of the status quo. He is now augmenting his own self-esteem from within, rather than asking for social approval from outside. Recognizing this, both the old left Communists from the 50s and the New Left protesters from the 60s, the old homophobic McCarthyists and the *Newt* Right of Newt Gingrich were—and are—terrified of the gay tribesmen around them, whether they are readily identifiable or not.

As a "throwback" within society, homosexuality presented many problems. For centuries Europeans thought that primitive peoples were more inclined towards "debauchery," "degeneration," and other "sodomistic" states. Europeans had to *work like the Devil* to get sodomy out of their colonies. In North and South America they murdered thousands of native peoples for various sexual and sodomitical "crimes." Part of this anti-homosexual hysteria was the fear that the natives had not had this part of themselves reformed by European inhibitions. So, along with converting the natives to Christianity came the added White-Man's-burden of setting them "straight."

But the other part of the problem was that European colonialists realized how easy it might be for them to "go native" and *de*volve back to their own "unnatural" instincts. Once away from wives, families, and the Church, there were many temptations. Therefore, for them to stay "natural" (as opposed to "unnatural"), they had to exercise a great deal of restraint. Eventually many colonialists and their colonies became even more repressed than the folks back home, as sexual repression became synonymous with the civilization of Europe. Although we have embraced, somewhat, a return to tribalism among indigenous peoples, it is still almost impossible for industrialized societies to see gay tribalism as a part of other tribal peoples, or to recognize *gay* tribalism among Western gay men. At the same time, many of these societies can understand gay consumerism—queers as a ready market—but cannot deal with the idea of men hungering for a deeper, organic closeness with each other.

### Women and the Tribe

Within the gay tribe are many women, both genetically female women and men who, either as drag queens or transgendered men, take on female forms and dwell within the characters of women. Whereas in heterosexual tribal societies women are a volatile presence who must be repressed and dominated—even through genital mutilation—within the gay tribe women often represent a safe area, a resting place from what can be a wearing, combative intimacy with other men. For this reason, women are often worshiped as divine totems (divas), goddesses, or mother-saint figures.

Within the tribe, from a safe distance, women are nourishing and supportive. However, too much closeness with women dilutes the closeness men in the tribe need to have with each other, and it also neutralizes much of the natural calming female godliness that women represent. The result, then, is often a feeling of distrust and resentment between gay men and women, whether lesbians or straight.

In ancient times, goddesses, like the Sumerian goddess Inanna, had many homosexual devotees, as did Aphrodite (Venus), the Greek goddess of beauty, and Artemis (Diana), the Greek virgin huntress goddess, 187 whose cult for centuries after Christ merged with that of the Virgin Mary and attracted many homosexual men. During the Middle Ages, the cult of the Virgin had much appeal to same-sexualized men, since it was a convenient mask to hide behind. The Virgin was pure, she was lovely and peaceful, and to be her follower meant that one could, with no questions asked, refrain from sexual contact with women.

The Virgin Mary's cult became identified with the cult of female virginity, and many noble (and secretly homosexual) knights celebrated the purity of their ladies, which they had few intentions ever of breaching. As long as they were attached to the Virgin, or their own virgin ladies, these knights were also celebrated as pure and were never identified with "perversity." They were also often known to be "perfect friends" with other knights, which meant that these friendships—pledged in "blood-brother" oaths—could not be dissolved. They were henceforth "twinned" to each other.

Within the gay tribe, opera singers and pop divas now take the place of goddesses. Drag queens have also taken on the role of being intermediaries between the great goddesses (Dietrich, Davis, Garland, Monroe-from the past; Ross, Madonna today) and "the boys." By taking on the character of the diva (the "divine one"), a man assumes her power and conveys her sense of grandeur and peace. In the global and psychic landscape of our tribe, the hunters—killers—are seen as heterosexual men, who must kill to protect their families and give them meat. Although we may envy and admire this skill, it usually turns our stomachs.

Women, though, in the form of divas and deities—women, in other words, who are bigger than normal—bring us peace. They bring us back to the image of the powerful, healing Mother (another component of the Male Companion) that we want. It is for this reason that many gay men find the presence of women in their lives absolutely necessary. They will marry to keep them there. They will rarely love (or desire) women with the intensity that they love men, and the need they have for women will rarely be as urgent as their need for men, although they may spend much of their lives repressing this need.

Although it is gratifying to contact the tribe through ecstatic sex, it is possible to renew your connections with our tribe spiritually on a more constant basis. This does not negate a real need for physical contact, but it produces a different, more introspective form of connection. Spiritual renewal can come from reading the works of authors who were undeniably linked with the tribe, such as Walt Whitman, E. M. Forster, Christopher Isherwood, Ralph Chubb, Edward Carpenter, or poets like Allen Ginsberg (who linked himself with Whitman and the great English spiritualist poet and artist William Blake) and James Broughton. There are Biblical passages where a link with the tribe still glows directly at us, even though they are often denied by homophobic interpreters. These include the stories of Jacob's dream, where he wrestles with an angel; the story of

Jonathan and David; and Christ's relationship with John, the "beloved apostle."

Within the tribe, I also call to mind the story of Abraham's servant approaching Rebecca, who, unbidden, gives him a sign that God has chosen her for Abraham's son Isaac. Unbidden (that is, unasked for) gifts are very much a part of the gay transaction of recognition: that we recognize the importance and wisdom of unbidden kindness, compassion, courage, and good will.

What is necessary is that you sense your own inner reality—that spiritual gyro that keeps us balanced—linked in a way that directs us through the tribe and the mythos to the Male Companion. This linking brings us to that spiritual Fatherhood whose final essence is, in fact, genderless, that we seek. It is vitally important to us.

Other links to the tribe can come through meditation or through meditative masturbation. This is done by projecting yourself, while masturbating, out to the greater spiritual presence of a man whose aura may be approaching you, even though physically he is unavailable. Many men have linked themselves through masturbatory experiences to the "body electric" spirit of Whitman, or directly to the Christ-like or Buddha-spirited Male Companion.

In a similar way, you may find yourself linking with someone whose lingering physicality you have denied because of death, or have blocked an imaginative sexual desire for because you felt desire was "inappropriate." The idea of allowing grief and physical desire to flood through the same sexual gates may upset some men—they have worked so hard to present their "mature" selves at all times—but repressing this part of our imaginative life can keep us from the tribe's great loving presence. In this presence we are all in contact with our own needs for love, closeness, dignity, and kindness: we understand these needs and know they can be met. So, basically, the tribe does not stand on static roles and ceremonies. In fact, it opens up roles and creates loving rituals.

Other masturbatory meditations you can use are having sex with yourself at an earlier point in your life—initiating yourself into sex as a young man; sex with a person who as a younger man you felt was unapproachable or were awkward with, what I call "curative fantasy sex"; or sex with figures charged with your own personal sexual mythology—therefore, reaching outside your own attempts to censor yourself or clamp a sexual "type" on yourself.

As a child, I remember having vivid centaur fantasies, of being picked up and carried off by one of these gorgeous half-man/half-horse creatures, who combined maleness, strength, and beauty. As a young teen, I drew pictures of centaurs, and remember masturbating thinking about them. As an adult, I have relived these fantasies, linking me back to the realities of my own repressed teen sexuality and to the startling sexuality of classical Greece. Other personal sexual mythologies are Egyptian, Biblical, Norse, the homoeroticism of knightly friendships; the American mythologies of the West, plainsmen, "the open road," the Indians; and other underground streams that feed our consciousness, which can include leather brotherhoods, "bear" cults, and African tribalism.

These mythologies do not have to be entered in a masturbatory way, although there is a sweet, intimate vividness to entering them this way. But they can also be entered with friends who share such a mythology with you. Sharing mythologies can be an extremely hot and deep experience, but, again, some caution should be employed when you're involved with it. The shared mythology deepens your contact with each other and holds you together. The relationship can be either purely spiritual or spill into haunting, lovely sexuality; but try not to let this intimacy take you farther than it can. Here again, you are contacting the tribe, and the contact, because of its intensity cannot be continuous but must be renewed.

As I repeat over and over again, we live in a time of *emotional, spiritual, and psychological deprivation* and many gay men have acted upon this in terrible ways. Sometimes they are involved in a kind of sexual bulimia, having as much blind or promiscuous sex as they possibly can (either safely or unsafely), then "throwing it up" by completely retracting emotionally afterwards. Following them are men who are engaged in sexual anorexia, having no sex at all for extended periods of time, or purposefully seeking the least satisfying sex possible (such as anonymous sex in dangerous places, or humiliating sex with hustlers, "straights," etc.) and then following it with periods of sexual starvation.

Along with sexual anorexia has come a form of male physical anorexia, of taxing bodies to the breaking point at the gym, while adding a carapace of "solid" muscle over bone structures that can barely take it. (In America we have forgotten that the word "gym" comes from the Greek word "gymnos," or naked. The Greeks felt that the gymnasium was the place for aesthetic and spiritual renewal as well as athletic training.) This has all become the "ethos" of the 90s, as men get farther and farther away from the tribe and trade their gay sexuality on an "open market" that only *appears* to be ready for them.

## Reacting Against Internalized Homophobia to Contact the Tribe

The idea of gay tribalism itself will seem to many men ridiculous. As I have said often in this book, their own denial of self-worth is so ingrained that seeking emotional nourishment from (of all things!) other queer men seems absurd. They have cut themselves off so completely from this yearning, needful part of themselves that most visions of the tribe are impossible. So, of course, to maintain the validity of their own blindness, they would like for you to stay that way as well.

So how do you deal with a "community" of gay men who have constructed their alienation (or "alien nation") so well that your own natural needs to reconnect with tribalism offend them? Here are a few ideas that I have; but don't feel that they are the only ones. You may have some ideas of your own to answer this question.

- Keep your eyes open. Realize that what you are seeing on the surface is not what is really happening. That most of us still work within the tight framework of homophobic values that has been placed on us by our families, work places, friends and society. Fear is still the operative word here. You can recognize this fear—this constant poison of shame—but you do not have to swallow it. In other words, the very tainted recipe that others are giving you for "reality" does not make a cake you will eat.

- Question what is going on around you. Realize that your own loving heart is wise and important—so don't let your "smart" friends talk you out of what it is saying. Your heart—your own questing soul—will connect with the tribe. This connection is vital. It gives depth and luminosity to our experiences and relationships. This connection may come solely from within you, or with only *one* other person. But any true, loving connection between two people is stronger and more capable of change than the entire, starved environment of disconnection around us.

- Realize that gay tribalism, like any form of tribalism, is not, by its nature, "moral." It entitles no one to superiority or smugness. Within our tribe, as within any group, are monsters, scoundrels, and shits. There are also angels, lovers, philosophers, and saints. They all want and need the nourishment and support of the tribe. The question is who will find it, who will connect with it? Who will pass on its real value and worth?

"It is important for us to deal with the generalized depression around us
and survive."

CHAPTER 13

# Punching Your Way Out of the Dark:
# Re-creating Yourself

One of my favorite words in the English language is *recreation,* which
comes from an old French word *recreare,* to "create anew; to restore oneself." It now refers, according to *Webster's Collegiate Dictionary,* to the
"refreshment of the spirit after work." In my mind, though, *recreation* will
always refer to the idea of "re-creating" yourself, and therefore adding
renewal to your life.

In recreation, you are paying yourself back for everything that the rest
of what we call *everyday living* takes out of you. I think this idea of "re-creation" is really the answer to what I call "working through your own
depression"—a work that gay men now are often engaged in. When I recognize gay men as being especially engaged in this, I am saddened to see
that so much of the rest of the population has simply internalized its own
depression as "normal." Thus we have a mainstream population that has
chosen to live off junk food, junk television, junk books, junk music, and
even junk politics. This population lives in a constant state of low-grade
depression and barely hidden anger. Anger and depression like this tries
to resolve itself by endorsing heroes like Newt Gingrich, Jesse Helms,
Laura Schlesinger, and Pat Robertson, who in turn have turned mass-stu-
pidity itself into a new junk art form.

Although the situation is very sad, it seems to be left up to gay men to
remind ourselves that something is *really* stinking here. As the kids homophobically say, "it sucks." What has brought the general depression of this
period to a head with us is AIDS and conditions of homophobic violence
around us. In other words, we don't have to be hit over the head with a
mallet to realize that something "queer" and unnatural is going on around
us—so much so that often it is easy to feel that we are the only people
involved with what—in a more "normal" world—would be natural.

It should not be *natural,* for instance, to walk over the bodies of people
sleeping in doorways and just pretend that they are not there. Neither

should it be *natural* to rant on about "family values" and know that every fifty minutes a child in America is beaten or brutalized to death (usually by his parents, a caretaker, or a guardian). Nor is it *natural* to see that as more and more people are making less money in real wages, a smaller group is bringing in unlimited amounts by manipulating a very dangerous economic environment.

For us, then, re-creating ourselves becomes important. It is important for us to deal with depression and survive. Although gay men have been surviving for centuries by hiding or pretending, too often their survival has meant learning to live on the poison around (and inside) them: their own internalized homophobia. My own generation of gay men, then, has been the first to see this homophobia and to realize it is not "natural." This has not been easy, since self-hatred is a "natural" element in our world and has become, like air pollution, something you don't see until it kills you.

The idea behind depression (as I said in the chapter on homophobic violence) is that we are made to feel smaller: we have contracted inwardly from pain. We are only letting out the smallest parts of ourselves to the outside world. We are recoiling inside, and burying important aspects of ourselves in the process. Although it has become standard operating procedure among therapists to say that depression is masked anger—and often this is the case—among the other aspects of ourselves buried in depression are our own feelings of beauty, joy, and the power of *creation* going on about us. Like any other natural happening, this creative power contains within it its own sadness, rage, vitality—and joy. I say this because frequently people ask me, "How can you be happy in the face of AIDS?" Or they say, "I find so much of your work sad—and depressing—because it deals with sadness." To these people I say: *Depression is not caused by acknowledging what is sad, but by covering up those feelings. By drowning real feelings in muteness, banality, and boredom. By giving in to the vacuousness of the commercialized world around us.*

My own remedy, then, has been to try to understand and be sensitive to what is going on around me, without censoring it. And, conversely, to try to re-create myself, both in the creative process and by coming into contact with others. I feel that for the most part you cannot "re-create" yourself alone (although much of the work of re-creation has to be done that way), and that is why, again, we need each other. Another important aspect of this re-creation for gay men comes from our need for recognition: for others to see us, for us to "come out" of what is often an imposed silence, to journey towards the Male Companion and the tribe. Then we can exercise our abilities to recognize hidden, tender situations and empathize with others (both important aspects of the gay work). But to do this, we have to leave our own pain and depression.

Much of this sense of re-creation comes from exploring my own self. Since this "self," this inner core, is something that I can go into, I see it as separate from the part of me that is walking around and working at paying the "daily toll" of the world. The inner core, then, is that thing which gives me the strength to pay this toll. Some people would say, "Are you talking about your own soul?" And in some ways it might be true: this core that I go to for "re-creation" might be comparable to a soul; but, unlike our more generalized concepts of a soul, this inner core is very much a part of the here-and-now. The everyday. It is, truly, the *real*, functioning part of myself.

What we want to do in re-creating ourselves, then, is to set aside some moment when our daily problems are laid aside and a real "newness," or renewing, is welcomed. The process that does this is directed and, yet, simultaneously, in a Zen way, undirected. Just as Zenists ask themselves questions that have no "real" answers, but that radiate through the sub-conscious to bring up answers (the most famous include "What is the sound of one hand clapping?" or "Where does the ice go in the summer?"), in re-creating yourself you *invite* this real core to extend itself to you. By doing this, the core will manifest itself to your conscious mind and bring you a feeling of relief. Of restedness. And a genuine lifting of the spirit from depression. At the same time, you are coming into contact with your real "creative" self. It is this self that constantly re-creates and enriches you.

Here are some methods I have used for this, and that have for worked for me and others.

∞ Allow yourself the pleasure of thinking without censoring your thoughts. Go into parts of your mind's "house" that give you pleasure, that delight you, that you rarely get a chance to visit. These visits can be triggered by memories, fantasies, or landscapes that you create yourself. What is important is to recognize the voluptuous, calming "uselessness" of these forays. That you are not thinking out problems or "taking care of business." Instead, you are allowing your mind to heal itself as it would by taking a pleasant walk.

This has become one of the hardest of all things to do: actually to admit thoughts into your head and "watch" them, experience them moving through your "mind space." To be able to do this, even for five minutes a day, is for many men a great luxury. To have just five minutes of your *own* thoughts: not concentrating on business plans, goals, problems, your schedule, your *normal* anxieties, but actually to engage your own thoughts and then to "watch" them, in a lovely, calm way, as they take physical form, as they travel across the "screen" of your mind.

I find this one of the most beautiful experiences in my life, and I find myself resenting any infringement on it. People have this idea that because you are only *sitting there*—not plugged into a machine, not listening to music that's been inflicted on you, *not* having things sold to you in some TV commercial or magazine ad—that you are doing "nothing." Some men are terrified of this, and can't spend a moment doing it. Instead, they will rush to their checkbooks, which must be balanced *right now*, or go out to rent a video.

In many ways, this inability to listen to your own thoughts reflects on our inability to listen to other people unless a structured situation is involved. We cannot listen to the beauty of words coming out of another's mouth; the simplicity of someone else's thoughts directed at us. There is the idea that every thought requires an answer, a rebuttal, a place in someone else's agenda. This has left many people running to therapy, since therapists are currently the only people who can, or will, listen to the thoughts of strangers.

I find listening to my own thoughts such a remarkable pleasure that I schedule a time to do it. The nicest times are at home in the middle of rain, fog, or the quiet of night. It is the simplest, most exquisite pleasure— and it makes riding on trains or long plane rides wonderful, unless there is too much noise around to "listen." At listening moments, even having insomnia can be delightful—that is, if it is not brought on by caffeine, stress, or anxiety. In these "night thoughts" it is possible to give physical form to your thoughts and "watch" them moving in the darkness, either over your head or in front of you. If you feel that this idea is crazy, remember that the first people who read letters projected on a movie screen had their sanity questioned, and some doctors felt, at the earlier turn of this century, that "moving pictures" could lead to "nerve" problems. It did not seem natural for people to be reading words that were not actually there.

∞ Exercise, meditation, and affirmations. In these methods of "punching out of the darkness," we are in various ways moving aspects of ourselves around. In exercise, this is done physically; in meditations and affirmations, it is done psychically. Exercise stimulates the production of adrenaline, which is both a natural antidepressant and a natural antihistamine. I bring this up because moving your body actually causes a surge of other body chemicals, including important hormonal rushes. Runners talk about having a "runner's high," produced by raising the flow of endorphins to the brain. But part of this high is also caused by releasing blocks of tensions, angers, and anxieties that become physically stored in the body. They are reuniting, in a safe manner, the natural relationship of physical and emotional elements that in the course of the day we try to divide. We try to divide our angers and frustrations from our rational, operating selves, but they remain, locked within both the muscles and the psyche itself. This is the reason why when we are doing things that cause us pain or frustration—drudge work at the office, boring housework, being stuck in traffic, etc.—old hidden furies can pop up. You're stuck in traffic and you can't figure out why suddenly you're furious at your boss—for something that he did a month ago! You've pushed down the anger and tried to divide it from your "adult" self. Now, suddenly, it comes back up again.

In running and other forms of exercise, these knots of tension rise naturally and ease themselves out. Even though activities like running, in-line skating, and fast walking are great forms of exercise that you can do on your own, getting involved with group sports such as volley ball, soccer, or baseball can also pull you out of depression, as long as the play aspect takes precedence *over* the competitive one. Fierce competition is very much a male trait, one that many gay men repress in themselves, and although enjoying the high of winning can be another release, absorbing the guilt for losing does nothing for drawing you out of troubled periods. Therefore, if you are going to become involved with group games, either in a gay team context or in any other way, remember that the ultimate goal must be your own self-development, not simply winning. Part of this self-development can mean grabbing hold of the "maleness" of competition (like I said, something that many gay men repress) and actually enjoying the competitiveness on a sensual and satisfying level. In many ways, straights do this in sports, even if they cannot consciously admit to the sensual (and sexual) aspects of sports activities.

An important aspect of exercise at any age is the idea of reclaiming your own body. Often we give up on it and feel that after a certain age things go downhill and are meant to be that way. Thus, growing a pot belly or a bay window, knowing that your endurance is half of what it was ten years ago and that your balance is off, all seem to be part and parcel of getting older. They are not. *What does happen with age is that the body no longer readily mends and cares for itself.* You have to do that for it. You have to take care of your own body, and in doing this you also learn to love and respect it. I will talk more about this important sense of physical self-love further on.

Meditation is an exercise of the mind, requiring its own discipline and protocol. This means not only doing it often, but also establishing a place and time to do it. There are many different avenues towards meditation, which include the use of breathing exercises, establishing mental pictures, and special words or phrases, known as mantras. One of the misconceptions about meditation is that it is a way to "blank" your mind, and you must have your mind "blank" before it works. Neither of these ideas is true. You don't blank out your mind in order to meditate, and once in a meditational state, your mind is not blanked out at all. Instead, meditational states are closer to that state I described of watching your own thoughts and giving them a "physical" presence. It is a way of isolating thought patterns so that the most basic, calming, and authentic ones emerge.

Often the avenues of prayer and meditation become intertwined, and many religious people become involved with meditation first through prayer. One problem with prayer meditation is that it can be used to lead you away from yourself and to cover up real problems; it becomes, in other words, a mental fix. Therefore, using meditation as a solution to problems is not a good idea, and many religious people using this approach end up with alcohol and other dependency problems as well.

On the other hand, I have known many gay men who have come out through meditation. They have seen the light of their own selves in the meditational calm, and have used meditation as a way to integrate themselves sexually into a world that does not welcome them. Often these men have not been a part of the pressurized "gay world." They have also seen themselves only moving around the edges of various spiritualist movements, many of which, despite much "live-and-let-live" rhetoric, are basically sexist and homophobic. I've often thought that the reason so many spiritualist movements are sexist and homophobic is that many of them—from Eastern cults all the way over to evangelical or fundamentalist movements—still want to play well on American campuses and their image of American college students has not changed since 1955. In other words, spiritualism and religion still have to fit in in an environment of Coors Beer commercials. This has meant that a popular spiritualist movement that *openly* embraces gay men has not arrived yet.

Affirmations are a form of self-hypnosis that are incorporated into Twelve-Step programs, self-help movements, and many spiritualist structures. Basically you are telling yourself what you need to hear, until you believe it, internally—that is, on an unconscious level. Affirmations work. They can pull you out of depression. But, like any form of propaganda or advertising (in this case for yourself), they are pretty much two-dimensional and shallow. It is easy to say, "I am capable. I am beautiful. I am lovable. I will not let people hurt me or disturb these feelings," and for a time believe it. But this does not get you into contact with your real core self that needs to be changed by these ideas. Instead, a living "affirmation" should be to experience things through your own larger consciousness: through your own depth, strength, openness, and joy.

∞ Sex, nakedness, masturbation, and massage. I know these are probably things that you think you know a lot about. A lot of us feel that gays invented *sex*, at least the idea of *recreational* sex.

But how often do we use the experiences of sex, as well as nakedness and/or masturbation, as a way of escaping ourselves instead of as an avenue to lead us back towards our selves? To begin with, much of our ideas about sex have become firmly based in competition. We hear these messages all the time: "He'd never look at me." "I couldn't even approach *him*." "He's such a troll; if he even comes close to me, I'll hit him." "What would my friends say if they saw me with *him*?" "He's a loser." "I'm a loser." Etc.

We use sex as a way of affirming our own worth or status, and when sex is not there, our self-feelings are immediately lowered. In this way, some of the more successful media figures of this age (at least in the gay marketplace) have been porn stars, fashion models, or hustlers who have been able to make commodities out of their bodies and sex appeal. The idea that they have left many other important aspects of themselves out of the sexual arena does not register with us or bother us, except in the most cynical way. For instance, the death of a porn star through drugs or AIDS may prompt some of us to say: "So what did he expect?" We cannot see that this young man's needs to contact the gay tribe and be fulfilled by the mythos were never met. This is another example of the commercialization of sex not bringing us closer to other men, but only further away.

In the same way, our attitude towards nakedness has become that it's either purely exhibitionistic, aggressively sexual, or impossible because of our associations with body shame. Accepting the body for what it is—fat, thin, old, young—and then enjoying the beauty of nakedness itself seems foreign. Perhaps the ancient Greeks could do it, or "professional" nudists, but not us. Once you accept nakedness for what it is—joyous, free, and delightful—then you become clothed, while naked, in the very air around you: the air of being happy with yourself, of learning to like your own skin. In the late 70s I lived in Germany, and I was struck by the German attitude towards nakedness, which is that it is close to holy and also—very much—divorced from sex. Many parks in German cities feature *luft-baden*, or air baths, which are often, but not always, sexually segregated. There you can strip off your clothes and take a "bath in the air."

The highest form of nakedness, I feel, is learning to take a bath in *yourself.* This is not simply a nakedness of the body, but also of the soul and psyche. In this nakedness, you begin to luxuriate in the warmth and wonder, the beauty and delight of yourself. It is really coming close to your own sense of self-love, and also experiencing—truly realizing—the love others, including God, have had for you. You can feel yourself now being touched by this love and letting it hold you. Once you have allowed yourself to have this "bathing in yourself," you will be surprised at the changes that happen in your psyche: it's as if vast "switches" of well-being have been turned on. Suddenly others, too, start to glow. It is a powerful feeling, but one which you must be careful to use well.

To experience this sense of bathing in yourself, you can be naked—and being naked is a plus—but you can also be on a train, or an airplane, or at your desk. (I *don't* suggest doing it while driving.) Anyplace where you are free to feel the completeness of yourself. To have this freedom with another man is beautiful; but don't expect it. It is rare for that to happen, because too often people want and need attention to be paid to them; they feel rejected when suddenly you come into contact with yourself. This contact is not closed, in a narrow "narcissistic" way, but open, in a truly generous one. You are experiencing yourself free, and naked, and lovable.

In a way, you are falling in love with yourself—that is, with the real inner core of yourself. You are coming into contact with it, recognizing it, 199 and accepting it. It is like finding yourself at the end of a walk on the beach and then conversing, in a compassionate, loving way, with this self. Once you have experienced this inner core, it is best—and wondrously possible—to transfer this love to others. It is now part of the unbidden gift that only becomes more marvelous through its transfer.

This feeling of bathing in self-love is, in fact, much of the essence of spirituality and religion. It brings us into contact, once again, with the Male Companion, whose presence stands behind the mystery of gay work. This contact with our own "naked" self leads us to realize—in the shyest, most beautiful way—that the Male Companion is within us and is, at its deepest, *us*.

But staying stuck in this "mode" of soul nakedness and love of naked-ness and oneself can be dangerous, too. It is why I have said it is best to transfer this love, which happens as we approach the Male Companion and see our own lovers in the Companion's shimmering light. It is too easy to go from self love into the various mirrors of narcissism that our society places in front of us, and to confuse "finding" yourself with sim-ply finding another mannequin of yourself that you have "fallen" for. Very attractive, talented young people often do this when they find them-selves falling in love with their own youth and beauty. They have been praised for it and loved for it so often that, suddenly, it no longer seems even a part of them. It is only something that others can use and sell—and the young become quickly, cynically, aware of this. Tennessee Williams wrote brilliantly about this in his play, *Sweet Bird of Youth*, a story about people latching onto and selling the image of their youth, years after the real loveliness of it is gone. This chimera, or fantasy, of youth is regularly being dangerously sold to gay men at druggy, loud-volume "circuit" par-ties, where this sellable image makes most men feel only more insecure, only more rejected.

So it is important to use this form of "nakedness" to "re-create" your-self, and then go on. To use it to bring others to you, instead of using it to shield yourself from others.

I have talked about masturbation meditations as a way of contacting the gay tribe, but I think it is also important to use this "tool" as a way of contacting and re-creating yourself. This is the opposite of what goes on in most jerk-off club situations, where getting off—with the "right" per-son—is everything. In re-creational masturbation you are using the road of "self-love," or self-eroticism, as a way of getting into yourself. Of expe-riencing every part of yourself. Sometimes this can be done in a purely physical way, such as masturbating with your feet instead of your hands. This means massaging the sensitive head of your cock with the equally sensitive soles of your feet (which, by the way, have as many nerve end-ings as your penis head!).

You can experience sucking, licking, and massaging other parts of yourself, including your nipples, elbows, knees, toes, and the very sensitive places inside your elbows and knees. Or chewing on your biceps muscles. Or gently biting your wrists, forearms, etc. You can fuck yourself with your fingers or dildos. Sometimes dildos become fantasy figures that take you away from yourself, instead of into yourself, so it is important to watch out for this. Again, you can do masturbation meditations and re-creations with another man, or other men, but it is almost impossible then to stay centered on yourself—in the generous way towards yourself that you want to be.

The ultimate aim in masturbation meditations is to come in contact with the more forbidden but lovely parts of yourself that you have kept hidden in most sexual situations. Suddenly, you are now your own Master, and you can be hard on yourself and demanding; or your own Slave, and you can ask for mercy or softness. You are the sexual child that you were not allowed to be, when you were once caught "doing that" and made to feel shameful. You are walking among your dead friends and experiencing sex with them, gladly, without remorse or shame; or you are experiencing sex in the next life. The curtains are being opened upon your real sexual self: not the self who is so critical and self-critical that he can only "do it" with a "beauty"; or the self who censors various parts of himself as his partners change; or the self who has to walk through a mine-field of old put-downs and bad memories in order to approach another man sexually.

Once you have experienced regular *re-creational* masturbation (I'm using this term of "re-creational masturbation" to separate it from the sort of furtive, limited, "safe" recreational experiences most of us have in jerk-off clubs or in other on-site sex clubs), sex itself changes. It becomes more involved with your whole self and at the same time less involved with simply "getting off," which (as important as that can be) often leaves us with an "unsatisfied" feeling after casual sex. This does not mean that all sex has to be cosmic, mind-blowing, and make you instantly want to fall in love. It should not. That is not only dangerous and misleading, but foolish. As anyone knows who has used sex as a main route to falling in love, that route is laden with blind alleys. But again, we are talking about sex as a way of reclaiming, re-creating, and restoring yourself.

This leads us back to the original idea of sex as a re-creational tool, of drawing you back into yourself, and then allowing you to come out refreshed. For many gay men, this has become a primary motivation for sex. Simply put, it means *getting off* and away from the humdrum realities of life. But, in pursuing this, we usually don't connect with other men or ourselves. Part of this is that our own blocked needs to touch and be touched by another man are so great (after being routinely repressed for so long) that they override any real closeness we can attain. It means that sex with another man usually means that he is "the trick"—and not a par-ticularly holy one—and sex with him will be bound by very set rules. Emotional roadblocks will be set up as high as possible, as physical    201 boundaries are lowered. Or, in this day of "safe" sex, physical boundaries will also be raised ("Nothing not safe!") and emotional boundaries raised even further, unless "the trick" evolves into the "boyfriend." In that case, some "safe-sex guidelines" will be tossed, unfortunately, out the window, as other emotions start to wash in.

But in real "re-creational" sex, you can allow as much of yourself to come out as *you* feel comfortable, because the boundaries you are setting around the sexual situation include both you *and* your partner, but exclude the host of usual "romantic" feelings (or baggage) that so often we place around sex. These feelings include: "I want to please him as a way of getting him to like me." "I won't see him again, unless the sex is good." "I'm going to fall in love with him because he's so *good* in bed, which means that he is warm and loving and sincere."

(Please don't feel here that this means I am—and want you to be—"anti-romantic." I love "hearts and flowers." I have talked frequently about the bestowal of unbidden gifts, and how important they are to our needs for recognition. But what we refer to as "romance" is really often only symbolic of the unbidden gifts. Those gifts should come from that "core" that strengthens itself by giving. In other words, "unbidden" gifts are not bargaining chips that we use to "trap" someone else when we cannot give of our real selves.)

Most of these "romantic" feelings, then, come out of our own deeper needs, both sexual and emotional. Sex is then weighed down with them. They often go back to our parents, their relationship, and what they did or did not give us. Many gay men go into a sexual situation with these romantic needs in full display, and then they are hurt by them. They become more defensive, wary, and more in need of closeness and healing. The opposite are men who divorce sex completely from their feelings, and who believe that nothing real ever comes from *sex*, especially *gay* sex. (It's here that internalized homophobia really rears its snarling head: these men are bashing themselves and every sex partner.)

Men who feel that gay sex is completely worthless—except as a way of "getting off"—and that it has no emotional value or truth in it at all, often get their values from mainstream society, in which women (the female version of "tricks") are seen only as cunts, bitches, or whores (or in hip-hop parlance, *ho*'s). Gay men who come from working-class backgrounds are especially prone to these feelings, since many of their friends may still be straight. They feel closer to other men from their background than to the "gay world," which seems more like a "decorator room" out of a department store than something to do with their deeply held emotional lives, their work, and their families. Unfortunately, with much of the "gay world," they are correct.

But once these yearnings and feelings have been addressed to their own places, that is, either as fantasies or needs which will probably not be fulfilled sexually, and once we have placed ourselves fully in the sexual arena—without the usual competition (who is the prettiest, who will get off first, who actually deserves whom, etc.)—we can allow this real core of ourselves to emerge. And we will know that when it does, we will not be destroyed by its emergence. We will be able to see it as a richer part of ourselves, instead of something that (as it is now viewed by our commercially driven cultures) will handicap us.

We will, therefore, *not* fall hopelessly in love with whomever our partner is, but will come into a richer contact both with him and ourselves. We will see that it is possible to care about him (and love him) in the same way that it is possible to care about—and love—this core of ourselves.

When this happens, many of our expectations and demands about sex dissolve. These include the idea that you can't "get off" with someone unless he is of a certain height, race, coloring, muscularity, age—the full menu starts to look like something from one of those Big Boy restaurants. Instead, the two of you are now progressing further, as you go with more *safety* into yourself. You can see that these feelings are there for you to work through without being destroyed by them, which is often the present attitude. This does not mean that from now on you will suspend your needs for attraction, but that the scope of your attractions will really open up as your own feelings about yourself open.

As in other forms of quick or "flash" intimacy—and sex is certainly an example of intimacy flashing right in front of us—again we have a "let the buyer beware" situation. Because you are experiencing this lovely opening of yourself, it is easy to project these feelings of self-love onto someone else: someone who may not understand them or who may be geared to misinterpret them. This is often a good recipe for "infatuation," for foolishness masquerading as love. Suddenly, like Titania, the fairy queen in Shakespeare's *A Midsummer Night's Dream*, who, under a spell, falls in love with the first thing in her view—who just *happens* to be a fool wearing a donkey's head—you could do the same thing. (This is a perfect example, in therapy, of "transference." Because you are opening yourself up, you fall in love with your therapist.) Likewise, because you seem so open, warm, and truly loving (which you are), *he* may feel that you have fallen in love with him: which you have not. For a man who is desperate for love, to meet someone like you may be overwhelming. You are, in the parlance of Twelve-Step programs, becoming "self-actualized," and he is not. So don't allow his *fantasy* to take you places you're not prepared to go, but be sensitive to the needs of other vulnerable men as well.

The last of the physical means I spoke about is massage. Massage is immensely relaxing. It enables you to have a feeling of warmth, contact, and being taken care of, which can be a wonderful relief from depression. But giving a massage can be good for the giver as well: here you are touching someone, exercising your own  muscles, and going back into a nurturing role that is important for gay men. Massage has helped many gay couples to stay together, and it is also an excellent icebreaker with 203 strangers. It can lead into sex—or not, depending upon how far you want to take this form of closeness.

Taking a massage course and learning to give a massage is important. There are right ways and wrong ways to massage someone—muscles can end up tensing up under the wrong type of pressure—so you should know something about it if you are going to give as well as receive a massage. But even the lightest, simplest forms of touching mean that you are bridging the lonely voids between men that we normally keep in place. One thing is certain: men like to be touched. They are often frightened about who will do the touching and what it can mean—will it mean a "submission" they are not ready for and cannot control? Will it mean that they are now "gay." (As if the label itself will absolutely cripple and destroy them!)

This touch starvation is constantly with us, especially since Americans and other English-speaking people come from an Anglo-Saxon culture that glorifies "sportsmanship" at the expense of affection. Infants are known, clinically, to die without being picked up, held, and touched. This makes you wonder how much of this need to be touched and held stays with us throughout our lives. It has also been proved clinically that little boys find hugging more important than being praised. Early on, they start to see distant fathers who will only shake their hands as competitors and not as friends. So massage is like feeding that touch hunger inside us, a hunger that is really not fed through sex—although good sex should include a lot of full-body contact.

Again, since we live in such a touch-phobic, sex-phobic culture, gay and straight, massage has become basically the province either of hustlers or of professionals who "clinicalize" the experience so that it becomes only "therapeutic," and any emotional response to it is stopped. Although most gay men like massage, few see it as a vital activity of the tribe. It is. It would be wonderful to see more massage groups and fewer groups for "sexual compulsives," who are "addicted to getting off," instead of being "normally" nourished by touching. We need to normalize these very human activities of sex, nakedness, masturbation, and massage, and see them as part of our necessary environment of wholeness. Without this, depression—the shrinking of the psyche itself—has become the "normal" environment we live in.

Allowing yourself to re-create yourself, through various forms of recreation, is immensely important. For many of us, it can mean the difference between being able to go on living and not. I have held out one last re-creational method that may, in the long run, be the most important. Very simply, I would describe it as:

∞ To allow yourself to become involved with something which is
much bigger than you are.

To allow, without reservation, all of your childlike sense of wonder to come out, and your (very important) adultlike sense of responsibility—and understanding—to go with it. To go both deeper and wider into this pursuit, and to allow this involvement to mature as you do.

This can be dance, sports, history, music, literature, art—and the vital spirituality that holds us to these things. It can mean an involvement with others, with close friends, children, the elderly, with other "queer" men and women, or simply people who need you and whose need will bring you into contact with the Male Companion within yourself. It can mean an involvement with nature, or the nature of cities: both are important parts of the environment of the gay tribe.

This should not simply be a hobby, but a *passion*. And it should belong only to you. Sure, you can share it with others—with your friends or a lover—but if you don't, don't keep that from letting you luxuriate even deeper in your pursuit. Gay men who do not have these passions really dry up. Tragically, as our society becomes more economically pressured, our passions become crowded out of our lives. They seem like luxuries (the "quality time" that we can marginalize or dispense with), instead of necessities. But I feel that in our own gay lives, they are the necessities. They open us up to ourselves. As Goethe said, "In play, man becomes human," and it is in our deepest, most enduring passions that we really find ourselves.

"I believe in the 'Gay Feast,' the inner banquet for gay men."

## CHAPTER 14

# Twelve Great Dishes for the Gay Feast

Okay, I know you feel that I've done enough dishing in this book. I've dished everyone from therapists to the "gay world" to the Twelve-Step programs that are keeping many of us alive. (Or at least keeping many of us in a direction other than killing ourselves.) But the following are different dishes. These are dishes that lead towards inner nourishment, something that is one of the hardest things to have in this "winner-take-all" period in which we are living.

Inner nourishment is what is needed to survive a difficult outside world. And the Gay Feast is one place where we can get this inner nourishment on our own terms. There are other places where we can obtain *some* inner nourishment, and I have no argument against these places in our lives. They include many churches and other outlets of "organized religion" (an institution many of us find repugnant, even though eventually most religions—including our currently fashionable New Ageism—become organized). Other places are in support groups, therapy groups, or therapy itself (when not tearing us apart, it can feed us), and in some gay groups, such as the faeries, gay naturism, and gay affinity and leather groups that work towards gay tribalism.

But what I want to stress in this chapter is having something that you can connect with yourself. *Alone*, if you must. This is becoming very important as we become even more disconnected from other people or those moments of closeness (like those free moments of "hanging out," which once brought many of us together) that our national corporate "culture," in its desire to milk a dollar out of everything, destroys.

Since we have, for the most part, now done away with the home culture and the family culture, many men look towards their jobs—and the closed corporate life that goes with them—as normalizing aspects of their lives. In other words, no matter how rough things get, they still have their jobs and the identities that go with them. This has left many people—gay and straight—trying to live, breathe, and find happiness in a dry, lifeless world. A world in which they are professionally "on" all the time.

It ain't no feast.

They're lucky if they get to choke down a kid's "value" meal at McDonald's.

I want something other than this. That is why I do believe in the "gay feast," the inner banquet for gay men, and I want to bring some dishes of my own to it. It is strictly—like some of the really great meals of this life—a potluck affair. What you bring to the feast (and how you share it with others) is important. One of the lovely aspects of our own gay lives is that we *can* improvise so much of it. Sometimes we are forced to do this, in that there is so little pre-patterning available to us. So we've had to learn to figure out things for ourselves.

The lucky among us arrived at this openly. We realized that we had an opportunity here, and we could run with it. The less lucky see this only in homophobic terms: that there is still no set "gay culture"—that we are still not a part of advertising's slick world. So if, somehow, they are fortunate enough to get to the Gay Feast, they'll have to schlep their own silverware. Their parents, most probably, will not provide it. They will have to fight to establish an identity. And part of that fight, for many homophobic gays, will be to establish that identity away from—and very much apart from—other gay men.

This is not what the Gay Feast is about. And yet some of these "dishes" will involve a certain keen sense of direction: you are here to nourish yourself, and not allow others to starve you. So you may find some of these dishes a little sharp, a little tangy. But I hope I have followed that sense of candor throughout this book.

But how do we go about setting up this gay banquet? Where do we find it?

In many ways, gay men have taken on, again, the role of monks; that is, we are the preservers of civilization, faith, and, for the most part, good times. This attitude was publicized in *Monk* magazine, which was a "mobile magazine" started by two men living in a "R.V." that they equipped with a solar-powered Macintosh computer. Each issue of the magazine spotlighted a certain location and tried to pull from it an attitude that the "monks," Jim Crotty and Michael Lane, considered "monk-like." This was a free attitude of fun and a connection to a real world that was not listed on the New York Stock Exchange. *Monk*, in short, became the prototype for many home websites today, in which people say, "Come into our homes and heads. Now, if we can just find some sponsors to pay for the guest towels."

In many ways, Jim and Michael really understood (*Monk* has gone the way of many magazines from the late 80s, although the monks themselves surface from time to time) that the gay feast is a traveling *inner* experience. It is almost impossible to pin it down, and yet we know it's there. In many ways, these "monks" were neo-hippies. And in the same way that doomed the old hippies, they were for the most part *apolitical.* Politics was messy. Ugly. Not *groovy,* and no good for sponsors or advertisers (whom, as I mentioned, you can no longer get around, no matter how soulful you are . . . I get the feeling that the Marriage at Cana would now be sponsored by Star-Kist Tuna). *Monk* also tried never (or hardly ever) to be overtly gay. They wanted the magazine to be "gay-friendly," but not openly gay. Open gayness was hardly a turn-on to "alternative" advertising. The alternative was not going to *alternate* to it.

So, on the contrary, I want this Gay Feast to be *gay.*

I want it to be *overtly* so. I feel that only in this way can it be the source of nourishment that we need. So I will not try to "universalize" it. I would prefer that it calls directly to us, and that it answer many needs that *we* have. To make it less so, to "de-gay" it—is to geld it. To make it merely palatable instead of *wonderful.*

I feel that by recognizing it as *gay* (or whatever term you want to use for yourself, for the self that is same-sex loving, that is self-reinforcing), we will take from this Feast the nourishment we need and then go out and give some of it to the world.

So, here are twelve goodies for the Gay Feast. They're twelve that I like to bring along. But don't feel that they are the only twelve. Let's make the banquet table *endless.* Let's make room for everyone of us, those alive as well as those who are, in the parlance of our time, "no longer with us." They *are* with us, and we want them there as well. So, at the end of this list, I hope you'll add some dishes of your own. Bring them along—and the next time you're planning your own Gay Feast, invite me.

1)    Allow yourself some compassion: compassion *for* yourself. This may be a hard thing for you to do, to feel compassion for yourself. And for *ourselves.* But it's necessary. To see that we are in pain. That we are fighting some very hard fights. That we're often alone. That often we are being sacrificed in various wars of "appearances" (Bill Clinton's "Don't ask, don't tell" capitulation—that sold out gay and lesbian soldiers—is not even an outstanding example of this; it is merely *one* example). It is necessary for us to see and understand these things—and to realize how much compassion we need. Not to see this is a great mistake. We need this compassion *now.* And no one is going to show it to us but *us.* So start with *yourself.* And, along with the compassion that you'll bring to the gay feast, bring a sense of self-love and happiness—and the kind of feistiness that is necessary to defend both. As I said in the chapter on defending yourself against homophobic attacks, we have a right to be here. And that sense of compassion must stand behind that right.

2)    Bring an understanding of the *beauty* of imperfection. The Japanese refer to this as *shabui.* It means valuing natural individuality    209

over the formal coldness of what we pass off as "beauty." For some of us who are getting older (and experiencing physical changes or illness), this understanding means that we can see these changes in a good way. And also that we can eroticize differences and aspects of aging and experiences, instead of the slick, canned, commercialized "ideal" that is being sold to us.

3)     Reserve judgment on yourself. Realize you don't always have to *save, salvage,* or *maximize* every situation. In our networking society, maximizing has become a religion. Every situation is a selling one. Perhaps it is time to stop selling yourself to others, and to "buy" yourself—for yourself—again.

4)     Learn to celebrate yourself. I mean, not just *tolerate* yourself or ask for the toleration of others, but truly to *celebrate* yourself. Allow yourself to be a center of joy.

For many of us living closeted (and, often, perilous) lives in homophobic settings, being given any amount of tolerance has been enough. We have pushed ourselves into a corner of gratefulness and self-abnegation. In turn, we are selling our birthright of celebration—and for what?

The early "homosexual rights" or homophile movement pathetically asked for tolerance. It asked psychiatrists for it. And psychoanalysts, psychologists, lawyers, politicians, ministers, priests, and rabbis for it. It gave all of these people the right to define and judge us—for nothing. The tolerance that some professionals showed us did nothing for most of these professions. It did not change them at all. (Old-school psychiatry is a perfect example of this; they never wanted to murder us, just screw our heads back on. The fact was, we didn't really need *their* screwing!) It wasn't until after the Stonewall revolution—which radicalized the gay movement—that we began to celebrate ourselves. We began to see the beauty in our lives and energies.

We need to continue doing this. I have known men who, dying from the scourge of AIDS, with their last breath told me that they still *celebrated* their lives, that they still believed in themselves as gay men. I am awed at the liberation of this, at the sheer beauty and power of it. Hold this celebration to you. And bring it to the Gay Feast.

5)     Recognize the importance, the excitement, and the attraction (which *is* sexual, if you allow it to be) of real interest in others. Of opening yourself up to the possibilities of a loving and engaged life. That story that I asked you in the beginning of this book to imagine yourself telling-the one that includes you and *him*—bring that to this Feast.

6)     Then bring forth your own *real* story. Something for you to tell at the right moment, to the right person. Don't allow it to become simply *another* routine. We live in the age of shallow confessions and empty

apologies. Don't become a part of this, so that your own story becomes just another "rap."

What is your own story? It's what is important to you. It includes your own real feelings about many things, not simply about sex (which many men can talk about at the drop of a baseball hat) but about your job (an important part of your life), about God, and the place of your own history—your own living "myth"—within your life. What's important to any story is your own attachment and feelings towards it. If these are not there, it becomes another piece of *Melrose Place* or the latest TV movie, which is just a smattering of fiction placed between commercials. It means nothing, so why bring it to the Feast?

7)     Bring the treasures of friendship and people you are close to. These are the ultimate rewards of life—and your ability to see people wholly will determine the real value of these treasures.

8)     Allow what *renews* you into your life. Welcome it and give it the importance that it deserves. But realize that much of your ability to renew yourself must come from your own self. So don't get stuck on a merry-go-round of hobbies, pastimes, home decorations, travels, collections, and "outside interests" that cease being nenewing and become only treadmills in themselves.

9)     Don't discount things because they come in the *wrong* package. We are so used to buying the package rather than the contents that we now denigrate things because the packaging does not turn us on. Some of the most elegant meals I've ever had have been simple and rustic. They were made with care and fresh, often homegrown ingredients. Some of the worst meals I've ever had have been "elegantly" served with silverware so heavy that you developed biceps with the meal. The food was a second cousin to garbage, but the service was superb. Likewise, some of the smartest, most moral people I've met have been outside the usual "norms" of morality. Neither did they resort to the kind of "higher" vocabulary that we often confuse with intelligence.

The reverse of this is that we expect "holy" people to be sexless. Or to come in a package that is without humor. Or human appetites or vices. They're packaged as "saints" for a "market" that would not recognize one. When we find out that this is not the case, and that even saints get erections (a fact that Bill Clinton may be able to swear to), all of our feelings for these people come into doubt.

Part of this may be that the packaging—or publicizing—effort, from organizations like the Church or our political parties, is so intense that we cannot see the people under it. But another part of it is that we still can't or won't go beyond the package. Even writers, a group in the past never judged for their high "moral" values, today are judged on their personal "correctness," as opposed to what they have to say. This means that we     211 have to keep sanitizing our thoughts, our pasts, our appearances, to stay within currently fashionable expectations. It puts a burden on the gay leaders among us that is unbearable.

10) Don't be afraid of those moments when you turn yourself off. When you go inward and can take no one else with you. These are precious moments. Younger people are often frightened of moments without "cool" diversion. But a part of maturity is being able to face these lonely nights of the soul—both the dark ones and the ones filled with moon and starlight—and wander around in them and then come out better for it.

11) Realize that joy is *not* always something you can share. Real *joy* is a release of all that we hold dear: love, sadness, sex, kindness, touching, holding, trust, and even fear. Joy has many components and personal ingredients. It is a different feeling from the hysteria, the "high," of many group activities. So allowing someone else to share your joy is a thing of real intimacy—and trust.

12) Don't bring guilt to the feast, but bring a sense of responsibility. Bring the deep sense of character that you have developed over a lifetime of dealing with life. Don't apologize for this part of yourself. Often gay men feel apologetic and embarrassed by character. Part of our oppression has been to be hit over the head with accusations that we lack character: that we live in a "moral vacuum." Individually, this has never been the case, but the commercialized "gay world" is not in the business of either caring for your character or working with you to develop it. You have to do this on your own. To leave character outside this feast—because it is a *Gay Feast*—is a mistake. You will never truly enjoy it if you do.

Now that you have some of the dishes assembled, how do you partake of them? *Joyfully*, you can do this by yourself. You don't have to look your best to do it; you don't have to clean up the house for the other guests—although you may decide actually to have a party and talk about it. One of the things I have discovered while writing this book is that many men I've talked to have found the ideas here *fascinating*, but they don't want to deal on a personal level with them. The sound bite is nice, but all they're interested in is a *bite*. This does not work with a real banquet.

A real banquet is a feast—a celebration—large and wondrous. It's a special, enriching time. Once you've had it, you may not want to go back for a while. But it's great to know that it's there. It's inside you. It is the Gay Feast of your life, and it will nourish you in your need to survive and to come to love your *own* gay life.

"There are still so many things to understand about our own gay stories. Each of us has one, and we have really only scratched the surface of them."

EPILOGUE

I have lived with this book for a long time. I have been amused, moved, frustrated, perplexed, and even delighted by it. The easiest thing in the world to give is advice, and the hardest thing to transmit is wisdom. What I've wanted you to do most of all is ask questions and know that there are answers, although they may not come from the standard sources. For the most part, they will come from your own experience. But the hard thing is to put the information your life has given you into some kind of order—and to allow it actually to enlarge you. That is what I have wanted to do in this book—and I wanted to enlarge myself while writing it. The hardest part of the book was writing about myself and my going forth into a "gay world" that as a young gay man in the mid-60s I was allowed to know almost nothing about.

The nicest thing was realizing how deep my influences have been: that as a gay man I do have deep roots. And these roots have very little to do with my biological family, but with my emotional one. These are the connections I have with other men who are gay, and who've also felt these connections.

There are still so many things to understand about our own gay stories. Each of us has one, and we have really only scratched the surface of them. I know that many people will find a lot to argue about in this book, especially my feelings about the gay world, our community, and the tribe. They will also question the things I have said—in the same way that I have questioned them myself—about heterosexuality and homosexuality, the mainstream world, and the various roles of women, class, and ethnic groupings in our lives.

What I wanted to present in this book is the sense that there is a platform that we, as gay men, can stand on. That we have a foundation and strength for ourselves. That there is something binding us together that is more than just "sexual preference," that we really do need each 213 other as enriching factors in our own gay lives. That we need men of many different backgrounds and ethnic, physical, and emotional characteristics. That there is an underlying gay consciousness that we can tap into for connectiveness and support, and that this consciousness should be recognized and honored. That there is, in fact, a *work* and a destiny for us to take part in.

And what I want to say about that, is that the work has just *begun*.

# Perry Brass

Although Perry Brass was born in Savannah, Georgia, he has spent most of his adult life in the Northeast. He edited *Come Out!*, the first gay liberation newspaper in the world, published by New York's Gay Liberation Front, and with two friends founded the first health clinic for gay men on the East Coast. His poetry and essays—some of the most influential in the early years of the gay movement—were published in alternative papers in the U.S. and in Europe. His work has been included in *The Male Muse, Angels of the Lyre, The Penguin Book of Homosexual Verse, Gay Roots, Gay Liberation* (from Rolling Stone Press), *Out of the Closets*, The *Bad Boy Book of Erotic Poetry, Grave Passions: Tales of the Gay Supernatural*, and *The Columbia Anthology of Gay Literature.*

His 1985 play, *Night Chills*, one of the first to deal with the AIDS crisis, won the Jane Chambers International Gay Playwriting Contest. He has collaborated with many composers, including Chris DeBlasio, who set *All the Way Through Evening*, a song cycle based on five poems from which "Walt Whitman in 1989" was spotlighted in the groundbreaking *AIDS Quilt Songbook*; Ricky Ian Gordon, who set Brass's "The Angel Voices of Men" for the New York Gay City Men's Chorus's "Stonewall 25" Carnegie Hall appearance; and Craig Carnahan, who set "Waltzes for Men," also for the NYCGMC, under a commission from the Dick Cable Musical Trust.

His first book of poems, *Sex-charge*, was published in 1991. *Mirage*, his gay science fiction thriller, was nominated for a Lambda Literary Award for Gay Men's Science Fiction. Its sequel, *Circles*, was described by San Francisco Bay Times as "a shot of adrenaline to the creative centers of the brain." *Albert or The Book of Man*, the third book in his SF series that deals with the planet Ki, was described in *Men's Style Magazine* as "part of a saga, comparable to Tolkien's *Lord of the Rings* . . . a rich and complete imagining of a whole world." His novel, *The Harvest*, a gay "science/politico" thriller, nominated for a 1997 Lammy in Gay and Lesbian Science Fiction/Fantasy, deals with the coming brave new world of cloning and the market in body parts. His second book of poetry, *The Lover of My Soul*, published in 1998, was favorably compared by long-time gay activist Jack Nichols to two of Brass's forerunners in the gay tribe, Whitman and Ginsberg.

Perry Brass currently lives in the Riverdale section of New York City. An accomplished public reader and exponent of gender and gay-related topics, he is available for public appearances.

# Index

198-200

Other Books by Perry Brass

# SEX-CHARGE

" . . . poetry at it's highest voltage . . ." Marv. Shaw in **Bay Area Reporter**.

*Sex-charge*. 76 pages. $6.95. With male photos by Joe Ziolkowski.
ISBN 0-9627123-0-2

# MIRAGE
## ELECTRIFYING SCIENCE FICTION

On the tribal planet *Ki*, two men have been promised to each other for a lifetime. But a savage attack and a blood-chilling murder break this promise and force them to seek another world where imbalance and lies form Reality. This is the planet known as Earth, a world they will use and escape. Nominated 1991 Lambda Literary Award for Gay Men's Science Fiction/Fantasy.

"What we've got here is four characters in two bodies . . . a startling historical perspective on sexual politics . . . intelligent and intriguing." Bob Satuloff in **The New York Native**.

*Mirage*. 224 pages. $10.95
ISBN 0-9627123-1-0

# CIRCLES
## THE AMAZING SEQUEL TO *MIRAGE*

"The world Brass has created with *Mirage* and its sequel rivals, in complexity and wonder, such greats as C.S. Lewis and Ursula LeGuin." **Mandate Magazine**, New York.

*Circles*. 224 pages. $11.95
ISBN 0-9627123-3-7

# OUT THERE

STORIES OF PRIVATE DESIRES. HORROR.
AND THE AFTERLIFE.

". . . we have come to associate [horror] with slick and trashy
chiller-thrillers. Perry Brass is neither. He writes very well, in an elegant and easy prose that carries the reader forward pleasurably. I
found this selection to be excellent." **The Gay Review**, Canada.

*Out There.* 196 pages. $10.95
ISBN 0-9627123-4-5

# ALBERT

## or THE BOOK OF MAN

Third in the *Mirage* trilogy. In 2025, the White Christian Party has
taken over America. Albert, son of Enkidu and Greeland, must find the
Earth mate who will claim his heart and allow him to return to leadership
on Ki. "Brass gives us a book where lesser writers would have only a
premise." **Men's Style,** New York
"Erotic suspense and action. . . . a pleasurable read." **Screaming
Hyena Review**, Melbourne, Australia.

*Albert.* 210 pages. $11.95
ISBN 0-9627123-5-3

# Works

## AND OTHER 'SMOKY GEORGE' STORIES
## EXPANDED EDITION

"Classic Brass," these stories—many set in the long-gone 70s, when, as
the author says, "Gay men cruised more and networked less"—have
recharged gay erotica. This expanded edition contains a selection of
Brass's steamy poems, as well as his essay, "Maybe We Should Keep the
'Porn' in Pornography."

*Works and other 'Smoky George' Stories* 184 pages. $9.95
ISBN 0-9627123-6-1

# THE HARVEST

## A "SCIENCE/POLITICO" NOVEL

From today's headlines predicting human cloning comes the emergence of "vaccos"—living "corporate cadavers"—raised to be sources of human organ and tissue transplants. One exceptional vacco will escape. His survival will depend upon Chris Turner, a sexual renegade who will love him and kill to keep him alive. "One of the <u>Ten Best Books of 1997</u>," **Lavender Magazine**, Minneapolis. "In George Nader's *Chrome*, the hero dared to fall in love with a robot. In **The Harvest**—*a vastly superior novel*, Chris Turner falls in love with a vacco, Hart256043." Jesse Monteagudo, **The Weekly News**, Miami. Finalist, Lambda Literary Award, Gay and Lesbian Science Fiction, 1997.

*The Harvest.* 216 pages. $11.95
ISBN 0-9627123-7-X

# THE LOVER OF MY SOUL

## A SEARCH FOR ECSTASY AND WISDOM

Brass's first book of poetry since *Sex-charge* is worth the wait. Flagrantly erotic and just plain flagrant—with poems like "I Shoot the Sonovabitch Who Fires Me," "Sucking Dick Instead of Kissing," and the notorious "MTV Ab(*solutely*) Vac(*uous*) Awards." **The Lover of My Soul** again proves Brass's feeling that poetry must tell, astonish, and delight. "An amazingly powerful book of poetry and prose," **The Loving Brotherhood**.

*The Lover of My Soul.* 100 pages. $8.95
ISBN 0-9627123-8-8

At your bookstore, or from:

Belhue Press
2501 Palisade Ave., Suite A1
Bronx, NY 10463
E-mail: belhuepress@earthlink.net

Please add $2.00 shipping the first book, and $1.00 for each book thereafter. New York State residents please add 8.25% sales tax. Foreign orders in U.S. currency only.

You can now order Perry Brass's exciting books online at www.perrybrass.com. Please visit this website for more details, regular updates, and news of future events and books.

About the photographer: Vince Gabrielly is a photographer living in San Francisco. His distinctive stlye of photographing men is gaining much attention in the art world. For more information, he can be reached at (415) 646-0883, or by E-mail at vince@ravengallery.com. His website can be viewed at www.ravengallery.com